BRESCIA COLLEGE
LONDON ONTARIO

PS 151
.F75

2002

Transformations of Domesticity in Modern Women's Writing

Transformations of Domesticity in Modern Women's Writing

Homelessness at Home

Thomas Foster

BRESCIA UNIVERSITY
COLLEGE LIBRARY

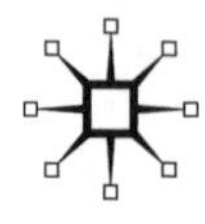

© Thomas Foster 2002

All rights reserved. No reproduction, copy or transmission of this publication may be made without written permission.

No paragraph of this publication may be reproduced, copied or transmitted save with written permission or in accordance with the provisions of the Copyright, Designs and Patents Act 1988, or under the terms of any licence permitting limited copying issued by the Copyright Licensing Agency, 90 Tottenham Court Road, London W1T 4LP.

Any person who does any unauthorized act in relation to this publication may be liable to criminal prosecution and civil claims for damages.

The author has asserted his right to be identified as the author of this work in accordance with the Copyright, Designs and Patents Act 1988.

First published 2002 by
PALGRAVE MACMILLAN
Houndmills, Basingstoke, Hampshire RG21 6XS and
175 Fifth Avenue, New York, N.Y. 10010
Companies and representatives throughout the world

PALGRAVE MACMILLAN is the global academic imprint of the Palgrave Macmillan division of St. Martin's Press, LLC and of Palgrave Macmillan Ltd. Macmillan® is a registered trademark in the United States, United Kingdom and other countries. Palgrave is a registered trademark in the European Union and other countries.

ISBN 0–333–77347–0

This book is printed on paper suitable for recycling and made from fully managed and sustained forest sources.

A catalogue record for this book is available from the British Library.

Library of Congress Cataloging-in-Publication Data

Foster, Thomas, 1959–
Transformations of domesticity in modern women's writing: homelessness at home / by Thomas Foster.
p. cm.
Includes bibliographical references (p. 188).
ISBN 0–333–77347–0
1. American literature – Women authors – History and criticism. 2. Place (Philosophy) in literature. 3. American literature – 20th century – History and criticism. 4. Women and literature – United States – History. 5. English fiction – Women authors – History and criticism. 6. Women and literature – Great Britain – History – 20th century. 7. Dickinson, Emily, 1830–1886 – Views on feminism. 8. Sex differences (Psychology) in literature. 9. Modernism (Literature) – United States. 10. Modernism (Literature) – Great Britain. 11. Homelessness in literature. 12. Women in literature. 13. Home in literature. I. Title.

PS151 .F68 2002
810.9'9287–dc21

2002074838

10 9 8 7 6 5 4 3 2 1
11 10 09 08 07 06 05 04 03 02

Printed and bound in Great Britain by
Antony Rowe Ltd, Chippenham and Eastbourne

BRESCIA UNIVERSITY
COLLEGE LIBRARY

Contents

Acknowledgements vi

1 What Comes after the Ideology of Separate Spheres? Women Writers and Modernism 1

2 Homelessness at Home: Placing Emily Dickinson in (Women's) History 26

3 'We Are All Haunted Houses': H.D.'s (Dis)Location 45

4 'A Place for the Genuine': Marianne Moore's 'Poetry' 63

5 The Grounding of Modern Women's Fiction: Emily Holmes Coleman's *The Shutter of Snow* 83

6 'Can't One Live in More Places Than One?': Virginia Woolf's *The Years* 98

7 'Dream Made Flesh': Sexual Difference and Narratives of Revolution in Sylvia Townsend Warner's *Summer Will Show* 115

8 From Domestic Grounding to Domestic Play: Problems of Reproduction and Subversion in Gertrude Stein and Zora Neale Hurston 137

Notes 155

Works Cited 188

Index 208

Acknowledgments

It is a pleasure to acknowledge the generous readings and responses I received in composing various drafts and sections of this book, from Joseph Allen Boone, Michael Cadden, Jonathan Elmer, Susan Friedman (under whose direction the project began), Lynn Keller, Mary Layoun, Jane Marcus (who first introduced me to the relation between feminism and modernism), James Naremore, Cyrena Pondrom, Judith Roof and Paul Strohm. I owe a special debt to the other students in Jane Marcus's experimental women's writing and feminist theory seminars at the University of Texas, who inspired the thinking that led to this project, especially Victoria Smith, and to the participants in Houston A. Baker, Jr. and Barbara Johnson's courses at the School of Criticism and Theory in the summer of 1987, especially Diana Fuss and Bill Martin. I'd also like to thank some of the people who lived through this project with me, including Catherine Wiley and Kari Kalve. Eva Cherniavsky is a continuing source of intellectual inspiration and personal support.

A shorter version of Chapter 2 originally appeared in the book collection *Engendering Men: the Question of Male Feminist Criticism*, edited by Joseph Allen Boone and Michael Cadden, and appears here by the permission of the publisher, Routledge. Chapter 8 appeared in *Modern Fiction Studies* 41.3–4 (Fall–Winter 1995), and is reprinted by the permission of the Johns Hopkins University Press.

1
What Comes after the Ideology of Separate Spheres? Women Writers and Modernism

If it was ever possible ideologically to characterize women's lives by the distinction of public and private domains ... it is now a totally misleading ideology, even to show how both terms of these dichotomies construct each other in theory and practice. I prefer a network ideological image, suggesting the profusion of spaces and identities and the permeability of boundaries in the personal body and in the body politic.

Donna Haraway (170; my emphasis)

This space [of money and commodities, of the marketplace] which established itself during the Middle Ages ... was by definition a space of exchange and communication, and therefore of networks.

Henri Lefebvre, *The Production of Space* (266)

There's many a ship 'twixt the cup and the lip, to paraphrase an old proverb.

Charlotte Perkins Gilman, *Women and Economics* (225)

My children play with skulls
and remember
for the embattled
there is no place
that cannot be
home
nor is

Audre Lorde, 'School Note'

1 A surplus of binary energies: deconstructing domestic oppositions

One purpose of this book is to reveal some connections between nineteenth-century domestic and sentimental writing, feminist versions of modernism, and postmodern theories of social space, in which clear boundaries and oppositions give way to a network metaphor. As Donna Haraway suggests, this postmodern redefinition of space poses a major challenge to the opposition between public and private spheres that structures modern concepts of gender, an opposition usually referred to as the 'ideology of separate spheres'. My argument, however, is that it is inaccurate to call this shift in concepts of space 'postmodern', since the oppositions between public and private, outside and inside, masculine and feminine begin to be unraveled at the beginning of this century. My focus will be on the ways in which modernist women writers reimagined domesticity in order to reject its positioning within the binary framework of the ideology of separate spheres. One result of this focus is to problematize some dominant periodizing concepts in both literary history and feminist historiography.[1]

The other main purpose of this book is interpretive. This introductory chapter establishes a theoretical, cultural, and historical framework that highlights the significance of the figure of 'home' for modern women writers, and the chapters that follow will demonstrate the new interpretive possibilities this framework is intended to open. How valid and how comprehensive is the ideology of separate gender spheres as a framework for explaining women's lives, activities, and literary productions? The focus on the ideology of separate spheres that characterizes most feminist work on the nineteenth century assumes that industrialization involved the severing of the home from the capitalist marketplace and the privatization of the middle-class home as a feminine space. To what extent is that mapping of gendered spaces still relevant, and to what extent was that mapping always an ideological illusion? If the opposition between masculine and feminine spheres is not an adequate mapping of gender relations, what other concepts of space might have coexisted with this dominant ideology, if only as a conceptual or imaginary possibility? These are the kinds of questions that haunt modernist women's writing, and these questions still pose a basic challenge to many of the methodological assumptions of literary and cultural studies. What does it mean to be 'homeless at home'? This phrase originates in the poetry of Emily Dickinson, and I take it to be a touchstone for the problems modernist women authors faced in defining their relationships to a history that categorized domesticity as a peculiarly feminine 'place'.

By turning to women's writing from the first half of the twentieth century, I intend to redefine domesticity by historicizing postmodern theoretical claims made about the recent emergence of new concepts of space. Haraway suggests that the network metaphor provides an alternative to the oppositional structure within which domesticity has normally been defined and to the binary categories that organize that structure. Michel Foucault is one of the major sources for this network metaphor. In arguing that 'the anxiety of our era has to do fundamentally with space' rather than time, Foucault sketches a set of shifts, from a medieval concept of the 'hierarchic ensemble of places' to an Enlightenment concept of extension or 'infinitely open space' and finally to the contemporary idea of the network, 'defined by relations of proximity between points or elements' ('Other Spaces' 22–23). I cite this posthumously published essay of Foucault's because it succinctly sums up the central argument of what is sometimes called the postmodern geography movement.[2] Haraway suggests that it should be possible to read this kind of argument for the transformation of spatial relations in the contemporary world back into earlier historical periods, but how is that process of historicizing the emergence of the 'network ideological image' to proceed? My thesis in this book is that modernist women's writing constitutes an overlooked resource for reconstructing the historical connections Haraway asserts must exist. Foucault's essay inadvertently exemplifies the need for making such connections, to the extent that it implies that the domestic ideology of separate gender spheres can be dismissed as obsolete or anachronistic. As Foucault puts it, oppositions between public (masculine) and private (feminine) spaces continue to exist only to the extent that the shift to a network model has not yet completely 'desanctified' older concepts of space (23). In particular, Foucault dramatizes the postmodern assumption that the network metaphor is fundamentally opposed to 'inviolable' oppositions between one type of space and another, which are replaced by Haraway's permeable boundaries (23). From this perspective, the network metaphor is used to justify a kind of amnesia about domesticity and, indeed, gender relations more generally.[3]

Modernist women's writing, I will argue, should be read as a transitional moment between nineteenth-century domestic ideologies and postmodern concepts of space, when those two sets of assumptions about space and gender can still be read in relation to one another.

This body of writing participates in the cultural work of transforming spatial relations that Foucault defines, but the result is also to redefine gender relations, since the concept of 'womanhood' took on 'a distinctive spatial character during the early stages of industrial capitalism' when the ideology of separate spheres was installed (Ryan 165). In the context of arguments like Foucault or Haraway's, this kind of analysis of the spatialization of femininity seems to take for granted the meaning of 'space.' It is not until the modernist period that space itself is called into question by women writers. In the modernist period, it starts to become apparent that 'home' figures what Foucault calls 'internal space', assumed to be 'a kind of void, inside of which we could place individuals and things' (23); but at the same time this concept of space is relativized, as only one possibility among others. Only recently has this shift in thinking about spatial relations begun to be theorized. Neil Smith and Cindi Katz, for instance, critique the assumption that spatial relations always take the form of 'absolute space', defined as the 'conception of space as a field,' a 'container', or 'a co-ordinate system of discrete and mutually exclusive locations' (75). But while they note that this concept of space provided the basis for 'a very specific tyranny of power' (76), they fail to identify the way in which nineteenth-century gender relations depended upon the figure of 'home' to define this concept of space as interiority, as container.

Nancy Armstrong has argued that domesticity provides precisely a model for the modern individual, defined by the inviolability of personal interiority – that is, by 'the juridical assumption of the individual body as the basic social unit' (Smith and Katz 75). Such arguments depend upon the 'surplus of binary energies' that gender categories gained when grounded in the notion of spatial segregation structuring the ideology of separate spheres (Romero 110). Binary gender categories and a concept of clearly bounded inner and outer spaces function as metaphors for one another; neither this concept of space nor this concept of gender could exist without the other. To the extent that this concept of gendered space and spatialized gender becomes generalizable, domestic ideology becomes not just a sociological phenomenon, but a 'technology of gender', capable of spinning off other sets of oppositions, which do not have to be explicitly gendered precisely to the extent that their structure remains homologous to the binary opposition of masculine and feminine spaces (de Lauretis). Gillian Rose defines this structural function when she identifies 'the rhetorical encoding of two different kinds of space as two different kinds of sexes' as a continuing problem within the postmodern geographical imagination ('Mirrors' 59). I intend to show that modernist women's writing stands as a key moment in the deconstruction of this kind of oppositional thinking about spatial relations. This body of work then problematizes the spatial metaphors prevalent within contemporary theories of subjectivity in language as well as feminist standpoint epistemologies or Adrienne Rich's politics of location, which define the basis for women's historical (rather than linguistic) agency.[4]

What consequences does a critique of spatial metaphors and assumptions have for thinking about gender? Armstrong's argument about the origins of modern individualism in domestic economy also includes an analysis of the ways in which nineteenth-century domestic fictions translated the complex, competing ways of representing human identity into a single binary opposition (253). The oppositions that organize domestic ideology and its accompanying literary forms had the effect of subsuming all social differences under the rubric of gender. The rethinking of spatial models of oppositionality that informs modernist women's writing begins to undo this reduction. That rethinking opens onto an acknowledgment of how race and class in particular operate within gender categories, and this rethinking is necessary in order to constitute as significant differences among women that the ideology of separate spheres tried to repress, since that ideology falsely universalized a model of home life that only seemed applicable to women who did not have to work outside the home. A critique of the boundedness of 'home' as the basis for femininity is necessary in order to either reveal the racial and class specificity of domestic womanhood or to define a more inclusive concept of gender. In the chapters that follow, I will document how white women authors became increasingly aware of the problem of their own relative racial and class privilege as a result of their increasingly critical perspectives on domesticity. Representations of race and class then become especially important as indicators of how far these writers are willing to go in undoing the spatial oppositions that define both domesticity and femininity, so that it becomes possible to articulate their perspectives on domesticity with those of working-class women and women of color. This analysis of how modernist women writers imagined transformations in domesticity makes it possible to understand the internal logic and the political impulse behind their representations of racial and class difference, which might otherwise seem marginal or irrelevant. To emphasize the way a focus on domesticity opens up onto these seemingly 'larger' issues, I will end the book with a chapter that connects experimental women's writing (Gertrude Stein) with a novel representing African-American literary traditions (Zora Neale Hurston).

While it may never have been entirely valid to 'characterize women's lives by the distinction of public and private domains', as Haraway argues, it is still necessary to account for the power that the public/private distinction held in the literary imagination, even after the impossibility of a strict demarcation between these gendered spaces began to become apparent. I agree with Foucault that modernism 'desanctified' nineteenth-century oppositions between a masculinized public sphere and a privatized feminine one, but what Foucault ignores is the fact that desanctification does not mean that these oppositions cease to circulate or to organize ideological formations and power relations. The common modernist themes of exile and expatriatism are an index to the ways in which the concept of 'home' began to be called into question in the first part of the twentieth century, in both European and American contexts. But for modernist women writers, it was not so easy to simply abandon that concept. Modernist women's writing therefore provides a record of a unique historical moment, which made explicit the already-existing contradiction between the dominant representation of all women's experiences in terms of the public/private distinction and the failure of such representations to account for the full range of women's activities. It is the emergence of this contradiction as such that distinguishes my readings of modernist women's writing from the rereadings of nineteenth-century domestic writing and the sentimental tradition that have taken place since Haraway's essay was published. But many modernist women writers still retained a relation, however ambivalent, to concepts of domestic space and the feminized, sentimental values relegated to the home. This continuing relation to domesticity distinguishes women authors' experiments with literary form from high modernism as it is typically defined, as a rejection of the supposed sentimentality of nineteenth-century Anglo-American literature after romanticism.[5] Modernist women writers use the cultural resources made available by such modernist critiques to redefine the meaning of 'home,' not to reject its significance entirely, as many male writers did in the modernist period.[6] This project of redefinition remains relevant today, given the postmodern tendency to privilege mobility over location, space over place, with 'home' still functioning as a metaphor for the very possibility of being 'placed'.

2 Counter-narratives of interiority: feminist interventions in domesticity

Haraway's argument that the ideology of separate spheres has become 'misleading' and oversimplified as a framework for understanding the construction of social space, even in the nineteenth century, is only a passing suggestion. This claim has been taken up in the last decade by a number of feminist historians and literary critics.[7] In the American context, the revaluation of domesticity has its origins in the groundbreaking work of literary critics like Jane Tompkins and Nina Baym and historians like Nancy Cott and Dolores Hayden, who argue that nineteenth-century domesticity provided the basis for 'a monumental effort to reorganize culture from the woman's point of view' (Tompkins 124). In other words, domesticity was not simply confining for women but a source of agency or 'sentimental power', to cite Tompkins again; in this view, domesticity embodies 'a reformist rather than conformist ethos' (Brown, *Domestic Individualism* 6).[8] This reading of domesticity depends upon accepting the public/private distinction as the basis for creating an alternative feminine culture, built on values excluded from the capitalist marketplace. In the British context, Martha Vicinus makes a similar argument when she describes nineteenth-century women as 'separatists by necessity' (8).[9] The anachronism involved in reading a contemporary form of feminist politics back into the nineteenth century highlights the similar assumptions about space which inform contemporary feminist politics.

For instance, the feminist 'standpoint epistemology' articulated by Nancy Hartsock argues that resistant forms of feminist consciousness and gender-based oppositional politics can be traced back to the ways in which women's 'immersion in the world of use' during housework or childrearing 'is more complete' than men's (Hartsock, 'Feminist Standpoint' 165). In other words, standpoint epistemologies depend upon a concept of women's *place* in society and argue that the 'ground for a specifically feminist historical materialism' (the title of Hartsock's major book on this topic) transforms 'women's own ground of expected domesticity' (Cott, *Grounding* 7) into a critical position.[10] But that possibility for critique and feminist consciousness-raising depends upon taking the boundary between public and private as a given fact, which has to be overcome, rather than examining how that boundary itself never entirely performed its ideological function of separating masculine and feminine spheres.

In contrast, a second wave of feminist work on domesticity insists on treating the idea of 'home' as a specific racial and class position for white, middle-class women, and therefore as an extension, of or at best a supplement to, the capitalist marketplace, not an alternative to it.[11] This second-wave critique emphasizes how casting domesticity as a countercultural movement, on the basis of its exclusion from dominant economic formations, obscures the way domesticity reproduces other kinds of power relations, especially imperialism (Romero 3). In this second reading, it is precisely the reformist impulse privileged by earlier feminist critics as an unrecognized form of women's historical agency that is now understood as fueling a kind of expansionist or missionary project, characterized by rhetorics of expanding woman's sphere and of social or enlarged housekeeping, which often translated into projects of class socialization and the imposition of middle-class norms. This trope of social housekeeping is the best example of what Romero means when she refers to domesticity as promoting problematic forms of 'generalized oppositionality', Conceptualized as an extension of the domestic sphere, these reformist projects were typically aimed at the lower classes and at racialized or colonial others, and they tended to naturalize the relative privilege of white, middle-class women within the culture of domesticity.[12] The autonomy from the public sphere or state intervention that domesticity attributed to all homes was in fact a freedom reserved for the property-owning classes. In this context, the possibilities for women's agency enabled by domestic ideology are understood as secondary phenomena resulting from a process of class formation, with the concept of a separate domestic economy governed by women understood as a specifically gendered form of internalized self-discipline and middle-class self-fashioning, what Gillian Brown calls 'domestic individualism'.[13] These critiques of the way in which domesticity functioned to further the aims of capitalism and imperialism in the nineteenth century problematize the desire, exemplified by Hartsock's feminist standpoint, to treat women's domestic activities as the basis for a critical perspective on class society. However, these second-wave critiques of domesticity also depend upon spatial metaphors, to the extent that they present domesticity as a bounded position occupied by a specific race and class of women. The middle-class home's ability to securely underwrite the image of 'a self by definition already domesticated', because it is modeled on the interiorized space of the private home, is called into question in the modernist period (Brown, *Domestic Individualism* 7).

Romero proposes an alternative to the reading of domesticity as providing a spatial model for feminist 'oppositionality' by emphasizing how the discourse of social or enlarged housekeeping has unexpected consequences. That discourse redefined domesticity as 'an identity rather than simply as a fixed location for women's lives'. The result is not simply to allow domesticity to 'travel', with nineteenth-century women arguing that 'they continued to embody domesticity even when they left home'; more importantly, this extension of domesticity opened it to internal debates and differences, 'sites of social conflict and political struggle' over what groups of women would be included in what the ideology of separate gender spheres famously defined as the 'bonds of womanhood' (Romero 25; Cott). The contemporary significance of these debates about domesticity is confirmed by African-American feminist Bernice Johnson Reagon, who argues that separatist attempts to create 'nurturing' or 'home' spaces, for women or lesbians only, result in the emergence of differences between women based on race and class. The result is that separatism's own dynamic generates a need for coalition politics (the 'home' starts to resemble the 'street'), and the opposition between public and private, difference and similarity, deconstructs itself (358–60).[14] Reagon's essay is useful for demonstrating that the emergence of a more polymorphous concept of womanhood is historically linked to the redefinition of social space as internally heterogeneous, a kind of space where two different things can occupy the same place.

I would argue, however, that Romero underestimates the extent to which the representation of domesticity as able to travel beyond the walls of the middle-class home had the ideological function of mystifying or suppressing the internal contradictions within the feminine sphere of domestic responsibilities. The link between women's movement into the public sphere and the emergence of internal differences within the category of 'woman' tends to emerge as such only in the modernist period.[15] The expansion of domestic responsibilities beyond the literal boundaries of the home and into the larger social realm often functioned as a mode of assimilation, an 'expansive, imperial project' (Wexler 15), which left intact the original assumptions of the ideology of separate spheres: domesticity is defined by its essential difference from the capitalist marketplace, and women's essential difference from men is confirmed by this opposition between home and market, as is the false universality accorded to the concept of an essentialized 'womanhood'. Domesticity's ability to literally and materially travel beyond the home does not in itself disrupt the ideology of separate spheres, in a testimony to the power of ideological and conceptual categories and metaphors to shape reality. One of the functions of domestic ideology was precisely to represent domesticity as having the ability to travel without risk to itself or to the racial and class privileges possessed by women whose lives centered primarily on the home. The contradictions of such representations only started to become obvious in the modernist period.

Specifically, it is in the modernist period that women writers begin to challenge the assumption Romero critiques in the scholarship on domesticity: the tendency to reproduce the binary spatial logics of the object of study, the ideology of separate spheres. Romero argues that domesticity has been understood entirely in terms of either 'capitulation or transcendence', women's assimilation to social norms and power relations or their exclusion from and opposition to them (110). Furthermore, this distinction has played itself out in constructions of literary history which associate nineteenth-century sentimental and domestic traditions with feminized forms of capitulation and associate literature's capacity for 'defamiliarization and social critique' (106) with masculine forms of 'authorial transcendence' (113). In the modernist period, these forms of transcendence or critical distance are literalized in the act of leaving home, when expatriatism and 'aesthetic gain through exile' (Kaplan 36) become the model for literary authorship. This model rejects 'cultural location as tradition and ... cultural context as a limit to the powers of the imagination' (Kaplan 43), and 'home' continues to serve as the primary figure for the idea of 'location' itself, with its connotations of specificity and particularity.[16]

3 Becoming 'homeless at home': domesticity as self-critique

Modernist women's writing, I argue, anticipates Romero's call for greater attention to political strategies that refuse to treat transcendence of place or freedom of movement as an indispensable precondition for resistance (113). In this book, I take the phrase homelessness at home from Emily Dickinson, to name one of the defining goals of modernist women's writing. This phrase offers a verbal formulation of the desire to resituate possibilities for 'defamiliarization and social critique' in relation to domestic settings and the feminine personae located there.[17] In the chapters that follow, I will examine representations of poetic speakers and fictional characters who embody the paradoxical characteristics of 'homelessness at home', and I will link these representations and their refusal of domestic oppositions to formal experimentation with some of the basic characteristics of lyric poetry (such as the opposition between 'I' and 'you', speaker and addressee) and the novel (the opposition of individual to society). In the phrase 'homelessness at home', home figures a claim to a gendered identity, while homelessness figures the writer's consciousness that this identity is neither completely determined and essentialized nor inherently spatialized in the ways that the ideology of separate spheres represents women as being. But this trope does not entirely reject the spatial figuration of femininity; in fact, the implication is that an alternate conception of space might empower a new feminist politics, as in Audre Lorde's poem 'School Note', where the speaker refers to herself as being 'at home' anywhere because no place 'is' home.[18] This book examines a group of women writers for whom the gender identity ideally grounded in the institution of the middle-class home as private space is shown to be inherently unstable and therefore open to redefinition through struggles over the social meaning of gender, struggles whose outcome cannot be predicted or specified in advance; this openness to change is one of the connotations of 'homelessness' in this context.[19] In the twentieth century the privileged or protected status of the private home became increasingly 'embattled' for all women, and not just for African-American or working-class women, whose relations to middle-class property rights had always been marginal and whose homes had always been liable to invasion by market forces.[20]

I will also argue that the trope of homelessness at home in the work of middle-class white women authors implies their rejection of any absolute boundary between their positions and those of other races and classes of women. One meaning that homelessness at home can have is the recognition that women who are relatively privileged by race and class can and should imagine the possibility of connecting their specific experiences with those of other women, without assimilating those other experiences to a white middle-class model in the way that the ideology of separate spheres universalized a specific kind of feminine experience (the 'freedom' to manage a privately owned home) to cover all women. On a more literal level, the trope of homelessness at home contains the historical trace of women's relatively precarious relation to structures of private property throughout much of the nineteenth century, a reminder of the ways in which domestic ideology never realistically represented women's experiences.[21] But this trope also marks a recognition of the need to imagine connections between different types of feminine experience as part of a process of self-critique (indeed, a critique of the dominant model that defined the self as interiorized or domesticated) for white middle-class women. This cultural work of reimagining and opening up the domestic model of feminine identity is distinct from actual coalition-building, but it is a precondition for participation in that form of feminist political work.[22]

The generalized 'embattlement' of the figure of 'home' in the modernist period anticipates the recurrent postmodern theme of the breakdown of boundaries between public and private spheres that results from the spread of mass media after the Second World War.[23] However, it is also necessary to consider the new dangers posed by such a generalized displacement of the status of 'home' as a fixed location. As part of her critique of the 'generalized oppositionality' attributed to domestic culture, Romero warns against the conclusion that 'if white women had possessed the wherewithal to challenge patriarchy then all of the other forms of inequality present in ... society that radiate outward from the patriarch's word would unravel in the process' (112). In other words, if domesticity embodies a form of racial and class privilege, then it is tempting to conclude that self-critiques of domesticity by white, middle-class women authors might also 'unravel' racial and class politics, as well as gender. The danger here is that such self-critiques will reinstate gender difference as the central social conflict, under which race and class can be subsumed, and thereby place white, middle-class women at the vanguard of social change while remarginalizing other women.[24] The same danger is clearly present when modernist women writers represent themselves as being in the process of becoming 'homeless', of detaching themselves from domestic ideologies, or rather detaching domesticity from femininity. For this reason, it is important to note that the concept of 'home', of a specificity of location and position, is not abandoned by modernist women but relativized, relocated outside a binary structure of opposition. Differences still matter, but they are not absolute.

For white middle-class women writers, beginning with Emily Dickinson, the double positionality of being both 'homeless' and 'at home' assumes that domestic or 'true' womanhood can be removed from its pedestal without effacing the history of privilege these women are contesting, defined as a continuing relation to 'home'. Romero is certainly right to warn against using domesticity to recenter white middle-class women and remarginalize working-class women and women of color within feminism. But it is equally true that the historical operation of the ideology of separate spheres did universalize and normalize a white middle-class model of domestic womanhood in ways that affected all women in the industrializing countries, though in different ways.[25] From this perspective, the modernist women's writing I examine in this book can be read as anticipating the responses of contemporary feminism to critiques made by women of color. To the extent that the trope of homelessness at home implies a narrative of unlearning the construction of home as a separate space secure in its internal homogeneity, modernist women writers can be understood as participating in a process of 'reconstructing [white] womanhood', to use Hazel Carby's phrase, a process taking place alongside the specific representational struggles of African-American women novelists in the late nineteenth century that Carby's book describes. While this process is quite different for white, middle-class women, these modernist writers were also attempting to de-universalize 'true womanhood'. While modernist women writers were not universally successful in unlearning their own privilege, the record of the attempt to do so that I find in this body of work is just as important for the way in which it demonstrates the limits of such self-critique.

The modernist period included its own particular motivations for such self-critiques among women writers, especially the fact that the general modernist 'fantasy of escape' from domestic containment through expatriatism often expressed itself through 'the exoticization of another gender, race, or culture' (Kaplan 45). But on the other hand, the nineteenth-century embrace of domesticity as 'generalized oppositionality' also resulted in reproducing the civilizing mission of imperialism under the sign of feminist social reform and 'enlarged housekeeping'. In the early decades of the twentieth century, then, white women writers faced the danger of reproducing race and class privilege whether they embraced or rejected home. There were no simple either/or answers. The modernist writers that I will discuss attempt to negotiate this double bind, with varying degrees of success, and the trope of homelessness at home marks their attempts to imagine this bind differently.[26] As Romero points out, neither domesticity nor its rejection are automatically either progressive or coopted in advance by the status quo (9–10).

4 Modernism and the 'abstraction' of space

In their attempt to rethink the meaning of 'home' outside binary logics, modernist women writers had resources available to them that nineteenth-century women did not. As Stephen Kern puts it, 'from around 1880 to the outbreak of World War I a series of sweeping changes in technology and culture', including 'the telephone, wireless telegraph, x-ray, cinema, bicycle, automobile, and airplane' as well as 'the stream-of-consciousness novel, psychoanalysis, Cubism, and the theory of relativity' created distinctive new modes of thinking about and experiencing time and space' (1).[27] Though left unstated in Kern's book, the best example of an old mode of thinking about space is the ideology of separate gender spheres. Critics of modernism often tend to emphasize the historical rupture created by such 'sweeping changes', as Marshall Berman does when he generalizes Marx's phrase 'all that is solid melts into air' into a touchstone for the modernist emphasis on flux and the resultant challenge to fixed boundaries, material or conceptual. Traditionally, this change has been conceptualized as a move from the fixity of spatial location to the fluidity of temporal process, exemplifying the persistence of naturalized assumptions about space as 'container' that Smith and Katz critique. In *Postmodern Geography*, for example, Edward Soja explicitly argues that it is only with the shift from modernism to postmodernism that we find a sensitivity to 'the spatiality of social life' that is comparable to the modernist sensitivity to temporality (11).[28]

To understand the ways in which modernist women writers prefigured this supposedly postmodern sensitivity to transformations in social space, and to avoid this dichotomizing of time and space, modernism and postmodernism, it is necessary to place in relation to one another two distinct historical narratives of the changes and transformations characteristic of modernity. If modernism generally can be defined as a cultural crisis in philosophical, political and economic modernity, then I would define women's modernist writing as the specific crisis that results when these two normally distinct historical narratives are perceived to contradict one another. The first of these narratives is the one I have referred to already as the ideology of separate spheres: a story about the effects of the transition to industrial capitalism in both England and the US and the remapping of home and marketplace, private and public spheres, as gendered spaces that takes place during that transition. For my purposes, the main effects of this new ideology are its association of gender identity not with space in general, as is more commonly asserted, but with a particular, reductive concept of spatial relations, defined as clearly bounded and mappable rather than as a permeable network. The distinction between inner and outer spaces seemingly carved out by the four walls of the private home came to serve as a metaphor for this concept of space.[29]

Neither feminist critics and historians of the nineteenth century nor critics of modernism and its transformations in time and space have paid sufficient attention to another narrative of the development of capitalism and its spatial relations. I refer here to Henri Lefebvre's *The Production of Space* and his analysis of capitalist development as the progressive 'abstraction' of social space. For Lefebvre, the key element in the transition to industrial capitalism is the transition from the immediacy of 'absolute space', whose origins are 'agro-pastoral', to the 'abstract' space of commodity relations and communications networks (234; 266).[30] From Lefebvre's perspective, the ideology of separate spheres *results from* but is *not identical to* the abstraction or dissociation of space from place. The ideology of separate spheres is *produced by* the capitalist abstraction of space as one moment in its development, but that very process of abstraction leads to continuing transformations in social space which *undermine* the separation of public and private, masculine and feminine spaces. Initially the separation of marketplace from private home corresponds to the abstraction of space from place, with the market being defined by abstract spatial relations best represented by Haraway's 'network' metaphor and home being associated with the lived immediacy of place. At the same time, though, the progressive abstraction of space from place leads to an emergent counter-tendency to the ideology of separate spheres within the development of capitalism, and this counter-tendency can be measured by the difference between the rhetorics of 'abstraction' and 'separation' in these two historical narratives.

The abstraction of social space involves more than the simple separation of space from place, and of the alienated social relations of the marketplace from the supposedly more immediate sentimental, emotional, and moral relations located in the domestic sphere during the nineteenth century. Instead, 'abstraction' refers to the *transformation* of place into space and the *replacement* of attachment to place by more tenuous and 'abstract' spatial relations, perhaps most easily visualized in terms of the space created by communications networks as opposed to that of face-to-face conversation (as Avital Ronell puts it, in a discussion of the cultural effects of the telephone, such communication technologies 'can barely abide an outside'; 94). In this sense, the abstraction of space from place stands in contrast to the maintenance of clear distinctions between public and private spaces, which are necessary to the ideology of separate spheres. Lefebvre's narrative then defines the way in which capitalism's general development is at odds with the very principle of the separability of public and private spheres, which the specific stage of industrial capitalism produces.[31] It is this contradiction within capitalist development that makes it impossible 'to characterize women's lives' exclusively in terms of the 'distinction between public and private domains', as Haraway suggests, even before the postmodern shift toward network images and 'permeability of boundaries' (170).

The modernist period can thus be understood as a moment of crisis when the contradiction between the separation of (gendered) spaces and the general abstraction or shift away from concepts of fixed locality became culturally explicit. As a result, the function of 'home' as a spatial metaphor for what Lefebvre calls absolute space becomes problematic. As Smith and Katz argue, such 'spatial metaphors are problematic in so far as they presume that space is not' (75). The trope of homelessness at home functions as a strategy of literalization which destabilizes the 'taken-for-grantedness' of the assumptions about space that underlie such metaphors (80). Those assumptions are thereby opened to critical scrutiny, and it becomes possible to develop alternative concepts of space that are capable of taking into account the diversity of spatial relations in modern life (80).

5 The place of subjectivity and the language of inner space

I have already indicated the extent to which the feminist political discourses depend upon the spatial metaphors of the standpoint and the politics of location, metaphors that need to be situated in relation to the 'surplus of binary energies' that Romero argues we have inherited from the ideology of separate spheres. This critique will be especially relevant to my readings of women novelists from the 1930s who attempted to reimagine the genre of social realism and the theme of feminine agency in the aftermath of high modernism (Chapters 5–7). As Smith and Katz point out, however, another theoretical site where outmoded spatial metaphors persist is the discourse on subjectivity in language (they cite Foucault and Althusser), with its rhetoric of 'positionality' (68).[32] This critique of structuralist and poststructuralist theories of subjectivity in language will provide the context for my readings of modernist women's poetry (Chapters 2–4).

The problem of spatial metaphors necessarily appears as these theories of subjectivity shift away from a humanist notion of the *self* toward a concept of the subject as *place*. Jacques Lacan, for instance, rewrites Descartes' 'I think, therefore I am' as 'I think where I am not, therefore I am where I do not think' (*Ecrits* 166), as implying that 'the question "who is speaking" can only be answered by shifting the grounds of the question to "where am I speaking from?"' (Fuss 30). This formulation sums up the way in which a particular notion of space, of '*where* I am', has been generalized within theories of subjectivity.[33] Judith Butler's influential theory of gender performativity challenges the spatial assumptions that typically underlie such formulations, by questioning the cultural sources for the language or rhetoric of 'inner space' and the association of femininity with interiority. Butler asks 'from what strategic position in public discourse and for what reasons has the trope of interiority and the disjunctive binary of inner and outer taken hold? In what language is "inner space" figured?' (*Gender Trouble* 134). My answer to this last question is that 'inner space' is articulated through the language of domestic economy.[34] While postmodernism is often defined in terms of challenges to the romantic distinction between the interior space of the self and the exterior space of the world, like the one Butler articulates, modernist women writers pose the same questions through their interrogation of how 'home' figures a securely interiorized space, a precondition for the romantic aesthetic of self-expression. The term 'expression' itself implies a spatial distinction, in which inner thoughts and feelings are imagined to exist before their social communication and their projection outward.[35] These questions emerge as a result of both modernist resistance to romanticism (the replacement of the aesthetic of expression by a modernist aesthetics of impersonality or dehumanization)[36] and early twentieth-century feminism's resistance to the nineteenth-century conflation of femininity and domesticity.

Carolyn Burke suggests the self-consciousness modernist women writers possessed about these questions when she argues that the central characteristic of innovative writing by modernist women, especially in the genre of poetry, is a tension 'between [the] desire to write from within a female subjectivity and [the] consciousness of the problems surrounding subjectivity itself' (132).[37] Burke emphasizes modernist writers' understanding of subjectivity as a function of language, so that subject position refers to the 'subject of the sentence or statement, with no fixed existence beyond its linguistic habitation' (131). I take this analysis a step further by examining how the problem of subjectivity is inherent in the spatial metaphors that Burke herself reproduces when she describes women writing 'within' female subjectivity, or refers to 'the problems *surrounding* subjectivity' and to language as a 'habitation'.

One of the founding texts on domestic economy as a language of gendered interiority is American writer Catherine Beecher's 1842 *Treatise* on the topic, which links a system of domestic organization and housekeeping with the policing of the distinction between public and private and with a regime of mental hygiene for women. Domestic economy is presented as a set of techniques for stabilizing feminine subjectivity, producing a 'peaceful mind, and cheerful enjoyment of life', and dispelling the 'secret uneasiness' which mirrors domestic disorder on the psychic level (32). The key point in this text is the analogy it establishes between feminine subjectivity and domesticity.[38]

This process of using the figure of home to figure a securely bounded form of subjective interiority for women has to be read in relation to Foucault's more general historical model for the process of subject formation in the period of the modern democratic nation-state. During the nineteenth century, to the extent that the private home became 'the proper locus for the exercise of female individualism' (Fox-Genovese and Genovese 327), the institution of the private home was posited as the only place where women could either speak or act in ways that were culturally intelligible as 'feminine' to other people. To use Foucault's term, the private home became the only legitimate 'enunciative modality' available to women. 'Enunciative modality' is Foucault's term for particular discursive formations grounded in various social institutions (the hospital, the prison). These formations or modalities define various objects of knowledge (illness, criminality), but more importantly they also define who has the authority to speak about those objects, to function as the subject of such a discourse (*Archeology* 50–55). Foucault's theory defines the historical and institutional basis for different speaking subjects in modern society. Women's authority derived from the institution of the private home.[39]

The main difference between Foucault's model and the institution of domestic femininity is precisely the ideological conflation of feminine subjectivity with a *single* institutional location. Foucault argues, in fact, that this theory of subjectivity as produced through the enunciative modalities specific to different social institutions requires us to imagine a dispersed rather than an expressive subject – that is, a subject defined by its 'exteriority' rather than its interiority. He defines discourse as 'a space of exteriority in which a network of distinct sites is deployed', a type of social space in which 'the dispersion of the subject and his discontinuity with *himself* may be determined' (*Archeology* 54–55; my emphasis). This passage exemplifies the (post)structuralist tendency to continue to define subjectivity in relatively familiar spatial terms, even in the course of rejecting the interiorization of subjectivity in an autonomous or alienated individual. Where poststructuralists like Foucault (and others who emphasize the subject's displacement or decentering within preexisting linguistic and discursive structures) reject the romantic and humanist interiorization of subjectivity, they continue to imagine space in terms of bounded locations; Foucault's 'dispersion' consists of a multiplicity of distinct institutional sites for defining speaking subjects, and does not contest the assumption that space functions as a container called for by postmodern geographers like Smith and Katz. On the theoretical level, then, this passage from Foucault demonstrates precisely the problem modernist women writers had with the modernist aesthetic of impersonality: it privileges exteriority over interiority, rather than deconstructing that opposition.[40]

Catherine Beecher explicitly defines domesticity in contrast to the dispersion and fluidity that for Foucault characterizes modern society. Beecher describes how, in democratic societies, 'every thing is moving and changing... . There are no distinct classes, as in aristocratic lands, whose bounds are protected by distinct and impassable lines, but all are thrown into promiscuous masses' (40). Domesticity functions then as a way to reestablish the spatial certainties and stabilities of feudal societies, where 'all ranks and classes are fixed in a given position' and 'the dwellings, conveniences, and customs of life, remain very nearly the same from generation to generation' (39).[41]

Beecher's purpose is to present domestic economy as a way of imposing coherence on 'the whole current of life' and resisting the confusions of democratic life by creating an interiorized space of both familial and personal stability. This project of domestic economy can be distinguished from the project of modernist feminism most sharply by contrasting Beecher's 1842 *Treatise* with Virginia Woolf's famous essay on 'Modern Fiction' (originally published in 1919), an essay that embraces the flux implicit in Beecher's 'current of life'. Woolf privileges impressionistic techniques and stream of consciousness narration precisely as a way of *undoing* the illusion of coherence provided by such spatial distinctions between interior self and outside world. As Woolf puts it, 'the mind receives a myriad impressions ... . From all sides they come, an incessant shower of innumerable atoms; and as they fall, as they shape themselves into the life of Monday or Tuesday, the accents fall differently from of old' (287). Woolf goes on to urge writers to 'record the atoms as they fall upon the mind in the order in which they fall' and to 'trace the pattern, however disconnected and incoherent in appearance' (288). In a move typical of women modernists, Woolf ultimately has recourse not only to spatial but explicitly to *domestic* metaphors, to define the transformation she seeks in modernist fiction. Her essay urges readers to distinguish the 'sense of being in a bright yet narrow room, confined and shut in', produced by conventional narrative techniques, from the sense of being 'enlarged and set free' that she finds in impressionism (289).[42]

This shift from Beecher's domesticated subject to Woolf's open boundary between self and world is best theorized by Julia Kristeva, since her book *Revolution in Poetic Language* situates the kind of dispersed and 'exteriorized' subject Foucault defines in relation to the forms of bounded subjectivity historically associated with the figure of the private home. Kristeva refers to such bounded or interiorized modes of subjectivity as the 'thetic', and she defines modernism as an exploration of how such interiorized subjects can be textually dissolved or 'put to death' through a 'revolution in poetic language' (43, 70).[43] Combining Kristeva's theoretical model with Foucault's more historical insistence on the institutional production of speaking subjects makes it possible to more fully understand both the effects of the discourse on domestic economy in the nineteenth century and the disruption of that discourse in the modernist period. From this perspective, domesticity appears to be a historically specific version of Kristeva's thetic position.

I want to argue that modernist women's writing offers a third position, beyond Kristeva's opposition between the thetic and its dissolution, the symbolic and the semiotic, or a dispersed, exteriorized subject and an expressive, interiorized one. Nineteenth-century domestic ideology produced its own version of these two alternatives, domestic womanhood and its exteriorization as enlarged or social housekeeping. Gayatri Spivak sums up these alternatives when she argues that Western women in the nineteenth century had available to them two main modes of self-fashioning. Spivak calls these two positions 'domestic-society-through-sexual-reproduction cathected as "companionate love"' and 'the imperialist project cathected as civil-society-through-social-mission' ('Three Women's Texts' 244). The first of these position corresponds to Beecher's program of rationalizing domestic economy and family life, while the second corresponds to the reformist project of expanding 'woman's sphere'. These alternatives define the context out of which modernist women's writing emerges, and women's modernism defines itself by its attempts to create a third space for representing femininity, the space designated by the phrase 'homelessness at home'. Despite the remarkable prefiguration of this third position in Emily Dickinson's poetry, this new possibility begins to emerge explicitly only at the end of the nineteenth century, in the work of feminist writers like Charlotte Perkins Gilman.

In a passage from *Women and Economics* (1898), Gilman begins to define the contradictions inherent in the concept of a separate domestic economy as the basis for femininity. This passage offers a counter-narrative of domesticity in terms of the spatial relations of global capital, relations which do not easily lend themselves to distinctions between interior and exterior spaces:

> human nutrition is a long process. There's many a ship 'twixt the cup and the lip, to paraphrase an old proverb. Food is produced by the human race collectively, – not by individuals for their own consumption, but by interrelated groups of individuals, all over the world, for the world's consumption. This collectively produced food circulates over the earth's surface through elaborate processes of transportation, exchange, and preparation, before it reaches the mouths of consumers; and the final processes of selection and preparation are in the hands of woman (225–6).[44]

In this passage, Gilman reveals the opposition between public and domestic spheres to be contradictory, since the domestic labor that resides exclusively 'in the hands of woman' is also necessarily implicated in world-historical processes of production and distribution. Gilman therefore anticipates Jurgen Habermas's analysis of how 'the reproduction of life in the wake of the developing market economy had grown beyond the bounds of private domestic authority' (Habermas, 'Public' 52).[45] This passage returns us to Lefebvre's argument about the long-range incompatibility between the capitalist production of a separate domestic sphere and the more general capitalist abstraction of space, in its move toward Haraway's 'network ideological image' with its 'permeability of boundaries' (170). Gilman's discussion of this theme makes the reference to 'the hands of woman' ironic, since the global economic processes described make it difficult to essentialize femininity in the way that previous uses of the rhetoric of 'woman' would have. Through her evocation of women's hands and what they may or may not be able to contain, Gilman problematizes the definition of the female body as container for a feminine essence at the same time that she problematizes the definition of domesticity as such a location.[46]

This passage from Gilman only becomes paradigmatic for the *modernist* traditions of women's writing I am interested in defining when the passage moves beyond the content of its analysis to make an intervention in language at the level of the signifier, as Gilman rewrites conventional wisdom (there's many a slip 'twixt the cup and the lip) through her pun on 'slip' and 'ship'. Similarly, the opening statement, 'human nutrition is a long process', rewrites the cliché of 'women's work is never done', but turns duration in time into extension in space. The result is to use the temporal incompleteness of housekeeping (the fact that it must continually be redone) to challenge the assumption that domesticity can be spatially delimited.[47] While this play with language remains relatively marginal within Gilman's text, it points toward the more consistent and programmatic projects of twentieth-century experimental writing, which will link attempts to rethink women's relation to domesticity with attempts to rethink women's relation to language.[48]

The situation that Gilman articulates for women resembles Julia Kristeva's more general description of how the continuing changes in social relations caused by the global expansion of capitalism insure 'that human experience will be *broadened* beyond the narrow boundaries assigned to it by old relations of production and yet still be *connected* to those relations, which will consequently be threatened by it' (*Revolution* 105). Only such a situation, Kristeva argues, makes possible the modernist project of transforming preexisting discursive structures and the subject positions already established within those structures, including gender positions. Gilman's text therefore suggests a possibility that neither Beecher nor the reformists who wished to widen 'woman's sphere' could imagine, the possibility of calling into question the grounding of both women's agency and women's speech in a domestic identity. This possibility becomes the project of the modernist women's writing discussed in the chapters that follow.

To show how significant the cultural framework of domesticity was for the development of modernist women's writing in the first three decades of the twentieth century, and how consistently these writers turn to the project of transforming domesticity's spatial metaphors, I have chosen as diverse a group of writers as possible. The works discussed span a period extending from the mid-nineteenth century through the 1930s and include representatives of both the British and American national traditions and examples of the genres of poetry, fiction and prose poetry. Some of these authors remained 'at home' all their lives (Emily Dickinson and Marianne Moore in the US, Virginia Woolf and Sylvia Townsend Warner in England), while others were expatriate travelers (H.D. and Emily Holmes Coleman both moved from the US to England and Europe). I have also chosen to include both canonical and relatively unknown authors from the period.

Among the poets, Dickinson, H.D., and Moore are well-known, though in each case I discuss a mix of poems, some often anthologized and others likely to be less familiar to students of modernism. While I include a chapter on Woolf, I focus on one of her most neglected novels, *The Years*, and the other two chapters on fiction discuss two modern fiction writers whose work has been almost completely overlooked, Coleman and Warner. Both Gertrude Stein and Zora Neale Hurston are well-known, though Hurston is seldom contextualized as a modernist.

With the exception of Hurston, I have, however, chosen to focus on white, middle-class authors. If feminist modernism can be defined as a cultural and literary project of problematizing the oppositional structures of nineteenth-century domesticity, the women with the greatest stake in that project are women for whom the legacy of domestic womanhood loomed largest, women for whom that legacy was not already lived as problematic. The implication, however, is that modernist women's writing imagines this process of problematizing domestic ideology as the basis for a convergence of interests between women who are positioned differently by the structures of race and class. By turning to Hurston at the end of this book, my goal is to suggest how my argument about white modernist women writers opens up onto issues relevant to women with different relationships to domesticity. At the same time, it seems necessary to turn to a writer like Hurston in order to measure not only the way critiques of domesticity make it possible for white women to begin to articulate gender with race and class, but also to measure the gap that continues to exist at the end of the modernist period between these different groups of women, as that gap is perceived by at least one woman of color.

I begin to trace this increasing self-consciousness about the role domesticity has played in suppressing the connections between gender, race and class in the three chapters that follow this introduction. These three chapters turn to the poetry of Dickinson, H.D. and Moore. The focus in these chapters is on how these poets use the figure of 'home' to define their relation to language, through the acts of rhetorical self-fashioning by which they authorize their assumption of the position of speaking subject, in the form of first-person lyric voice.[49] While each poet reimagines a feminized domestic space in terms of a more 'permeable' boundary between public and private spheres, each poet also begins to situate that new space of femininity in relation to other figures of social difference (from Dickinson's drunken working-class man to H.D.'s blackface performers to Marianne

Moore's African elephant). The refusal to separate off the feminine domestic sphere, however, also increases the temptation to appropriate figures of racial or class difference in order to resist the assimilation of the domestic to the public, and these three chapters also trace this ambivalence in the work of each poet.

Chapters 5, 6 and 7 focus on three novels, by Coleman, Woolf and Warner. These novels emphasize women's roles as subjects of history rather than enacting women's relation to language as speaking subjects. But the novels are similarly structured by the double necessity of claiming and problematizing a positionality figured in terms of domestic space. The novels' representations of women's relation to domesticity show how an 'emphasis on sexual difference' can open up 'a critical space – a conceptual, representational, and erotic space – in which women could address themselves to women' (De Lauretis, 'Sexual Indifference' 155). In other words, the novels are interested in the ways in which the opposition between the private domestic sphere and the public world, a sexual difference according to the ideology of separate spheres, can be transformed into what Rita Felski calls a feminist counter-public sphere (164–74; it is this interest in address that links the novels to the poetry, which emphasize representations of women's speech). The emergence of differences among women in such a counter-public sphere effectively deconstructs the opposition between gendered spaces and problematizes the construction of the feminine domestic sphere as a distinct narrative standpoint.[50] All of these novels struggle with the problem of how to narrate the redefinition of domesticity by white, middle-class women without privileging gender as the basis for a narrative of liberation and thereby reproducing the tendency for domestic fiction to subsume other social differences into its framework of 'generalized oppositionality'.

The concluding chapter then sums up the argument of the book by contrasting the experimental tradition of feminist modernism, exemplified in its most extreme form by Gertrude Stein's prose poems *Tender Buttons*, with a classic African-American feminist novel, Zora Neale Hurston's *Their Eyes Were Watching God*. On the one hand, the purpose of this contrast is to demonstrate some of the connections between the white, middle-class women authors discussed in the other chapters and the writing of African-American women in the same period. On the other hand, I also read Hurston's novel as a commentary on some of the limitations of the tradition of modernist feminism that Stein epitomizes. Hurston situates herself ambivalently in both African-American and feminist modernist traditions, in part through the representation of how her black female protagonist experiences domesticity as a process of being 'classed off' from other black people and through the narrative's emphasis on travel and mobility as a structural feature of the main character's life story. Hurston's novel suggests some problems that result from the redefinition of domesticity as a performative process rather than a bounded location,[51] and in this way *Their Eyes Were Watching God* defines the ways in which white, middle-class women's self-critique of their own centrality to the definition of domestic womanhood constitutes only partial, but real, progress toward a more inclusive and internally diverse feminist politics.

2
Homelessness at Home: Placing Emily Dickinson in (Women's) History

In a letter written to her close friend and future sister-in-law Susan Gilbert, Emily Dickinson anticipates the challenges that her poetry continues to pose for contemporary feminist critics at the same time that she prefigures important themes that would reappear later in the poetry. Dated 11 June 1852, when Dickinson was 22 and about ten years before she began to produce the main body of her poetic work,[1] this letter closes with an important warning to its reader and to Dickinson's readers generally:

> Now, farewell, Susie, and Vinnie sends her love, and mother her's, and I add a kiss shyly, lest there is somebody there! Dont let them see, *will* you Susie?
>
> Emilie–
>
> Why cant *I* be a Delegate to the great Whig Convention – dont I know all about Daniel Webster, and the Tariff, and the Law? Then, Susie I could see you, during a pause in the session – but I dont like this country at all, and I shant stay here any longer! 'Delenda est' America, Massachusetts and all!
>
> open me carefully

My topic in this chapter will be the ways in which Dickinson's poetry demonstrates the inadequacy of the ideology of separate spheres to explain this woman poet's deployment of the language of domesticity. In particular, I will focus on how Dickinson's poetry redefines the relationship between public and private and authorizes the linguistic construction of a feminine poetic voice by locating that voice within this alternative textual space. The result, as I will show, is to problematize not only the relationship between public and private spaces, but also the relationship between the categories of space and time or history.[2] The passage quoted from the letter is one of the earliest articulations of the condition that Dickinson will later coin the phrase 'homeless at home' to represent.

I will begin, however, by establishing how a series of issues raised in this letter are relevant to this reading of Dickinson. First, the letter provides all the terms necessary to understand the relationship between Dickinson's situation as a woman writer and her seeming lack of interest in historical and social issues, as attested by her infamous, self-enforced seclusion within her father's home. Second, the letter's injunction to 'open me carefully' suggests that the perennial debate over Dickinson as 'private poet' can be understood in terms of our habits of reading rather than the author's individual eccentricities or any external historical determination of her life's choices.[3] Finally, in its address to another woman, this letter enacts the dynamics of identification and the importance of the intersubjective space between women in the construction of femininity. But the letter goes further, to confront dramatically the difficulties women writers face in finding a *space* where women can speak and have their speech legitimated as a historical event, a space that would represent both a social position and a textual position of enunciation. Dickinson, however, departs from the models of domestic womanhood current at the time she wrote, in her willingness to imagine new experiences of space that associate it with fluid possibilities rather than certain confinement.

I will examine how Dickinson's poetry conceptualizes this space as specifically domestic, while at the same time she resists the dominant representation of the home as a separate and subordinate feminine 'sphere'. I will argue that implicitly in this letter and more explicitly in the poems, Dickinson uses domestic space to figure the contradictions between her assignment to a bounded subject position, one that limits public recognition of women's various activities, and the resources that her gender position gives her to resist that assignment. As a site of contradiction, the home becomes a space of possibility for Dickinson, rather than an ideologically naturalized ground for feminine identity.[4] By turning first to this letter as an introduction to problems of reading Dickinson and to the demands for interpretation that she makes on her readers, we can then more fully understand the relevance of nineteenth-century representations of domestic space to Dickinson's poetry and finally see how the poems themselves resist those dominant discourses.

1 'Open me carefully'

Dickinson's letter to Susan Gilbert shows the writer becoming progressively more aware of how the act of writing creates possibilities for public discourse – that is, the possibility that her words might be read by persons other than the letter's individual addressee – while at the same time the conflation of femininity and domesticity functions to contain and privatize those possibilities. On the most obvious level, the letter's postscript voices a sense of exclusion from the public world of politics, law and finance dominated by men. But Dickinson's objection to that exclusion takes the form of claims to knowledge about 'Daniel Webster, and the Tariff, and the Law'. Those claims can be read either as the basis for Dickinson's inclusion in that public world or as being based in her exclusion from them, as claims to equality or as assertions of difference, and this ambiguity between inclusion and exclusion is the dominant motif in the passage quoted from the letter. For instance, the knowledge of law Dickinson asserts could reflect either her claim to equality with lawmaker Daniel Webster or the self-consciousness unique to those who are subjected to laws without having had the opportunity to participate in authoring them, even indirectly, through voting for the officials who do. Equally significant is the metaphorical meaning of 'tariff': as an economic obstacle to the passage of goods across national borders, tariffs can also stand for the border between domestic economies and the larger marketplace, women's work and men's, and the penalties that enforce that separation. Finally, Webster's reputation was as a public speaker, and here it is significant that Dickinson claims to 'know' Webster, not know how to emulate his accomplishments. In each case, the knowledge that Dickinson claims to possess can either undermine the boundary defining the feminine space of domesticity or reestablish that boundary as uncrossable.

Earlier in the letter, Dickinson writes that her father has been chosen to serve as a delegate to the 1852 presidential nominating convention of the Whig party. Dickinson reacts to her exclusion from this scene of official American history, the kind that gets into the history books, by imagining herself in her father's role as delegate to the national convention. A break in the postscript, marked by the second dash, interrupts this fantasy and shifts it toward a different scenario, presumably in reaction to the author's recognition of the impossibility of her being admitted to a political convention at this time, whatever her qualifications. In this second scenario, Dickinson reacts to her exclusion from the Whig convention not by fantasizing her simple inclusion in the public sphere as an equal or by retreating into a privatized domestic sphere of feminine authority. Instead, she rejects the structure of American politics as it rejected her, by calling for its destruction ('"Delenda est" America, Massachusetts and all!') and announcing her desire to go somewhere else, as if those two things depended upon one another. Dickinson's reference to not staying in 'this country' is especially startling for a poet who is notorious for seldom leaving the house, much less the country, especially since if she were literally imagining leaving the country then it would be unnecessary for America and Massachusetts to be destroyed. Destruction then seems to be a metaphor for how radical a social change Dickinson thinks it would take before women like herself could participate in running the country: America would have to cease to be, in its present form.[5] At the same time, she suggests how destabilizing it would be for domestic women to abandon their roles. In this reading, not staying 'here' becomes a metaphor for future change at home rather than a literal statement of a desire for travel; in this sense, the passage deliberately blurs the categories of space and time. Rather than destroy America, what Dickinson wants in this letter is to destroy what it means to stay in a place, be it a nation or a household. It is this cultural work of simultaneous destruction and transformation of the conventional meanings of space that aligns Dickinson with the modernist movement.

However, in the course of explaining the first scenario, in which she would merit inclusion in the Whig convention, Dickinson subverts her imagined appropriation of masculine prerogatives by inverting the usual priorities: she wants to get to the presidential convention primarily in order to spend time with another woman, not to enjoy the exercise of political power. In this sense, the convention is encoded as a feminine space of affective relations between women, a potential always present in the idea of a separate domestic sphere. Another possibility is that Dickinson can see Gilbert only during a pause in the proceedings because Gilbert, unlike Dickinson herself, is imagined to still be excluded from participation with the men, with the result that Dickinson takes on masculine qualities and prerogatives with respect to Gilbert, in an act of textual cross-dressing.

Before Dickinson creates a textual space of defiant opposition to the ideas of America and home in the postscript to the letter, she has already eroticized the typical nineteenth-century rhetoric of intimate female friendship by playfully insisting that Gilbert keep the kiss Dickinson adds to the letter a secret and thereby suggesting that the kiss is itself a kind of transgression.[6] The emphasis on secrecy also plays on the quality of privacy attributed to the domestic sphere. Both these overtones become more explicit in the final fragmentary caution, 'open me carefully', which marks a convergence of sexuality and textuality. This final phrase indicates the need for interpretation to 'open' a text whose meaning may not be exhausted by the immediate message it conveys; the phrase implies a need to go beyond the letter, the object in Susan Gilbert's hand as well as the literal denotation of its words, to reach that 'me', the figure of the woman as author, produced and mediated by her own textual practices.

Dickinson's 'open me carefully' figures reading or interpretation itself as both sexual and potentially violent or aggressive, but in either case being 'opened' seems inevitable; the possibility for control lies in how the opening will be performed, not whether it will happen. In other words, Dickinson ends her letter in the hope that Susan Gilbert will not take a potentially hostile position in relation to her text, and that reaction is figured as that of a male reader, not just because of the overtones of sexual violence, but also because the postscript imagines how the letter might be read by an intruder into an exclusively female scene, a private and feminized (private *because* feminized) textual space. The anticipation of such intrusions mean that this textual space is already 'open' and permeable, not securely bounded. In contrast to the emphatic '*I*' of the postscript, Dickinson's addition of that final 'me' points to the way that she claims autonomy by self-consciously making herself and her own subjectivity the object of her discourse. At the same time, this lapse into the status of grammatical object suggests Dickinson's insight into the nature of discursive power itself, by implying that ultimately there is no escape, no way to avoid exposure to the interpretations of others except by abdicating language entirely. Interpretive violence always remains a possibility. Nevertheless, that final phrase also leaves open the possibility that discursive appropriation can be countered by another act of interpretation, a different, more 'careful' form of inquiry. By avoiding the opposition between active reader and passive text, it is also possible to disrupt the conflation of interpretive and sexual violence, since that conflation depends upon an analogy between textual and feminine passivity. However, for my purposes here, it is also important to note that this quality of textual passivity or vulnerability derives from the assumption that a text is merely a container that has to be opened to get at the meaning inside. In other words, the analogy between interpretive and sexual violence depends upon the reductive spatialization of both textual meaning and femininity, and by suggesting an alternative mode of reading Dickinson begins to call into question the social assumptions about the spatialization of domestic womanhood that were naturalized by the ideology of separate spheres.

Now, after the publication of Dickinson's letters and poems, I believe the phrase 'open me carefully' should also be understood as a warning to male critics of her work. This final enigmatic phrase extends the plea that Gilbert protect the privacy of the women's figurative kiss ('Dont let them see'), to ask that the same protection be given to the body of the letter itself. But the injunction to 'open me carefully' also anticipates the letter's exposure to a possibly voyeuristic intruder who nevertheless forms part of the textual scene of the kiss.[7] The previous reference to not letting 'them' see encodes this intruder as a male figure who is at once excluded from the physical circuit of the women's intimacy and included, at least to the extent that his existence is acknowledged.[8] The possibility of applying the phrase 'open me carefully' to a reader other than the letter's addressee enacts the capacity of writing practices to transgress the boundaries of the public and the private, in a social context where public and private correspond to the gendered spaces of the marketplace and the home.[9] Dickinson's letter positions me by exclusion, as a male reader. But it also includes me by addressing the possibility of my gaze, if indirectly. The letter then provides an allegory of my responsibility to women's texts, while at the same time it clearly indicates that its primary concern is with relations and possible conflicts between women.[10] The letter provides a textual model that retains sexual difference but not as an absolute distinction.

Dickinson's letter therefore makes it clear that its writer does not simply identify with her gender and with other women like Gilbert. The textual space this letter creates between the two women is more complex than simple identification or group solidarity, a complexity indicated by the phrase 'open me carefully'. That phrase poses the letter as a space of potential difference between women, a potential that creates the necessity for 'careful' attention.[11] Moreover, Dickinson rejects, in the strongest possible terms, the limitations imposed on her by gender identity, especially confinement within a horizon of domesticity and a teleology of motherhood, both associated with the social and cultural hegemonies she names 'America' and 'Massachusetts'. Dickinson's poems rewrite the ideological conflation of domestic space and an inevitably maternal femininity; home comes to figure the instability or double gesture that both affirms and negates a gender identity founded on the idea that women's social location can be empirically determined and thereby taken as a given fact. Dickinson's use of domestic imagery makes possible a materialist reading of her poetry, while it also redefines oppositional practice by deconstructing the spatial logic that underlies binary gender categories. This double gesture, I will argue, underlies Dickinson's designation of women's contradictory social position as 'homelessness at home'.[12] In Dickinson's poems, female identity is an open question: 'Who occupies this House?' (*P* #892).[13]

2 'Necessary economies'[14]

The moment of Dickinson's greatest poetic production, the decade of the 1860s, marks the historical completion of the transition to industrial capitalism in the US and the installation of the ideology of separate sphere as naturalized common sense.[15] Despite the considerable critical attention Dickinson's domestic and spatial imagery has received, the dominant tendency in the criticism has been to read that imagery as purely metaphorical and divorced from the material circumstances of domestic life, in part because Dickinson's famous seclusion in the home and her choice of poetry as a genre both suggest a retreat from historical exigencies. Joanne Dobson indicates the contradiction involved in taking Dickinson's immersion in domestic life as a flight from history when she argues that Dickinson could just as easily be criticized for taking her domesticity not as an escape but 'unusually seriously', as a historical imperative, to the extreme of literalizing and living out an 'ideal' of domestic womanhood which was unrealizable for most women (Dobson 232, 237).[16] Dickinson might then be understood as testing domesticity to destruction; she both acts out the historical materiality of domestic ideology and exposes its inability to fully realize itself, to fully account for any woman's experiences.

In life, Dickinson realized the alternative outlet for historical agency that she imagined in her 1852 letter to Susan Gilbert only by remaining inside her family home and making it a site of poetic production. But the 1852 letter also suggests that Dickinson's action in situating herself within those four literal walls actually constitutes a rejection of 'home', given that the meaning of 'home' as 'one's own country' is included in the definition found in Dickinson's cherished lexicon, fellow Amherst resident Noah Webster's *American Dictionary of the English Language*. For Dickinson's declaration that America must be destroyed ('"Delenda est" America, Massachusetts and all!') only mirrors and reveals the violent effacement of the gendered body that underlies the elevation of a masculine privilege, full rights of citizenship, to the neutral universality of the pronoun 'one'. However, Dickinson's lexicon also defines home as 'the present state of existence', glossed as being 'at home in the body'.[17] To be 'at home' in a female body was to be dispossessed metaphorically, in terms of political participation, and literally, in terms of property rights and home ownership.[18] By dramatizing these contradictions, Dickinson transforms her own internal exile – her choice to remain at home – into a counter-hegemonic space that both functions in the present *and* embodies the promise of a different future: the textual space of the poems.

The success of the domestic novelists who were Dickinson's contemporaries meant that they were literally 'displaced' from a fixed location in the private home, even though they typically remained 'unable in their own minds to leave' that conventionally feminine space (Kelley 111). In contrast, I would argue, Dickinson refused to choose between the option of remaining domesticated or accepting the consequences of publication, being placed 'beyond female boundaries' in being placed beyond the home (Kelley 111). Instead, Dickinson paradoxically chose to treat the domestic sphere as a place where she could 'operate from displacement as such' (Spivak, 'Displacement' 186).[19] In the previous chapter, I argued that this third alternative emerges explicitly as a collective, feminist project in the writings of Charlotte Perkins Gilman at the end of the nineteenth century, but Dickinson explored that same possibility of a more fundamental resistance to, and transformation of, domestic ideology decades earlier, albeit in a more oblique and fragmentary manner. Dickinson can thereby also be read as resisting not only domesticity but one of the central antinomies of bourgeois thought in general. The ideology of separate spheres can in fact be understood as the model for such dualistic habits of thought, given the fact that 'in both theory and practice, domestic economy offered a social representation of the internal and the external, public and private, ordering principles derived from an acceptance of absolute property' (Fox-Genovese and Genovese 318).

The thematics of the home in Dickinson's poetry invites comparison to these 'ordering principles' of capitalist society and makes it possible to see how Dickinson's poems attempt to radically restructure the typical relations between time and space, inside and outside, public and private spaces, within modern industrial societies.[20] One way that Dickinson resists the spatialization of women's lives within the home is by associating the experience of domesticity with qualities more typically associated with the experience of temporality. Dickinson's concept of the female subject in its relation to the social order is characterized by the trope of prolepsis or anticipation, in which the future is represented as already present in some form, a trope which can be read as both spatializing linear temporal sequence and temporalizing the space of the present. For Dickinson, this trope functions critically and negatively, to delegitimate existing conditions by suggesting alternatives and raising the possibility of change within existing structures, much like her reference to metaphorically leaving the country or destroying it, in the letter I quoted at the beginning of this chapter.

For example, in *P* 1489, 'A Dimple in the Tomb / Makes that ferocious Room / A Home', a woman's condition after death is presented as an extension of the social role of homemaker that was presumed to constitute women's lives in general, in a satirical mimicry of, and implicit commentary on, the power of domestic ideology to colonize other spaces and to turn even the ferocious emptiness of the tomb into a domesticated and habitable 'Room'. The poem reproduces the domestic ideology that defines domesticity as an essential quality of femininity, so that the mere presence of a woman's body (for which 'dimple' is a synechdoche) possesses a transforming influence (in this case, on the tomb in which her body is placed). The identity of 'tomb' and 'home', however, is actually shown to derive from the private and unrepresentable nature of death, which domestic ideology attributes to 'home' by asserting its separation from the public world. In this sense, the poem seems to provide an image for what I suggested earlier was Dickinson's own autobiographical project of testing domesticity to destruction by taking it to its logical extreme, since these opening lines imply that domestic ideology can only realize its ideal of absolute privatization in death; in this reading, through an ironic reversal of terms, domestic ideology turns 'rooms' into 'tombs', life's openness to change into a death-like closure.

I would like to qualify this critique of domesticity's spatial logic, however, by locating a more utopian meaning in this poem. On another level, the image of the tomb can also be read as an image of a different future in which radical transformations in domesticity and its relation to society might be possible, a future whose difference from the present functioning of domesticity as Dickinson knew it would be as absolute as the boundary between life and death. In this sense, it is possible to read the poem as simultaneously collapsing the future into the present status quo and imagining the reality of that present state as fundamentally incomplete or partial. The poem then both acknowledges the inescapable power of domestic categories and suggests their absurdity and inappropriateness. The use of death as an image for a different future measures the negativity of Dickinson's critique; a society in which domesticity might really have a transformative power was not possible within women's lives as they were structured at that time. But as Sharon Cameron has shown in her analysis of poems structured proleptically by a speaker recounting the story of her death in the past tense, Dickinson's poems continually attempt to enter a space beyond her own (domestic) life and to define the positive value and social content of such a space (*Lyric* 112–121).[21] In the more detailed readings that follow, I will try to show how the trajectory of these attempts can be reconstructed.

3 Homelessness at home

In a poem written after the death of her mother in 1882, according to Thomas Johnson's attribution, Dickinson presents the result of her loss as an existential transience:

> Fashioning what she is,
> Fathoming what she was,
> We deem we dream–
> And that dissolves the days
> Through which existence strays
> Homeless at home.
>
> (*P* 1573)

These final, elegiac lines demonstrate a self-consciousness about the position shared by Dickinson and her mother within the home as constructed by both patriarchal and capitalist social relations. The mother's death necessitates the (unmarried) daughter's reflection on what it means for her to succeed to the role that her mother had previously played in the organization of their family's domestic economy.[22] The daughter/speaker fathoms how her own life has been fashioned into a dreamlike repetition of her mother's. The mother's literal absence in death, the difference between 'what she is' and 'what she was', only reinforces the speaker's sense of their figurative identification on the basis of their domestic roles, which dissolves the boundaries separating them. In the absence of the other woman, the differences between them collapse. The speaker therefore refers to herself in the plural as 'we', in a sudden, surprising enactment of enforced gender identification. As if the older woman were still a presence and the speaker simultaneously reduced to a ghost or a dream, they are represented as haunting or wandering like sleepwalkers within a space not their own, in a 'home' that is also a condition of homelessness or alienation. In this condition, women's 'existence' lacks any narrative structure; the 'days' dissolve into one changeless Now without temporal divisions and without any prospect of change.

Although the poem's condensed language consistently supports this critical reading of a reproduction of mothering within which the speaker remains caught, the ambiguities here seem intended to suggest an alternative to this situation. Existence may seem unreal in the mother's absence, and this unreality may reflect dominant ideologies of femininity whose pressures the daughter now bears alone for the first time, as I suggested above. But the very presentation of those ideologies as unreal, as our culture's collective dream of true womanhood, already begins to demystify them. The poem, however, does more than just indicate the negative effects on women of the dominant social construction of motherhood. It also suggests the positive effects of redefining the domestic sphere as the basis for bonds between women. Dickinson implicitly critiques the masculine gender narrative by which men achieve public identity through separation from the mother and the domestic space associated with her – that is, through becoming 'homeless'.[23] The poem suggests the possibility of dissolving the boundaries that circumscribe the speaker's life and those of women generally by dissolving the assumption that women's destiny resides essentially within domestic roles and that the only alternative to the reproduction of mothering is to take up a masculine position within the public sphere by leaving home.[24] This critique of the oppositional structures that define masculine and feminine spheres makes it possible to imagine a transgressive and critical 'straying'. The poem can be read as anticipating the 'days' when the signifying chain that associates women with the space of the home will have been 'dissolved' – that is, as anticipating a time when the ideology of separate spheres is history, not nature. In that reading, the historicizing of women's spatial identification with 'home' points to the possibility of a female 'existence' that would be characterized by both temporal transience and spatial freedom of movement, a condition conceptualized in the speaker's present as vagrancy and internal exile. The temporal experience of 'days' becomes inseparable from a spatial experience of 'straying'.

Dickinson had already affirmed a similar sense of homelessness and transience in the early 1860s, as attested by 'Forever – is composed of Nows' (*P* 624). This poem refers to a 'different time' characterized by a 'Latitude of Home' in which 'Months dissolve in further Months'. A later poem (c. 1865) elaborates the phrase 'Latitude of Home':

> Up Life's Hill with my little Bundle
> If I prove it steep –
> If a Discouragement withhold me –
> If my newest step
>
> Older feel than the Hope that prompted
> Spotless be from blame
> Heart that proposed as Heart that accepted
> Homelessness, for Home –
>
> (*P* 1010)

The final line revises the traditional marriage plot, in that the speaker gains maturity by leaving her parents' home for 'Homelessness' rather than a household of her own. The representation of marriage as a 'newest step' implies that women's initial acceptance of their role as objects of exchange in kinship relations will be compensated for by the autonomy they could exercise in the privacy of their own homes. This 'newest step' thereby only reproduces an old story of women's dependence on men. The poem is about the difficulty, the 'Discouragement', of thinking women's agency in terms external to that story. The final lines draw on marriage imagery – 'Heart that proposed' and 'Heart that accepted' – to reveal how this exchange means not freedom but alienation for women, alienation from 'home' considered as the site of connection between the daughter who speaks in the poem and her mother. According to this reading, in the final lines the speaker would be saying that neither her husband, 'Heart that proposed', nor she herself, 'Heart that accepted', are personally to blame for the sexual division of labor and the traffic in women. The self-deprecating reference to her 'little Bundle' would then mark the hierarchy of values that subordinates domestic work to productive labor in modern economic systems.

However, like the poem written after the death of Dickinson's mother, 'Up Life's Hill with my little Bundle' also envisions a transformation of gender positions, in addition to a critique of them. The combination of old and new in the steps the speaker is taking raises the possibility that the two hearts in the penultimate line do not belong to two different people, but instead both belong to the speaker at different times. The difference between old and new, the heart that proposes and the heart that accepts, would then define the difference between an oppressive present and the speaker's capacity to imagine the transformation of those oppressive conditions. This transformation would mean that women's biological capacity for childbirth, represented here as carrying a 'little Bundle', would no longer be accepted as naturally mandating women's confinement to domestic roles. The speaker would then be figuratively wedded to the idea of women's autonomy, as a personal and political goal. This political reading is also suggested by the speaker's refusal to 'blame' or disown the impulse, the 'Heart', that motivated her exchange of 'Home' for 'Homelessness'. Only if 'Homelessness' is read figuratively, as representing the gap between women's capacities and the positions that Dickinson's society made available to women, does it become clear why the speaker would accept the apparent flight from domesticity that is represented in overwhelmingly negative terms at the beginning of the poem. Though Dickinson never literally and physically traded home for homelessness, through the act of writing this poem and expropriating vagrancy as a trope for a woman's life struggle she literally assumes the position of the 'Heart that propose[s]' trading homelessness for home, while acceptance or realization of that proposal on any large scale still lies in the future of the women's movement. The poem thereby suggests that it is not necessary to transcend or devalue domesticity, only to redefine women's relationship to it from the inside. It is this possibility that I would designate with the phrase homelessness at home.

'How many times these low feet staggered' (*P* 187) emphasizes present limitations by showing how imagined alternatives to domestic confinement remain ineffective as long as they are ideologically contained within the private sphere.[25] Like 'A Dimple in the Tomb', 'How many times' makes this point by using the boundary between life and death to represent the boundary between domesticity and the public world. The first stanza of the poem describes the dead body of a woman in terms that emphasize her inaccessibility to our desire for knowledge of her everyday life. The second stanza of 'How many times' implies that death places the woman beyond the traditional home industries; her 'adamantine fingers' 'Never a thimble – more – shall wear'. The epithet 'adamantine' asks us to consider whether it refers to the rigor of a dead body or to the quality of endurance demanded of such a worker during her lifetime; thus her condition starts to prefigure a living death, buried within the space of the body described after death as a condemned, locked-up building ('soldered mouth', 'awful rivet', 'hasps of steel'). This implicit critique sets the stage for the reversal in the third stanza, when death appears as an escape from household labor:

> Buzz the dull flies – on the chamber window –
> Brave – shines the sun through the freckled pane –
> Fearless – the cobweb swings from the ceiling –
> Indolent Housewife – in Daisies – lain!

This 'escape' necessarily renders inaccessible to both speaker and reader the unrecorded history of 'how many times [her] low feet staggered', a story 'Only the soldered mouth can tell'.

In the final stanza the poem moves toward a satiric tone as this woman's death makes it possible for the speaker to assume a perspective usually encoded as masculine, a perspective external to women's work and lives. From that male perspective, even death is no excuse for a woman's departure from an identity defined by adherence to, or neglect of, her household duties. The final reference to the dead woman as an 'Indolent Housewife' points to the possibility of women redefining their lives in terms external to domesticity as presently constituted, a redefinition that can only appear negatively, as 'indolence', from a perspective that remains confined within the assumptions about both femininity and domesticity that were current at the time Dickinson was writing. That same final line also demonstrates the speaker's ability to distance herself from a male perspective even as she assumes it, just as the poem ends with a more than satiric assertion that female identity persists even outside the boundaries of domestic life. The ending risks being taken as a reassertion of domestic standards, but it also raises the possibility of women transgressing the traditional boundaries of the feminine without conforming to the paradigm of the 'sprightly gentlemen' in *P* 54, who keep the external world of both commerce and nature 'bustling' even 'When we with Daisies lie'. One mark of that nonconformity would be 'indolence' as a measure of the incommensurability between an economy based on use or need and one based on profit and exchange, the different aims of the former appearing as a failure to produce when placed in the context of the latter.[26]

Significantly, the possibility of transgression in 'How many times' is linked to an undecidability between interior and exterior spaces, figured by the flies on the window in the final stanza. Are they inside like the cobwebs and buzzing to get out, or are they outside, like the sun, trying to get in? Are they 'dull' because they are dying, trapped in the house, or is their sound dulled because the speaker hears it only through the window, from the inside? In both cases, the speaker continues to locate herself *within* the housewifely space even as she blurs its boundaries.

In a more comic mode, a similar inversion and transgression occurs in 'Alone and in a Circumstance' (*P* 1167).[27] In that poem, the speaker tells us a spider 'on my reticence' grew 'so much more at Home than I' that 'I felt myself a visitor / And hurriedly withdrew'. While the speaker's 'reticence' is presumably the result of her domestic location, that silence is figured as a 'Home' in which she is made to feel like a visitor – made aware that her relation to the home is not inevitable but contingent on social determinations. The speaker's 'withdrawal' or dispossession by the spider leads her into the public sphere, the 'street' where 'the Law' applies and legal 'redress' can be found. Her departure from the metaphorical 'Home' of her imposed silence represents a refusal to be limited to domestic work, indicated by the fact that her leaving permits the spider to fill the house with webs, like the cobwebs left by the 'Indolent Housewife' of the earlier poem. The poem's comic effect is produced by reversing this causal relation and playing with representing liberation as eviction, so that the spider's filling the house with webs is presented as the cause of the speaker's sense of estrangement from her 'Home', which in turn is presented as the precondition for her claiming the right to speak and to tell this story. The very fact that the poem confronts us with a *speaker* reveals an inherent instability in the condition of both female 'reticence' and female domesticity, an instability already structurally present even before the poem narrates how the speaker became conscious of it.

The window often figures the simultaneous possibility and impossibility of the textual inversion of public and private spaces.[28] That figure remains implicit in the opening lines of an early poem:

> At last, to be identified!
> At last, the lamps upon thy side
> The rest of life to see!
>
> (*P* 174)

The transposition of an article of household furniture (the lamps are later revealed as a trope for the dawn) into the outside world effects a reversal of inside and outside. The poem achieves this effect by alluding to the way a person inside a lighted room can only see her reflection in a window when looking out, but someone on the darkened side can see in, a trope for the masculine privilege of moving from the public world into the home while the inverse movement is denied to women. These lines imagine that the act of bringing the light of public recognition into the private sphere will allow a speaker located in the home to at least see 'the rest of life'. The question that the poem leaves unanswered is whether seeing constitutes a form of participation or merely detached observation of a 'life' the speaker cannot have.[29]

'I heard a Fly buzz – when I died' (*P* 465) offers one of the clearest examples of how Dickinson links the imagery of windows and death, in the form of a speaker who proleptically narrates her own death as a challenge to the boundaries established by the architecture of the private home. The speaker tells us in the first line that she is already dead, and the poem ends at the moment of her demise:

> There interposed a Fly –
> With Blue – uncertain stumbling Buzz –
> Between the light – and me –
> And then the Windows failed – and then
> I could not see to see –

As Sharon Cameron notes, the doubling of darkened windows and the darkness that falls over the eyes in death, echoed in repetition of the word 'see', suggests that some form of perception and consciousness or interiority might survive death, that it might somehow be possible to still see within the darkness that is death, since it remains necessary to close the eyes even within that darkness. Though the grammar of the final lines denies that possibility, the speaker's very ability to make such a statement about her own death in the past tense implies otherwise (*Lyric* 115).

However, the phrase 'the windows failed' can also be read as a failure to shut the speaker *in* any longer, an image of release from confinement, and the doubleness Cameron specifies might function as part of that release since it distinguishes one interiority (the consciousness in the body) from another (the domestic space of the home) and implies that they are not necessarily linked as content to container. The ending leaves open the question of whether this death is to be taken literally (meaning that the speaker's voice would be emanating from beyond the grave) or whether it functions as a metaphor for a possible *liberation into* the public world. This undecidability operates, then, to combine a radically critical perspective on the exclusion of women (free only in death, if then, from confinement) with the anticipation of possibilities for change (the windows fail to keep the outside world at bay).

The contradiction between death as a vehicle of change through the absolute refusal of hegemonic norms and death as a finality after which no change is possible pervades Dickinson's poetry, and the very fact that it is never resolved indicates the extent to which she escapes the ideological limitations of the period. Dickinson's poems lay bare the violence with which a social order attempts to justify or conceal the gender relations structuring a division of labor oppressive to women. The proleptic structure of this group of poems exemplifies this exposure of the violence underlying social taxonomies. Like *P* 1489, 'A Dimple in the Tomb / Makes that ferocious Room / A Home', the effect of such a poem depends on the indeterminate status of their central categories: is 'Tomb' a metaphor for 'Home' or vice-versa? Is the poem a critique of the deadening effects of domestic confinement on women, or does it measure how much domesticity must change in order to escape the oppositional structures that defined it in the nineteenth century? Such textual oscillations encode the contradictions of domesticity itself as Dickinson experienced them.

4 'I lingered with before – '

Dickinson is notorious for never literally expanding the circumference of her values and consciousness beyond the 'feminine' confines of her father's home in Amherst. Her rejection of that limitation took the form of 'homelessness at home'. Only in her poems does Dickinson follow the line of flight articulated in her 1852 letter to Susan Gilbert ('I shant stay here any longer!'). Finding herself located within a domestic perspective, in her poems she proleptically treated a future state of greater freedom as if it were already present and by doing so foregrounded the contradictions and potential for resistance already present in women's lives.

Both the value and the limits of this process of reimagining social relations by reimagining the separation of gendered spheres become apparent in poem #1645, 'The Ditch is dear to the Drunken man'. The speaker begins by asking if the ditch is not 'his Bed – / His Advocate – his Edifice?,' and goes on to both praise and gender the ditch as feminine: 'How safe his fallen Head / In her disheveled Sanctity'. Erkkila briefly cites this poem as expressing Dickinson's 'own fear of a "democratic mixing" of classes' (4) and as an example of how 'the multitude and the common man are consistently demonized' in Dickinson's poetry (14). While Erkkila reads this revulsion as a 'class act' (7) and a marker of how Dickinson writes from within racial and class privilege, it seems to me that the poem instead demonstrates Dickinson's awareness of the consequences of moving outside that privilege, the consequences of de-idealizing domestic femininity, which leaves the 'Sanctity' of true womanhood 'disheveled' alongside the drunken man. The question is whether the poem presents that situation negatively or positively. At times, Dickinson certainly seems to draw back from the proximity to people of other classes and races that seems likely to result from her own critical attitude toward the segregating spatial logic of domestic ideology, as in the anti-immigrant comments Erkkila finds in some letters and the primitivizing racial imagery that appears in some poems (9–12). In 'The ditch is dear' this reading might be supported by the characterization of homeless men as drunken, if that state is taken as a reflection of what happens when people are deprived of the civilizing moral influence located by the ideology of separate spheres in the hands of women and in the home.[30]

But a close reading of this poem would note the tone of acceptance that characterizes the poem's depiction of feminine proximity to the 'masses'. In this reading, we would note the apparently approving reference to the 'disheveled Sanctity' of the feminized space of the ditch, a space that is both public and private, a liminal or border space rather than a container defining an inside and an outside. This image of 'disheveled Sanctity' surely suggests an alternative to the domestic rhetoric of putting women on a pedestal, without entirely rejecting or devaluing the concept of domesticity and embracing a purely metaphorical form of homelessness, which would erase the historical and social differences between middle-class white women like Dickinson and homeless men of other classes and races. 'True womanhood' here has the chance to get her hands dirty in history. When the speaker ends the poem by referring to 'Honor' as being 'leagues away', Erkkila would presumably read that as a derogatory reference to the 'drunken' man's dereliction, but it seems to me equally plausible to read that final line as referring to the feminine figure in the poem, who is imagined as no longer being concerned with having her 'honor' protected by enclosure within the domestic sphere. The figure of the drunken man in Dickinson's poem points to the limits of domestic individualism as a model for feminine self-discipline.

Through these attempts at self-critique, Dickinson's poems demonstrate the prefigurative potential Sheila Rowbotham locates in feminist organizational forms, which are not utopian, she writes, because they 'seek both to consolidate existing practice and release the imagination of what could be' (*Beyond the Fragments* 146). In Dickinson's 'What shall I do when the Summer troubles' (*P* 956), the time of the speaker's discontent is also the proleptic anticipation of a time 'when the Eggs fly off in Music'. This figuration of a future condition of freedom combines the speaker's desire to leave the nest of domestic confinement with her desire to resist separation from that feminine space of connection to the mother.[31] The same characteristic gesture and the same temporal structure appear again when a speaker declares both 'I lingered with Before – ' and 'I Years had been from Home' (*P* 609).[32] Dickinson's 'Before' is also an 'after', a point in time that Dickinson herself never reached, a point when she would leave home. The word 'before' encapsulates the transformation of fixed spatial categories into relational categories more closely resembling traditional notions of temporal process. A model of the linking of moments in time replaces a model of mutually exclusive spatial boundaries. The modernist women poets who would follow Dickinson attempted to expand the alternative and unstable terrain of poetic subjectivity that Dickinson opened through her interrogation of the categories of space and time.

3
'We Are All Haunted Houses': H.D.'s (Dis)Location

A member of the original Imagiste group, formed in London under the auspices of Ezra Pound, and therefore a key participant in the first modernist movement in Anglo-American poetry, the American-born H.D. (Hilda Doolittle) is as famous for leaving home as Emily Dickinson is for staying there.[1] H.D. is also notorious for the visionary style that dominates her later writing, and her mysticism is usually understood as another, more metaphorical form of travel, in this case beyond the limits of the body itself rather than the domestic sphere.[2] For both these reasons, it is therefore typical to find H.D.'s work, especially her later long poems, characterized in terms of a desire for transcendence: H.D.'s goal is to 'open the boundaries of the self to another reality, not in order to deny its operations but in order to claim and be claimed by them', in an act of 'transcendence, a breakthrough into a new dimension' (Morris, 'Concept' 429). As this reference to a 'new dimension' suggests, H.D.'s literary project involves the development of new spatial metaphors, but these metaphors are usually understood as a clear alternative to the home she left behind, not a transformation of the domestic sphere, as I will argue.[3] Where in the previous chapter I had to show how Dickinson's poetry contained a critical perspective on the domestic life she led, in this chapter I will have to show how H.D.'s metaphors of travel can be contextualized in terms of domesticity, despite H.D.'s having left the feminine sphere behind. In the memoir she wrote about her sessions in therapy with Freud in the 1930s, H.D. reflects that 'leaving home was not always an unhappy matter' (*Tribute* 166). As the rather convoluted use of the double negative suggests, H.D. is more ambivalent toward the process of 'leaving' and more attached to forms of 'home' than her personal history and literary reputation would suggest.

It is no coincidence that this suggestion that leaving home is sometimes an unhappy process comes in the aftermath of H.D.'s encounter with Freudian psychoanalysis. These sessions led H.D. to write an unpublished autobiographical narrative entitled *The Gift* during the years 1941–43, and this narrative provides an indispensable resource for understanding the significance of domesticity for H.D. and the work her poems do to transform the spatial metaphor of 'home'. *The Gift* records H.D.'s memories of her childhood in Bethlehem, Pennsylvania toward the end of the nineteenth century, and shows H.D. applying the psychoanalytic model of recollection, repetition, and working through to the constructions of domesticity and gender that were still dominant at that early and impressionable stage of her life.[4] At the same time, this narrative shows considerable self-consciousness about the spatial metaphors for the psyche that structure Freud's thinking, and H.D.'s critical stance toward the privatization of women's lives in the domestic sphere is paralleled by her critical stance toward the privatization of the individual mind or self. As Susan Stanford Friedman points out, H.D. deliberately frames the narrative of her childhood in relation to the present moment of its composition in London during the Blitz, so that the domestic sphere of her childhood is juxtaposed not to 'the semidark cave of Freud's safe room' but instead 'a flat under constant bombardment from Nazi bombs' (*Penelope's Web* 330). This frame then enacts an oscillation not between one 'safe' and securely bounded maternal or domestic space (childhood) and another, metaphorical one (Freud's office), but instead an oscillation between this ideal of home and an actual place under continual threat of having its walls blasted open and being exposed to history. The result is to undermine any nostalgia for domestic security. Within H.D.'s text, in fact, threats to domestic stability seem indistinguishable from the promise of a cure, in a parallel to the therapeutic effects of psychoanalysis and its exposure of the workings of the unconscious. Like Dickinson, H.D. works to imagine destruction as transformation and specifically as a figure for a different experience of space.[5]

The nineteenth-century culture of domesticity is most directly invoked in *The Gift* through a scene in which H.D. remembers attending a stage performance of *Uncle Tom's Cabin* as a child and as a result learning to reinterpret domestic space as theatrical space. The implications of this redefinition of home are elaborated in the metaphor that serves as the title of the first section of *The Gift*, the 'Dark Room'. This metaphor links domesticity and the unconscious, both figured in terms of obscurity and inaccessibility.[6] Freud uses a similar photographic metaphor in *The Interpretation of Dreams*, to define what he calls 'psychical locality' as the 'point *inside* the [photographic] apparatus at which one of the preliminary stages of an image comes into being' (Freud, *Standard Edition*, Vol. 5: 536; my emphasis). 'Locality' here is synonymous with interiority and privacy, figured by H.D. as darkness. H.D.'s critique of such reductive concepts of space resembles Derrida's, who points out that Freud's technological metaphors imply that this supposedly private space of psychic interiority is already mediated by external forces, in this case photography, as a public, representational medium (*Writing and Difference* 228). The relevance of such critiques to H.D.'s redefinition of domesticity in *The Gift* is more apparent in a more recent text of Derrida's, in which he describes how Freud's technological metaphors for the 'psychical locality' of recollected images constitute the space of the mind as a '*domestic outside*' (*Archive* 19), a space that cannot be clearly divided along an inside/outside distinction.[7] Dickinson's metaphor of being 'homeless at home' imagines just such a 'domestic outside'.

The Gift, I am arguing, serves as a kind of interpretive key to the importance of domestic imagery and spatial metaphors throughout H.D.'s career, and I will prove this point by following my reading of *The Gift* with an analysis of the spatial imagery found in H.D.'s first book of Imagist poetry, *Sea Garden* (1916), especially that book's central contrast between the figure of the 'sheltered garden' and the 'sea garden'. This contrast itself enacts an 'opening' of gendered space, both domestic and subjective or psychic. As Rachel Blau DuPlessis points out, the phrase 'sea garden' itself functions like Dickinson's 'homeless at home' – that is, the phrase 'sea garden' is itself 'already oxymoronic for vast/contained or uncontained cultivation' (*H.D.* 12). In the context of H.D.'s reflections upon both the formation of gendered subjectivity and the status of the domestic sphere in *The Gift*, these poems dramatize the problem of defining a subject position for women that would be located somewhere between traditionally feminine enclosures and the masculine freedom of a public identity founded on the rejection of domestic and maternal spaces. This chapter will end with a discussion of the poem 'Pursuit', from *Sea Garden*, which I will read as allegorizing subjectivity in language and the use of spatial metaphors to represent the position of the linguistic or textual subject. In this poem, the instability of the first-person poetic voice stylistically enacts the problem of self-location on a more fundamental level than the other poems in *Sea Garden*. As the title suggests, 'Pursuit' tells a story of the speaker's desire for transcendence and her inability to ever finally achieve it.

1 'Heaven-is-my-home': redefining transcendence

As Friedman puts it, H.D.'s 'expatriatism was a spatial metaphor of interior difference, itself a geographic enactment of an inner alienation that was the precondition of her modernism' (*Penelope's Web* 218).[8] But what kind of a spatial metaphor is constituted by internal rather than external differences? This very suggestive interpretation of H.D.'s travels points to the redefinition of space itself that I want to elaborate. In the memoir of her time with Freud, H.D. redefines expatriatism as a process of being in two places at once, not a linear narrative of leaving one place for another: 'there were two countries, America and England as it happened, separated by a wide gap in consciousness and a very wide stretch of sea' (*Tribute* 32). The problematic nature of her positionality becomes apparent in this passage.[9] In this statement of the paradoxical imbrication of home and exile, H.D. defines her own version of being homeless at home, or at home in homelessness, and by doing so she problematizes the gendered connotations of these terms.

In a statement that echoes Dickinson's play with the boundary between life and death as a figure for the boundary between home and world, H.D. defines her desire for transcendence precisely as a desire for a different kind of home: 'we say ... when someone dies, he or she has *gone home*. I was looking for home, I think. But a sort of heaven-is-my-home.'[10] As H.D. notes, Freud encouraged her to reimagine both her travels and her spiritual researches as quests for a metaphorical home, by associating the process of analysis with feeling 'at home' (*Tribute* 146). More specifically, Freud encouraged H.D. to explore her bisexuality, the 'mother-layer of fixation' resulting from the fact that 'the girl did not invariably transfer her emotions to her father' (175). However, H.D. resisted the idea that she should resolve this ambivalence or pathologize the 'failed' transfer of affection.[11] H.D.'s conflation of 'home' and 'heaven' represents the same desire to have it both ways, to open the boundaries of home to what lies beyond it, that H.D. also articulates when she rewrites Freud's family romance in terms of a refusal to gender domestic space: 'the house', H.D. decided during her analysis sessions, 'in some indescribable way depends on father–mother' (*Tribute* 146). One of the things that is 'indescribable' about this idea of 'the house' is the redefinition of space as well as gender in terms other than a binary opposition between outside and inside, masculine and feminine.[12]

When H.D. goes on to conclude that 'we are all haunted houses'(146), she situates herself in the tradition established by Dickinson's poem

'One need not be a Chamber – to be Haunted – / One need not be a House' (*P* 670).[13] In the context of *Tribute to Freud*, H.D.'s statement obliquely rejects the idea that it is possible or even desirable to try to eliminate the potential for bisexuality that haunts the subject, especially 'the girl', in Freud's narrative of sexual development, and one result of using the figure of the house to represent this internal split is to challenge the gendering of home as a feminine sphere. In other words, the space of sexual and gender identity and the domestic sphere function as metaphors for one another in such formulation, since H.D.'s renarration of home in terms of the duality of mother and father also challenges the teleology of heterosexual development in Freud's thought. The trope of the subject as haunted house retains the figure of 'home' while complicating its definition as a container or barrier. At the same time, it also rejects the possibility of any final or absolute transcendence; it is home itself that continues to haunt H.D., even after she leaves. The fact that she had to leave and go 'looking for home' means that home itself was already lacking, already not itself, already its own ghost. But since H.D. defines dying as 'looking for home', the act of leaving also turns her into a kind of ghost, haunting the idea of home by searching for alternatives to it, as she does by ransacking her own memories in *The Gift*.

2 History's 'dark room'

In its focus on her childhood home, *The Gift* is H.D.'s version of the feminist project Virginia Woolf defined in *A Room of One's Own*: 'we think back through our mothers if we are women'(79). H.D.'s assertion that 'the house' depends upon 'father–mother' leads her to redefine this project as one of building 'a counter-world to that of both the fathers and the mothers' (Marcus, 'Thinking Back' 5).[14] In *The Gift*, H.D. directly thematizes the historical context for this project, the ideology of separate spheres, when she remembers her father as being 'outside this, he was outside everything, where was he?' (96). The final question points to the association of masculinity with both freedom of movement and the dispersion of subjectivity, in contrast to the association of femininity with localization. This definition of the father's being in terms of his being outside, in a space that seems to have no boundaries, to be no place in particular, is grounded in the father's occupation as an astronomer and in what H.D. refers to as his 'gift.' The narrative explicitly raises the question of why this paternal 'gift' cannot be passed down to his female children, when H.D. remembers overhearing someone say 'it's funny the children aren't gifted with such a brilliant father'; she then asks herself 'what was this gift? It took him out of doors, sometimes several different times at night after we were all in bed (96).' As the title of the narrative implies, H.D.'s goal is to somehow claim a right both to paternal and maternal gifts, 'my father's science and my mother's art' (*Tribute* 145–6), but to do so requires overcoming the separation of inside and outside that defines their difference.[15] H.D. also remembers an economics lecture that was structured by the ideology of separate spheres; she is told that if her father 'did not make money, where would you be, you wouldn't have a home' (104). But the lesson H.D. takes from this lecture is to ask herself what would happen if she took the rhetorical question literally: where would she be, if she rejected the distinction between male economic productivity and the feminine security of home? H.D.'s goal is to be able to treat her location as a question, not a destiny.

On one level, then, the trope of the 'dark room' refers to being walled off from this 'outside'. The darkness of the room resides in its incommunicability, the way it remains wrapped up in itself. H.D. plays with the pun on the photographer's dark room in at least two ways. First, she uses the photographic process in the same way that Freud does, as a metaphor for the process of psychic internalization. On the way to the theatre to see a production of Stowe's *Uncle Tom's Cabin*, H.D. contrasts herself to a group of rowdy 'university boys', who seem not to know how 'to see things in themselves, and then to see them as if they were a picture' (*Gift* 46). The suggestion here is that this process of representing things to yourself, implicitly compared to developing a photographic image, has the function of producing subjective interiority.

The narrative makes this point more explicit when it self-reflexively extends its photographic metaphors to the operations of memory that produce this autobiographical text itself. H.D. refers to how 'time' and 'the curious chemical constituents of biological or psychic thought-processes' combine 'to develop single photographs or to develop long strips of continuous photographs, stored in the dark-room of memory' (49–50). This process of development itself constitutes the mind as a room, as H.D. indicates when she describes how it allows her 'to watch people enter a room, leave a room, to watch, not only those people enter and leave a room, but to watch the child watching them' (50).[16] Note the way in which this room is defined by people's ability to enter and leave it, as well as the way in which there is a play between container and contained in this definition of psychic space. The 'room' referred to here is a space that (partially) contains these people (or

H.D.'s memories of them), but it is also a space that is contained within the theatre of her mind, so that this is a space that is both internal and external at once. It is that doubling and destabilizing of traditional spatial boundaries that permits 'people' to cross into and out of the room with such ease.[17] The shift from photographic to cinematic tropes, in the reference to memories as 'long strips of continuous photographs' is also significant for its introduction of temporal change into the 'dark room'.[18] The same point is made in a later passage in which H.D. returns to this metaphor of the 'dark-room of memory.' This passage describes how memories become unexpectedly associated by comparing such associative processes to the effects of a wind blowing through a door that has been 'left open' (84), using imagery reminiscent of Virginia Woolf's essay on 'Modern Fiction' (see chapter 1 above). The permeability of the boundaries of this 'room' leave it metaphorically 'open' to change. H.D. goes on to add 'Shut the door and you have a neat flat picture. Leave all the doors open and you are almost out-of-doors, almost within the un-walled province of the fourth-dimensional' (84).

The second way H.D. uses the photographic metaphor, therefore, is to pun on the idea of 'development' as the production of images and as openness to change. She suggests that this darkness is merely a necessary stage in a 'developing' process rather than a self-enclosed end in itself.[19] The darkness of the 'dark room' can then be read as a way of insisting on the indeterminacy and incompletion of interior, domestic spaces rather than their boundedness. This reading can be taken a step further if we take this indeterminacy as a mark of the multiple and sometimes contradictory stories or histories located within the social space of home, on the model of the irreducibly multiple meanings Freud attributed to dream images. One implication of this reading is that H.D. is not so much interested in eliminating the darkness as redefining its meaning. As the disapproving reference to the rowdy university boys suggests, while being trapped in the dark room is a problem, it is equally problematic to be purely 'outside', to lack the ability to 'see things in [ourselves]'. As H.D. puts it, her goal is to affirm that 'the darkness ... was my own darkness' (182), but she uses the photographic imagery to transform the meanings conventionally associated with darkness and with the interiorized spaces figured by domestic imagery in her text.[20]

The transformation of domesticity is made explicit in the description of H.D.'s reactions to seeing a theatrical version of *Uncle Tom's Cabin*, after which 'everything' seems 'different' (*Gift* 46). The story of this event is keyed to H.D.'s first memory of the crossing of gender boundaries, when as a child she learned that her mother taught music to an uncle rather than to the other female children in the family; the child's response is to ask 'can ladies be just the same as men?' (43). The child is then reminded of the existence of Louisa Mae Alcott and Harriet Beecher Stowe's books, as well as the fact that the child has seen *Uncle Tom's Cabin* performed. The key lesson H.D. takes from this experience is that 'If you take down one side of a wall, you have a stage. It would be like the doll house that only had three walls, and you could arrange the room without any trouble' (48). She also emphasizes this transposition of the architecture of the theatrical proscenium onto the domestic sphere by claiming that 'it', the experience of learning to view space theatrically, 'didn't stop there, because when we got home everything was like that' (48). This reading of domesticity reveals domesticity as both a social construction and as a site of significant social action.[21] After returning from the theater, it is not only her own home that is reimagined without its 'fourth wall'. The narrator describes how as a child she 'could see how the room had only three sides ... . You could think about it in bed. Everyone's house would be open on one side and you would see it all going on' (49). H.D. is then able to think of the home in the same way that she thinks of the theater: 'it was history' (47).

3 'Races – nurtured in the dark': the problem of race and gender

This insight into the possibility of transforming and opening domestic space and gendered subjectivity to alternative configurations might have been generated by any theatrical performance. I turn now to the significance of the specific performance H.D. remembers, a theatrical adaptation of Stowe's *Uncle Tom's Cabin*.[22] There is more to it than just the fact that the nineteenth-century American novel that spawned this theatrical franchise is the paradigmatic literary expression of the project of expanding woman's sphere into a reformist project of enlarged or social housekeeping. H.D.'s image of removing the home's fourth wall departs from this reformist model; it does not simply release women's supposed moral influence into society at large, but also opens the home itself to critical scrutiny. More importantly, the racial themes in *Uncle Tom's Cabin* constitute a test of the extent to which H.D. is able to elaborate the implications of her critique of domesticity, especially its implicit self-critique of white, middle-class women's relative privilege and the suggestion that they need to establish coalitions with women whose lives could not be so easily imagined within a domestic framework. In this context, H.D.'s trope of the '*dark* room' also evokes the conventional analogy between race and gender that Sanchez-Eppler identifies in the nineteenth-century suffrage movement, which appropriated slavery as a metaphor for the negative consequences of middle-class women's compulsory domesticity. Emily Dickinson seems to reproduce this analogy uncritically, in poems like 'Races – nurtured in the Dark' (*P* 581), and H.D.'s claim to define herself in terms of a metaphorical 'darkness' might be read in much the same way (*Gift* 182).[23] Does H.D. avoid this trap?

Unlike Dickinson, H.D. did develop direct collaborative relationships with African-American writers and artists in the late 1920s and 30s, such as Paul Robeson, relationships that Friedman argues led H.D. to reconceptualize her expatriatism as a kind of 'diaspora', moving her away from the modernist tendency to celebrate exile as the basis of an artistic style and toward a more political understanding of her situation (*Penelope's Web* 218). Friedman sees this move as evidence of H.D's 'identification with the different and dispersed' (Friedman, 'Modernism' 116).[24] There is no doubt H.D. felt this identification, but how does that process work? To what extent does H.D. turn to racial difference as a way to give political meaning to middle-class women's consignment to the domestic sphere, rather than conceptualizing her own racial privilege as a contradiction of her gender subordination and therefore as a form of bilocation for which she has to assume responsibility? Does identification with persons of another race as H.D. deploys it help to break down the universalizing of domesticity as model for all women's experience, or does it merely turn racial difference into an image in her own 'dark room', something she sees inside herself as if it 'were a picture?' (*Gift* 46).

In *The Gift*, these questions emerge most urgently at two moments when H.D. presents herself as identifying with black characters from the performance of *Uncle Tom's Cabin*. The first example occurs during the public procession of actors, in character, that precedes the performance itself. The procession includes a chain gang, about which H.D. remembers being reassured 'it's only a parade' and that 'they are as free as you are'. The child then goes on to reflect that 'the darkies tied together were as free as I was' because her father and uncle fought in the Civil War (44). The use of this particular racial epithet seems intended to extend the metaphor of the dark room, in a deliberate semantic echo. The emphasis on how the members of the chain gang are 'tied together' even suggests the typical language used to describe domesticity as 'the bonds of womanhood' (Cott), in a version of the appropriation of abolitionist rhetoric within the suffrage movement that Sanchez-Eppler analyzes. However, the reiteration of the statement about the 'darkies' being as free as the young H.D. herself opens a number of possible ironies. On the most obvious level, H.D. is being reminded that slavery is history, not present reality, despite the fact that chain gangs hardly disappeared after the Civil War. In this sense, her repetition of the statement is a reminder to herself that the 'darkies' are only actors in a play, and the people depicting them are not actually in a chain gang. From that insight, it is possible to move to a critical perspective on the stereotype of the 'darkie' itself as a made thing rather than a realistic representation, just as the play leaves H.D. with an insight into the fictional nature of domestic ideology. This reading is supported by the possibility that H.D.'s comment on the 'darkies' freedom might be literally true, if the chain gang actually consists of white people in blackface, as was often the case in these 'Tom shows'. In this case, the repetition of this statement about their freedom might indicate some self-consciousness about white appropriations of blackness and the recognition that actual black people are not as free as she is – that is, these actors are free because they are actually white like her. However, it is also possible that the spectacle of white actors performing blackness might inspire H.D. precisely to use images of the 'dark' to represent the situation of women, by showing her that blackness is appropriable by white people.

The key question is the extent to which H.D.'s acts of identification erase racial difference rather than lead to self-critique and the de-idealization or relativizing of domestic womanhood. This question appears again when H.D. tells us that the other children tended to identify with one of the more stereotypical African-American characters, Topsy, while H.D. was more interested in Little Eva, a white character, and Eliza, a black character (45). H.D. compares Little Eva to 'the princess in our fairy book who had long gold hair', so that she embodies the idealized image of white femininity promoted by domestic ideology (47). One key attribute of a princess is that she lives in a castle, after all, and H.D. seems to emphasize the princess's containment 'in' a book. But H.D. is equally fascinated by the famous scene in which Eliza is pursued by dogs while carrying her baby over the ice, even though H.D. emphasizes her awareness of the fictive nature of the scene, especially the lack of realism in the baby and the dogs, whom she sees as both 'terrible' and 'really very good dogs'.[25] The same question emerges here as in H.D.'s perception of the chain gang as both bound and free. Does the scene dramatize H.D.'s willingness to accept patently absurd depictions of African-Americans as 'true', in good minstrel show fashion, or her willingness to acknowledge real difference where others see only inferiority?[26]

Similarly, is H.D., either as a child or as an adult remembering these events, able to perceive any real difference between Little Eva and Eliza? Is Eliza no more than another potential blond princess in black-face, able to achieve 'freedom' only by assimilating to a white, middle-class mode of domestic femininity? Does Eliza's flight across the ice function as a metaphor for H.D.'s own desire to escape a domestic destiny? Or does Eliza here represent precisely the kind of historical experience that was never included under the heading of domestic womanhood, the kind of difference between H.D. and other women that can only be recognized when the identification of femininity and domesticity is rejected, when the boundaries of the house are opened so that 'you would see it all going on' (*Gift* 49)? Are the irreducibly different historical experiences of women of different classes and races among the things this critique of the ideology of separate spheres would allow us to see? It seems to me that H.D., while she may not be able to successfully avoid all the dangers of cross-racial identification, at least succeeds in staging these kinds of questions in her text, by representing a kind of primal scene of cross-racial identification as one component of the alternative spatial metaphors she develops in her vision of the private home opened to its own theatrical possibilities.

4 *Sea Garden*: 'Where would you be?'

One of the dominant thematic concerns in H.D.'s first book of poetry, *Sea Garden*, is the problem her speakers have in defining the place where they are standing as they speak. They often resemble the figure of Hermes: 'Dubious, / facing three ways' in a 'garden' between sea and shore (38).[27] H.D.'s speakers are typically located at the intersection of at least 'two mutually exclusive worlds', but they refuse to treat those spaces as mutually exclusive and instead try to exist in two places at once (Pondrom 88). One critical response has been to interpret this precarious perspective as a metaphor for the modernist sense of crisis and estrangement.[28] But this collection of poems is structured by the contrast between two conceptions of space, figured by the uncertain position of the 'sea garden' and the oppressive and confining security of the 'sheltered garden', which has all the qualities of the nineteenth-century domestic ideal. As a conflictual boundary space holding together 'two mutually exclusive worlds', the sea garden is defined in opposition to the homogeneity of the 'sheltered garden'.[29] In other words, H.D. sets up an opposition between a space defined by clear oppositions such as inside/outside, public/private, and a space that is not defined dualistically. The sea garden represents a space of indeterminacy where gender identity remains at issue, but cannot be easily mapped and taken for granted.

In the poem entitled 'Sheltered Garden', the speaker declares her dissatisfaction with her location within an enclosed space where every road is a dead end (*Collected Poems* 19). Her first words are 'I have had enough. / I gasp for breath'. This enclosure gives the speaker no room to breathe and implicitly inhibits speech as well. The lines suggest how women are essentially identified with the domestic space that circumscribes their lives and leaves them no room to operate outside of the canons of domesticity and true womanhood. But the same lines also imply that writing can create a textual space in which the speaker can express her dissatisfaction, when the possibility of speaking in an everyday social setting has been foreclosed. The act of writing the poem provides an alternative to the situation described in it, at least to the extent that this situation involves being unable to speak. H.D. here implies that the creation of a new position of enunciation is the precondition for her emergence as a poet and her claims to a public identity.

'Sheltered Garden' indirectly invokes forms of domestic labor associated with women, through images of food. The speaker asks 'Have you seen fruit under cover / that wanted light – / pears wadded in cloth, / protected from the frost, / melons, almost ripe, / smothered in straw? // Why not let the pears cling to the empty branch?' (20). These images recall the history of feminist critiques of the gendering of 'refinement', beginning at least with Mary Wollstonecraft: 'I wish to persuade women to endeavour to acquire strength, both of mind and body, and to convince them that the soft phrases, susceptibility of heart, delicacy of sentiment, and refinement of taste, are almost synonymous with epithets of weakness' (*Vindication* 9). It is in this sense that H.D.'s imagery possesses a political unconscious and that 'the store of images' she refers to as 'the common property of the whole race' appears in *Sea Garden* (*Gift* 50). At the same time, this implication of rhetoric like Wollstonecraft's in H.D.'s Imagist poems offers a different take on Pound's famous call for a 'harder' Imagist poetry against the sentimentalism of the nineteenth-century, as he saw it (*Literary Essays* 12).

In an image that H.D. would return to in *The Gift*, this 'sheltered' space is excluded from the light of day. However, these lines also challenge the conventional representation of the home as a haven in a heartless world, a representation that poses women as being in need of protection. While this space is 'sheltered' from the wind that would 'leave half-trees, torn, twisted, / but showing the fight was valiant', the majority of the poems in *Sea Garden* attempt to answer a question that might initially seem only rhetorical: 'Why not let the pears cling to the empty branch?' The transition from 'sheltered garden' to 'sea garden' attempts to define a feminine space which would be a site of struggle, struggles against women's subordination to male power but also struggles to determine or redefine meaning.

This struggle to redefine the meaning of conventional imagery emerges in the final lines of 'Sheltered Garden', which define the project of the whole book: 'to find a new beauty / in some terrible / wind-tortured place' (21). This statement has the ring of a typical modernist manifesto, but the gendered nature of H.D.'s modernism appears in two forms. First, the struggle 'to find a new beauty' is also a struggle to find a new 'place' from which to speak, a particular necessity for women writers due to the association of femininity with maternal or domestic spaces. Second, the poem's desire 'to find a new beauty' also implies H.D.'s desire to distance herself from the stereotype of the poetess, with all its connotations of sentimentality and cliché.[30]

The poem in *Sea Garden* entitled 'The Gift' is addressed to a woman who owns a 'sheltered garden' (*Collected Poems* 17). The speaker comments that 'The house, too, was like this, / over painted, over lovely – / The world is like this'. The speaker here critiques traditional domestic labor as a model for women's relation to the world in general; she refuses to accept the extension of 'woman's sphere' and instead points to the possibility of transgressing the boundaries of the domestic by criticizing the assumption that 'house' and 'world' could or should be identical. In addition, the deliberately and repeatedly vague word 'this' in these lines can be read as referring not only to the garden to which both 'house' and 'world' are compared, but also to the language that is used to describe the scene. The poem implicitly rejects both the domestic themes and the conventional diction associated with the poetess stereotype. H.D.'s concern to avoid that label provides one explanation for the absence of direct gender references, including pronouns, in *Sea Garden*.[31] This indirection and the poems' focus on the first-person voice, devoid of explicit gender markings, are part of H.D.'s attempt to establish an area of indeterminacy within the oppositional structure of gender identity that is represented in the poems in terms of implicitly gendered spaces. However, this apparent escape from or transcendence of conventional gender identity does not prevent H.D. from addressing, if only indirectly, the issue of her embodiment as a woman.

The poem 'Garden' provides a transition between confinement within a 'sheltered garden' and the imagined freedom of the 'sea garden'. This poem thematizes the struggle to redefine conventional poetic imagery, specifically the rose. This struggle is directly tied to the speaker's struggle to redefine her own gender position and her relation to language. The speaker apostrophizes the rose that she describes as 'cut in rock': 'If I could break you / I could break a tree. / If I could stir / I could break a tree – / I could break you' (24–5). The 'break' here is a break with inherited systems of meaning that present preestablished signifying relationships as if they were inscribed in stone. H.D.'s project is to activate what Jakobson describes as the potential of poetry in general: to reveal that 'the identity between sign and object' is never complete and that it is therefore possible to intervene in the determination of meaning ('What is Poetry' 175). That 'identity between sign and object', between the rose and our culturally determined expectations of what it signifies, is the 'rock' the speaker wishes to break.

However, these lines also present this intervention in language as the precondition for the speaker's gaining the freedom of movement, the ability to 'stir', that characterizes the 'sea garden'. The 'tree' that the speaker imagines she could break if she could break the rose figures the speaker's objectification by male discourses and male desire, and she is unable to stir because she is identified with the position of object for men that the tree represents. This objectification takes two forms. First, Ezra Pound's early nickname for H.D. was 'Dryad', and this conflation of woman and tree positioned H.D. as the romantic object about or to whom Pound wrote, rather than as the agent of her own writing. In H.D.'s fictional autobiography *HERmione*, the character who represents H.D. expresses a sense of alienation by accepting this objectification: 'I am in the word TREE. I am TREE exactly' (73). It was also Pound who gave Hilda Doolittle her writing signature of H.D., when he attached those initials to H.D.'s first published poems and sent them to Harriet Monroe. The desire to break the tree in 'Garden' suggests H.D.'s sense of the precarious status of her claims to subjectivity within language and the continuing possibility of her appropriation by male discourses, like Pound's on modernism.[32]

The second type of objectification represented by the image of the tree involves the cultural assumption that women's capacity for childbirth, for natural, biological creativity, is incompatible with more figurative forms of artistic or literary creativity. This problem also emerges in other poems that use the image of the fruit tree, like 'Orchard'.[33] In both cases, the tree implies the speaker's sense that her identity for others is conflated with her body, as object of male desire. 'Garden' links this reduction to the body with women's enclosure within the 'sheltered garden' of domestic identity, as two linked forms of immanence. But the poem also implies that the female speaker's transcendence of this condition of objectification and her formulation of an alternative to it depends upon introducing an element of indeterminacy into the inherited structure of linguistic conventions and the positions that are established there. This linguistic process of redefinition is the goal of many of the poems that describe the 'sea garden'. H.D. especially reworks the standard connotations of flowers by locating them on the borderline between sea and shore where they are exposed to the unpredictable effects of the elements rather than being contained with a 'sheltered garden'.

I have already suggested that her poem 'Hermes of the Ways' exemplifies the 'dubious' and conflicted place in which H.D. tries to locate her poetic voice in *Sea Garden*. This poem also implies that the transcendence of women's objectification results in a redefinition of gender identities and the gendered spaces in which those identities are grounded. In 'Hermes of the Ways', H.D. resists both enclosure within the domesticated space of the 'sheltered garden' and the appropriation of a masculine position of privilege and freedom.[34] The first section of the poem describes Hermes waiting, 'welcoming wayfarers', and standing on the borderline where 'sea-grass tangles with / shore-grass' (*Collected Poems* 37–39). The poem ends with the speaker claiming to be one of the wayfarers for whom Hermes waits. But she denies that the shadow of the twisted tree branches is 'the shadow of the mast head' or 'of the torn sails'. The speaker defines herself in contrast to the male sailor who seeks refuge on shore, as the poem alludes to Odysseus's voyages and his experience of being a castaway.[35] But the allusion also implies that the speaker is rejecting the role of Penelope, as well. The figure of Hermes provides an alternative to the role of the woman who waits to welcome the (male) traveler; Hermes both waits and travels, and it is in this sense that Hermes is a borderline figure, with one foot in each traditional gender role, as figured by the place where he stands on both the 'sea-grass' and the 'shore-grass'. The speaker of H.D.'s poems in *Sea Garden* attempts to occupy this same position. H.D. rejects the opposition between male power to travel and the spatialization of femininity within the home by retaining the 'garden' as a female space but opening it to the wind and sea.

5 'Pursuit': the (dis)location of H.D.'s poetic voice

The poem 'Pursuit' enacts the double gesture that characterizes *Sea Garden* as a whole, of defining a position of subjectivity without allowing that position to become fixed within an oppositional framework for gender identity. The result is the redefinition of positionality itself, as imaged by the 'sea garden'.[36] The process of the speaker's 'pursuit' in this poem represents this refusal of the static, spatialized position that is imaged by the 'sheltered garden'. 'Pursuit' is an account of how the speaker follows the traces left in the landscape by an unseen and unnamed person that the poem addresses as 'you':

> A patch of flowering grass,
> low, trailing –
> you brushed this:
> the green stems show yellow-green
> where you lifted – turned the earth-side
> to the light:
> this and a dead leaf-spine,
> split across,
> show where you passed (11).

The speaker's movement through space in pursuit of this other provides another version of the unstable or 'dubious' position of the speakers in the other poems of *Sea Garden*.[37] In Irigaray's words, the poem attempts to suggest how women can reclaim their identities from the stories told by men and still avoid essentialist claims to 'a territory of our own' that would only recontain and defuse the subversive implications of women's emergence as historical agents (*This Sex* 212).

The unstable position of the speaker in 'Pursuit' is also thematized temporally in terms of belatedness and loss. At the end of the poem, it turns out that the language of the poem has not just been generated by the speaker's 'pursuit' of a second person who is absent because always only a few steps ahead of her. Instead, she has been in pursuit of a transcendent figure, whose absence is less easily remedied. At the end of the poem, the person addressed has disappeared: 'some wood-daemon / has lightened your steps. / I can find no trace of you / in the larch-cones and the underbrush (12). In fact, I would argue that the speaker here is in pursuit of transcendence itself, rather than, or in addition to, a specific person capable of transcendence. Like H.D.'s desire for a 'home' that would be 'a sort of heaven-is-my-home', the desire for transcendence in 'Pursuit' is always denied and therefore is experienced in this world as loss. In 'Pursuit', the speaker remains embodied in the world, 'in the larch-cones and the underbrush'. However, her desire for transcendence, represented through mythological allusions like the 'wood-daemon', takes her outside the boundaries of the 'sheltered garden' of traditional feminine identity and her objectification as an object of male desire. The desire for a transcendence that can never be fully or finally realized in this life results in the redefinition of the speaker's subjectivity as an endless process of 'pursuit' rather than a bounded position.

This reading of how 'Pursuit' addresses the issues of both female embodiment and the transcendence of conventionally feminine gender identity is reinforced by the way the poem rewrites the conventions of romantic love. The speaker finds herself placed in the traditionally male role of active pursuer. In fact, the poem alludes to mythological stories like Apollo's pursuit of Daphne, when the speaker imagines the object of her search gasping '*wood-daemons grant life – / give life – I am almost lost*' just before she describes that person's disappearance.[38] However, as DuPlessis points out, the disappearance of the second person effectively 'prevents speaking or narrating being a form of possession of the "you"' by the female speaker, in resistance to traditionally masculine 'erotic and cultural powers to define stories of desire and desire for story' (DuPlessis, *H.D.* 13, 15). The poem departs from the masculine courtly love tradition and its convention of the female beloved whose absence generates the poet's language, but only to the extent that 'Pursuit' focuses on the instability of the speaker's position as a result of the second person's absence and not on the power the speaker gains over the beloved as a result of the beloved's exclusion from the poem's discourse. 'Pursuit' does not simply reverse the courtly love roles, so that H.D. takes over the male role and utilizes that 'erotic and cultural power' to address the beloved as other. In this poem, when the other disappears, so does the stability of the speaker's position. The speaker is empowered as subject, but subjectivity is not defined here in terms of power over an other against whom the subject can define herself.

H.D.'s use of apostrophe in 'Pursuit' foregrounds the problem of establishing subjectivity in language and assuming the position of the 'I'. 'Pursuit' dramatizes the failure of poetic voice, a failure that generates an endless 'pursuit'. But since 'pursuit' also means vocation or occupation, the poem suggests that H.D.'s poetics is founded on just such a failure of voice, imaged as a failure of 'home' to define a clearly bounded space in which a subject could be located. This 'failure' points to a redefinition of gendered subjectivity outside the oppositional frameworks of male and female, transcendence and embodiment, self and other, 'I' and 'you'. In the other poems of *Sea Garden*, these oppositions are shown to be grounded in spatial metaphors that distinguish insides and outsides and organize those spaces into separate gendered spheres, an ideological formation that H.D. depicts in *The Gift*. As a result of H.D.'s attempt to establish a position within language for herself as a woman that would not function as a mechanism of exclusion, her writing shows how these oppositional structures and spatial metaphors are constitutively 'haunted' by the outside or the other that they attempt to exclude in the formation of gendered identity.

4

'A Place for the Genuine': Marianne Moore's 'Poetry'

Biographically, Marianne Moore's relation to domesticity resembles Emily Dickinson's more than H.D.'s, Moore's friend and modernist contemporary.[1] Although Moore certainly established a prominent public identity as a writer and enjoyed a high-profile position as editor of *The Dial* from 1925–29, like Dickinson she never married and chose instead to live at home with her mother until her mother died in 1947. In fact, in 1933, Moore published a review of the 1931 edition of Dickinson's letters, in which Moore specifically singles out Dickinson's phrase 'homeless at home' for particular attention, in one of the more direct examples of the centrality of this trope to modernist women's writing. When we read those poems of Dickinson's in which a speaker proleptically narrates her own death as having already occurred, Moore argues, we are confronted with 'the sudden experience of unvaluable leisure by which death is able to make one "homeless at home"' (*Collected Prose* 291). Moore cites these poems as examples of how Dickinson's 'process of "interiorization" ... was not a dark one' (291). Like H.D., Moore seems here to use darkness as a metaphor for enclosure, and Moore's language suggests her understanding of the analogy that the rhetoric of domestic ideology established between the private space of the home and the interiority of feminine subjectivity. My goal in this chapter will be to establish the centrality of this remarkable reading of Dickinson to Moore's own poetic practice.

An earlier review of H.D.'s book *Hymen* (1921) shows how Moore herself saw more affinity between H.D. and Dickinson than their biographical circumstances might suggest. In this review, Moore reads H.D.'s poetry in terms of how H.D. has to negotiate the problem of defining herself as a woman poet without reproducing assumptions about gender difference that are grounded in the ideology of separate spheres. In a comment that alludes to the famous imagist lyrics of H.D.'s first book, *Sea Garden* (1916), Moore writes that 'the tendency to match one's intellectual and emotional vigor with the violence of nature, give[s] a martial, an apparently masculine tone to such writing as H.D.'s'. Moore goes on to reflect on the gendered habits of reading that are dramatized by such an ascription of 'apparent' masculinity, which Moore herself seems unable to avoid projecting onto H.D.'s work.[2] Moore argues that this gendered reading derives from the way that 'women are regarded as belonging necessarily to either of two classes – that of the intellectual free-lance or that of the eternally sleeping beauty, effortless yet effective in *the indestructible limestone keep of domesticity*. Woman tends unconsciously to be the aesthetic norm of *intellectual home life*' (*Collected Prose* 82; my emphasis). These two 'classes' represent traditionally masculine and feminine qualities. The 'intellectual free-lance' implies both rationality and freedom from any particular destiny – that is, the privilege of transcendence. In contrast, the 'eternally sleeping beauty' figures women's confinement within embodied particularity as well as the 'limestone keep of domesticity'. Moore suggests that both these options must be resisted by women writers.

Despite her focus on women as public intellectuals, Moore here analyzes the lingering effects of the ideology of separate gender spheres even after the historical breakdown of that separation and the emergence of significant numbers of women within the professional classes. The phrase 'aesthetic norm of intellectual home life' can also be read as Moore's characteristically idiosyncratic synonym for the stereotype of the poetess, whose 'sentimental' writing was expected to reproduce the moral values preserved within the home but absent from the competitive marketplace.[3] Moore sees H.D. as negotiating the double necessity of resisting placement within either a traditional feminine position of domesticity and immanence or a traditional masculine position of universality and transcendence, 'the intellectual free-lance'. Moore's final comment is that in H.D.'s work 'we have heroics which do not confuse transcendence with domination'. Moore thereby points to the possibility of redefining the oppositional categories of masculine and feminine, transcendence and immanence, self and other, categories that are hierarchically organized into structures of dominance.

Returning to the 1933 review of Dickinson's letters, we can now see that Moore reads the relationship between Dickinson's writing and her life in terms of the same double necessity that Moore identified in H.D.'s poems. Moore argues that Dickinson's poetry was 'enhanced by its separateness,' but at the same time Dickinson 'was not a recluse, nor was her work, in her thought of it, something eternally sealed' (291). In this context, the comment that Dickinson's 'process of "interiorization" ... was not a dark one' recalls H.D.'s redefinition of the 'dark room' of domesticity. Moore's 'Poetry' uses the spatial metaphor of 'a place for the genuine' to figure women poets' claims to authority over language, while at the same time she calls into question the construction of subjectivity through mechanisms of exclusion that depend on distinctions between inside and outside, 'I' and 'you', self and other, as H.D. did in her 'Pursuit', through images of travel and movement rather than placement.[4]

1 'A place for the genuine'

In its various versions, the poem 'Poetry' (1919) has long been famous as a statement of Moore's ambivalent relation to lyric poetry both as a set of generic conventions and as a cultural institution. Many critics have responded to the challenge posed by Moore's title and have read the poem as a paradigm for her modernist poetics, but 'Poetry' also can be read as an example of the implicitly gendered nature of modernist subject formation.[5] In a self-conscious performance of the generic conventions of lyric, 'Poetry's' first word is the first-person pronoun 'I', framed and set off from the rest of the sentence by the comma that immediately follows it: 'I, too, dislike it'. But the second word of the poem, 'I, *too*', begins to indirectly define the character of the 'I' collectively, in affiliation with others who are also assumed to dislike poetry and to share the attitude of 'perfect contempt' for it. Since these others are not specified, the poem is able to suggest the speaker's claims to participation in several forms of public identity. Moore's speaker implicitly defines herself as a modernist poet, as a populist opposed to hierarchies of cultural value, and finally she adopts a set of utilitarian values that would previously have been associated with masculinity and the public sphere, especially in the context of American history and literature.[6] The poem does not just stage a typical modernist moment of decreation or defamiliarization that dismisses previous poetic conventions in order to 'make it new'; in addition, the poem also implies that such an attitude constitutes a generic, and possibly gendered, subject position and so by definition cannot be completely 'new' or *sui generis*.

The poem therefore situates its implicit claims to a capacity for modernist self-invention in relation to the speaker's awareness that the identity she claims is already situated from the very moment that she begins to speak; this 'I' comes to us already classified in subjection to a variety of preexisting discursive taxonomies or structures of difference. With the phrase 'I, too', Moore's 'Poetry' begins by implicitly acknowledging the power of such structures to appropriate or 'place' the speaking subject. Only then does the poem go on to locate a capacity for resistance to this power, by allowing that 'a place for the genuine' can be found or made within poetry, if only when poetry is read with 'perfect contempt':[7] 'Reading it, however, with a perfect contempt for it, one discovers in / it, after all, a place for the genuine.' Of course, the final three-line version of the poem still leaves open the question of what 'the genuine' refers to; the poem deliberately refrains from prescribing criteria for inclusion within the boundaries of 'the genuine'. Even in the longer versions, complete with apparent examples, the category of 'the genuine' is shown to be inherently unstable, without any predetermined or essential content.

Preserved in Moore's note, the longer version of 'Poetry' goes on to represent the direct experience of an apparently ungendered body as 'genuine': 'Hands that can grasp, eyes / that can dilate, hair that can rise / if it must, these things are important not because a // high-sounding interpretation can be put upon them but because they are / useful'. But a referent for 'the genuine' is not as easily established as the syntax of the poem would suggest. Instead, Moore's examples quickly become just more 'derivative' representations of the genuine, so quickly that it becomes difficult to distinguish the original from the derivative: 'When they become so derivative as to become unintelligible, / the same thing may be said for all of us, that we / do not admire what / we cannot understand'. Similarly, the colon after 'we / do not admire what / we cannot understand' suggests that the further examples of the bat, elephants, horse, wolf, critic, baseball fan, and statistician all exemplify the 'derivative'. But on the contrary, the phrase that immediately follows this list, '*nor* is it valid / to discriminate against "business documents and / school-books"' (my emphasis), indicates that the various animals and people just listed are examples of 'the genuine' that are conventionally excluded or overlooked as topics for poetry.[8] The poem then unsettles its own definition of what is genuine and what is derivative; those distinctions are deliberately confused in the longer version of 'Poetry'. Rather than a neutral list, Moore's examples dramatize the way in which the categories of 'the genuine' and 'the derivative' are historical and cultural constructs rather than inherent qualities.

In the context of Moore's poem, the phrase 'the genuine' is paradigmatic of Moore's treatment of gendered subjectivity in that it functions not as an extra-textual ground for some fixed identity, but instead merely as a place-holder, like the 'empty' forms' Emile Benveniste argues 'language puts forth' in order to permit 'each speaker to *appropriate to himself* an entire language by designating himself as *I*' (226). For Benventiste, subjectivity in language refers precisely to such '"empty" forms', and as the word 'empty' implies this conception of subjectivity depends upon metaphors of space as absolute and as a mere container, defined by fixed boundaries between an interior and an exterior. The speaker of Moore's poem simultaneously mistrusts and grudgingly respects both the established conventions of poetic utterance and their apparent opposite, 'genuine' experience, and this complicated stance can be systematically related to Moore's position as a *gendered* speaking subject in relation to the ideology of separate spheres and its construction of exterior and interior spaces.[9] The point I wish to stress is that Moore's critique of the genuine is not just a critique of essentialism, but is also a critique of assumptions about space, about the *place* of the genuine or the genuine as a strategy for defining identity in terms of fixed places and positions.[10]

In the same way that poetry holds open 'a place for the genuine' without specifying in advance what experiences will come to occupy that space, poems of Moore's like 'Poetry', 'Silence' (1924), and 'Black Earth' (1918) redefine gender as a space of indeterminacy, a place held open for multiple determinations and new meanings, in opposition to established representations of femininity.[11] For Moore, the problematizing of 'the politics of location' that results from this redefinition of the category of space is directly related to the problematic status of poetic utterance itself.

2 'Silence': 'woman's place' in language?

Moore's poem 'Silence' poses women's relation to language and literary tradition as a question which recapitulates and displaces nineteenth-century debates about the status of 'woman's sphere' and its exclusion from the capitalist marketplace. If women must work through a language and a tradition from which they have been excluded and within which they are marginalized, then what is the appropriate response to that alienation from the language and literature of men? Should women writers try to create a language and a literature of their own, in which they can be 'at home', or should they affirm their displacement as the basis for rethinking language and literature and accept that language is no one's 'home' in the sense of being no one's private property? It is in this sense that 'Silence' gives a gendered meaning to Moore's typical techniques of quotation, which foreground the ways in which her language is not her own.[12]

'Silence' uses the figure of 'home' to represent the textual space of the 'I' that Moore attempts to appropriate; she authorizes that appropriation by drawing on the ideological association of women and domesticity, but at the same time she redefines domestic space. The first line of the poem introduces a quotation attributed to the speaker's father, and that quotation takes up almost all of the poem. The father speaks of the value he places on 'silence', or rather 'restraint', on the part of guests in his home: 'Superior people never make long visits / ... they sometimes enjoy solitude, / and can be robbed of speech / by speech which has delighted them. / The deepest feeling always shows itself in silence; / not in silence, but restraint'. The poem sets up an analogy between the position of these guests in the father's home and the position of the speaker in the poem: the status of the speaker as a guest in her own poem is implied by the fact that the poem consists almost entirely of the father's words. The speaker is forced to use a language that is not her own to make her point. This relationship to language encodes the daughter's ambivalent relation to the patriarchal authority that the father exercises over his home and to the silencing effects of that authority on her.

However, the speaker succeeds in appropriating the father's language in the final two lines by turning the father's favorite saying against him.[13] *She* responds to the invitation and warning extended by the father to his guests. The speaker comments 'Nor was he insincere in saying, "Make my house your inn"', and she goes on to have the last word: 'Inns are not residences.' These lines pose readers the question of what kind of intervention and appropriation is being performed. The lines could be read simply as a paraphrase or extension of the father's words by the daughter. On the other hand, in the last line the daughter inverts the grammatical placement of the words 'inn' and 'house' in the father's proverb, and replaces 'house' with 'residence'. The effect is to emphasize the negative that she introduces, in which she affirms that inns are not homes for anyone, in contrast to the father's assertion than his house is a home only for him. This rewriting of the father's words suggests that they are being used against him, or that the daughter is finding a meaning in those words that the father never intended and thereby demonstrating that the father is only a guest in his own language, which can be taken to mean something other than what he thought he was saying.

However, even if the final lines are taken as making a different point from that of the father's original words, the question remains: does this rewriting of the father's words constitute the construction of a separate counter-discourse, a discourse of the daughter against the father? In other words, has the speaker created her own linguistic 'home' in the final lines? Or is the speaker rejecting any notion of language as a metaphorical 'home' in favor of treating language as an 'inn?' By ending without resolving this question, the poem encodes the trope of 'homelessness at home' at the structural level, while it also renders readers 'homeless' and undecided between these two equally possible interpretations.

By accepting the father's definition of 'home' as an 'inn' the daughter's relationship to the father's house is no longer regarded as natural and essential, the basis of the daughter's identity. Instead of a space of confinement, the house is only a temporary and provisional point of stasis. On this level, the speaker also affirms a version of the 'homelessness at home' Moore found in Dickinson. By representing 'home' as an 'inn', Moore's poem reveals how that domestic space participates in and is produced by economic structures, instead of 'home' being defined by its opposition to the public sphere. 'Home' cannot then represent a pure space of freedom from economic or political constraints, a haven in a heartless world. 'Home' is the place assigned to women in modern, industrial societies. But Moore does suggest that the very fact of being assigned such a place creates possibilities for women to claim a certain freedom of movement, by resisting the representation of home as a purely private space. In 'Silence', 'home' becomes a borderline figure, neither public nor private, an 'inn'.

The condition of being 'homeless at home' is also performed by the wordplay on 'in', 'inn', and 'insincere'. By the end of the poem, both the home and the silence that the speaker finds herself trapped 'in' have become an 'inn'. The speaker thereby claims not only the capacity to transcend her position within the home, but suggests that she always existed in excess of the ideological definition of her feminine identity, an excess marked by the extra letter '*n*' that transforms a state of confinement into a statement of possibility. The home is revealed as only one limited position among others, and the father's sincerity, the genuineness of the sentiment he expresses, is revealed as an expression of the privilege assigned to the place he occupies within patriarchal social relations. Sincerity is a quality reserved for the insider, and that position of cultural insider is associated with possession of a securely bounded internal self, as the ground for and content of expression. When the speaker sees the father's position as such and comments on it at the end of the poem, she articulates an alternative perspective that allows her to see the limitations of the father's discourse and its authority, as if from the outside, as one who is 'homeless' and whose use of the father's language cannot help but be 'insincere', at least from the father's point of view, because these words cannot easily be located as belonging or not belonging to the subject who speaks them, since that subject is neither domesticated nor free, neither inside nor outside the father's language.

3 'Are you a jet-black Ethiopian Othello-hued?': Moore's 'Black Earth'

Ezra Pound poses this rhetorical question about Moore's race in a letter to her, dated 16 December 1916, with reference to a line from one of Moore's poems that had recently been published in England in *The Egoist*, though Pound does not name the poem (Pound, *Selected Letters* 143). As Cristanne Miller points out, in her reply on 19 January 1919, Moore herself took Pound to be referring to 'Black Earth', a poem 'written about an elephant that I have named Melancthon' (quoted in Miller, *Marianne Moore* 134; 'Black Earth' was reprinted in Moore's 1951 *Collected Poems* under the title 'Melancthon', but omitted, presumably at Moore's request, from her *Complete Poems*).

'Black Earth' is the 'first of the several animal portraits which become a trademark of [Moore's] verse (Miller, *Marianne Moore* 115), though 'Black Earth' is also unusual in that the fictional speaker of this poem is an African elephant. This adoption of the animal's point of view, in the form of its ventriloquized speech, stands in stark contrast to Moore's more typical techniques of external observation and description.[14] Though the poem does unsettle its own first-person voice by shifting back and forth between the elephant's use of 'I' and third-person references to the elephant (Hotelling 88), Moore's risks the pathetic fallacy of projecting her own viewpoint onto the otherness of the animal by assuming its voice at all, although it might be more accurate to say that 'Black Earth' explicitly stages a risk that is inherent even in seemingly objective descriptions of another entity. In other poems, the closest Moore comes to assuming and perhaps metaphorically colonizing the point of view of an animal is in the quoted remarks in the poem 'The Monkeys', but those remarks articulate precisely the creature's objections to the way that humans fail to respect animals' difference, the way that 'they have imposed on us' (*Complete Poems* 40). This atypical style and the way it complicates the poems of naturalistic observation that made Moore relatively popular might be one reason why she later omits 'Black Earth' from her official oeuvre.

In many ways, Pound's comment suggests a racialized version of T.S. Eliot's more notorious reference to the 'feminine' qualities of Moore's writing, in a 1923 review of her poetry (Tomlinson 51). Eliot puts the word 'feminine' in quotation marks when he uses it, as if to acknowledge what Gilbert and Gubar call Moore's techniques of 'female female impersonation'.[15] Pound seems to suggest that Moore similarly puts 'race' in quotation marks when she assumes the voice of a black African, elephant or no. It is likely that the lines that inspired Pound to ask Moore whether she is a 'jet black Ethiopian Othello-hued' are the elephant speaker's reference to its back as 'Black / but beautiful' (Moore, *Collected Poems* 46). Pound's effortless interpretive move from the elephant to the 'jet black Ethiopian' seems to reproduce the colonialist convention by which 'African natives can be collapsed into African animals' (JanMohamed 87), or rather Pound's question seems to assume that this collapse is what Moore's poem does, intentionally or not. It is important to note, however, that Moore's talking elephant inverts and literalizes this colonialist trope rather than simply redeploying it. In its colonialist form, the collapse of African person and African animal more typically involves presenting African persons as uncivilized and unintelligible brutes rather than presenting African elephants as articulate participants in philosophical debates about immanence and transcendence, which is what Moore's poem does.

The question here is whether 'Black Earth' indulges in the kind of 'romantic racialism' that Cristanne Miller locates in another poem of Moore's about an African animal, 'The Jerboa', or desert rat. Miller persuasively argues that this poem 'celebrates nomadic Africans as being like the desert rat' (*Marianne Moore* 138). The poem 'presents "the blacks" as *other* at the same time that it argues for the value of the unmaterialistic life [Moore] uses them to represent' (139). In other words, the poem exemplifies the exoticizing tendencies of 'romantic racialism' (139), in its modernist form, where supposedly 'primitive' cultures are taken to represent positive alternatives to the banality of middle-class life. The result is to preserve racist stereotypes of Africans as 'other', but simply to invert the negative connotations of those stereotypes into positive connotations. As I suggested above, 'Black Earth' seems both to take this process of identifying with (stereotypes about) primitivized others even further than 'The Jerboa', and also to suggest that Moore is trying to intervene in that discourse of romantic racialism and modernist primitivism. Her intervention would come precisely through mimicking or performing that discourse in such a way as to create some ironic distance from it.

Moore's 'feminine' voice is read as an ironic repetition or doubling of readers' likely cultural assumptions about gender, a 'playful repetition' that reveals gender to be performative, as an arbitrary construct rather than an essentialized identity.[16] 'Black Earth', however, raises the question of the difference in meaning between Moore's poetic acts of 'female female impersonation' as subversive strategy and the impersonation of racial categories, the treatment of race as a masquerade. John Slatin suggests that a kind of poetic blackface is a more general issue in Moore's poetry, and not just in 'Black Earth', when he points out that the words 'dark' and 'black' are key terms in Moore's writing, where they function in part as metaphors for Moore's infamous obscure, oblique, and opaque language (Slatin 6). This reading of Moore returns us to the questions raised in the previous two chapters, about the appropriation of figures of racial difference to represent the marginality produced for middle-class white women by their domestic exclusion from public life, what Moore calls 'the indestructible limestone keep of domesticity' (*Collected Prose* 82). In the context of this tradition, Moore's claim that Dickinson's 'process of "interiorization" ... was not a dark one' is especially significant in defining Moore's awareness of the problems that result from such appropriations (291). But we have also seen H.D. turning to a concept of domesticity as performative in a way that similarly raises issues of the connection between that redefinition of gender and the history of blackface minstrelsy.[17]

In the only extended discussion to date of Moore's representations of racial difference, Cristanne Miller argues that Moore 'was not captivated by, and did not fetishize, racial otherness' (*Marianne Moore* 140), or at least did not *always* indulge in racial fetishism. Miller justifies this claim by identifying a central tension in Moore's poetry, one that for Miller becomes clearest in poems focusing on racial and national identity categories. In this view, Moore's poetry oscillates between a classic liberal critique of racial inequality that focuses instead on 'individual idiosyncrasy or accomplishment' and a contrasting and often mutually exclusive acknowledgment of systematic or structural inequalities in the 'access to power' available to different social groups (131). This tension then translates into an internal debate between a pluralistic endorsement of irreducible difference and a liberal endorsement of a fundamental 'equality of spirit among all people' (141). Miller argues that this debate in turn often takes the form 'of philosophical discussion about the importance of outer trappings, the skin or other elements of the physical ... to the spirit' (141), with 'Black Earth' being one of the most explicit and most extended examples of this debate.

This analysis suggests the importance that the spatial categories of 'inner' and 'outer' have in Moore's poems about race, and what Miller seems to me to underestimate is the radical nature of Moore's critique of those categories. The exoticizing of racial difference as primitive 'otherness' depends upon treating racial difference as an external category, a mask that can be assumed by white, Western persons. Whiteness then functions very traditionally, as an unmarked or universal category. This kind of universal identity is synonymous with being unbounded or unplaced, so that to be universal is to possess the privilege of mobility across the boundaries of social differences; that mobility permits us to understand and subsume the perspective of our racial others in ways that they are presumed to be unable to do to us. From this point of view, it is important to note that Moore sometimes seems to reproduce this version of white privilege, since minoritized racial differences sometimes function in her poetry as examples of identities that are even more place-bound than gender. At the end of this chapter, I will turn briefly to Moore's depiction in 'The Hero' of an encounter between a woman tourist and a black man who functions as a local expert. But to focus on 'Black Earth' for now, Miller points out precisely this association of race and place when she suggests that 'the black elephant represents the subject *position* par excellence' (146; my emphasis). The elephant in this poem is also associated with the figure of 'black earth' from the title, as a metaphor for the elephant's rootedness and grounding in a specific place.

However, Moore does not simply take this relationship for granted, and 'Black Earth' in fact constitutes a set of reflections on the relation between place and placelessness within racial formations.[18] It is this tension, between home and homelessness, that seems to me to distinguish Moore's representations of racial difference from the modernist norm of exoticism and primitivism. Moore's self-consciousness about questions of location in relation to race and nationality is made explicit in her poem 'England'. This poem ends with a series of examples of supposedly inherent cultural qualities, including 'the sublimated wisdom of China, Egyptian discernment', and 'the torrent of emotion compressed in the verbs of the Hebrew language' (*Complete Poems* 47). But the purpose for this list is to refute the idea that these qualities are completely lacking in the American scene: 'if not stumbled upon in America, / must one imagine that it is not there?' The key word here is the preposition 'in', which as a metaphor for a particular conception of space as bounded is the source of the paradox in these lines. In contrast to that metaphor of space and the role it plays in grounding conceptions of identity, the poem ends with the speaker's assertion that 'it', this essential quality that defines national, racial, or ethnic difference, 'has never been confined to one locality'. There is no place for the genuine, if place has to be understood in terms of clear distinctions between inside and outside.

It is in this way that Moore extends her critique of domesticity, as a model for the construction of bounded 'localities' based on clear distinctions between interior and exterior spaces, to the topic of race and ethnicity. For Moore, the local is also translocal – that is, the local or 'home' is not a container that 'confines' a securely interiorized space.[19] It is precisely Moore's critique of domesticity that leads her to this critique of the spatial assumptions that identify locality with confinement. This critique also leads to an engagement with racial issues, to the extent that domestic ideology idealized and universalized a model of white, middle-class femininity. From this perspective, race emerges as a factor internal to the formation of gender norms about femininity, and the critique of domesticity can lead to a historical understanding of white femininity as a situated, racial category rather than an idealized and universalized category subsuming all women.

If 'Silence' articulates a challenge to the ideological conflation of femininity and domesticity, Moore's poem 'Black Earth' then responds to the ethical and political implications of that challenge and of the resulting necessity to redefine the category 'woman'. In 'Black Earth', Moore both claims as her own a position marked as traditionally feminine and claims the capacity to transcend that position, in part by marking her ironic distance from the speaker of her poem, an African elephant. As Miller points out, the poem 'allies' the figure of the elephant 'with the feminine' precisely because 'it is improbably unlike any notion of conventional female beauty' (*Marianne Moore* 115). But the poem also indicates that the claim to transcendence necessarily calls into question the stability of a feminine identity defined entirely by a gender opposition grounded in the opposition between the private home and the public sphere. The claim to transcendence opens for Moore the problem of women's relationship to structures of dominance other than gender, such as race and nationality.

This reading of 'Black Earth' primarily in terms of gender can be traced back to Bonnie Costello, who points out that 'Black Earth' moves between the twin themes of 'the limitations and the necessity of the empirical self' and the possibility of a self 'transcending discrete identity' (*Marianne Moore* 57, 61).[20] The limitations of the empirical self are represented by the first-person voice of the elephant. But initially at least, the elephant speaker is also an image for a self defined by its securely interiorized location within a body. Moore's thematics of transcendence in this poem then anticipates Simone de Beauvoir's gendered reading of the distinction between immanence and transcendence, even more strongly than H.D.'s thematics of transcendence did. Like whiteness, the category of transcendence is associated with the claim to an unmarked, universal, and therefore mobile identity, one unconstrained by the limits of its particular location or positionality. In Beauvoir's account, the state of immanence represented by both the body and the domestic sphere must be transcended in order for women to liberate themselves and gain access to the sphere of social and symbolic action. Moore's 'Black Earth' then poses the question of what happens when the rejected ground of such transcendence – the 'black earth' of the body – is seized as a site of linguistic agency. What Carolyn Burke calls the 'metaphysical dialectic of mind and body' in the poem is also an oscillation between the gendered positions of immanence and transcendence as Beauvoir defines them (Burke 142–3).

When the speaker of Moore's poem refers to 'this elephant-skin / which I inhabit, fibred over like the shell of / the cocoanut, this piece of black glass through which no light / can filter – cut / into checkers by rut / upon rut of unpreventable experience' (*Collected Poems* 46), it becomes possible to read the poem as a feminist protest against the familiar assumptions that female biology determines women's destiny and that feminine identity is necessarily determined by the 'unpreventable experience' of the female body. Such a reading is made possible by the speaker's sense of distance from the identifying marks of its species, the 'elephant-skin' with which the speaker does not identify but rather 'inhabits'. At this point in the poem, the speaker begins to sound like a person comparing her body to that of an elephant, and the way that our culture exaggerates the importance of body-image in women's self-definition is ironically and even humorously figured by the outsized body of the elephant. In other words, the figure of the elephant can be read as suggesting the way in which the speaker's body image looms large in her own thinking about herself, although it can also clearly be read as an attempt to expand the limits of femininity or feminine beauty, by combining 'elements that are unfeminine in conventional stereotype', such as size and physical power, with conventionally feminine elements such as irrationality or intuition, since the elephant praises its own 'beautiful element of unreason' (Miller, *Marianne Moore* 116–17; Moore, *Collected Poems* 48).

But this priority given to the body in the cultural construction of femininity has the effect of excluding women from the public sphere as the site of legitimate historical agency and consigning women to a condition of obscurity and darkness within 'this piece of black glass through which no / light / can filter'. The imagery here recalls H.D.'s trope of the 'dark room'. The ideological nature of this construction of femininity and the body is suggested when the speaker goes on to say 'Black / but beautiful, my back / is full of the history of power' (46). The category of 'power' comes before, pre-vents in the etymological sense, the category of 'experience' and thereby calls into question how natural any supposedly universal female bodily experiences actually are.

In 'Black Earth', Moore authorizes her assumption of the 'I' of the poem by posing as an animal who exists in a state of bodily immanence that resembles our culture's representations of the condition of the 'feminine', at least in Moore's version of what it means to be an elephant. It is logical, therefore, that the speaker's claims to transcend this state of immanence are enacted through a rejection of the first-person voice. With the statement 'the I of each is to // the I of each / a kind of fretful speech / which sets a limit on itself' (47),[21] the speaker of the poem dissociates herself from the elephant and begins to refer to the previous speaker of the poem in the third person: 'the elephant is black earth preceded by a tendril?' This shift produces a curious instability of voice within the poem; we are left to wonder just who is the speaker of these final lines, especially since that speaker ceases to use the word 'I'. Costello argues that this shift in voice marks a transformation in the 'limit' the speaker had previously set on herself and that the self in this poem has instead become 'an expansive term transcending discrete identity' (61).

This shift away from the identification of the elephant with the first-person voice of the poem problematizes the romantic racialism of Moore's implicit claim to speak from an African perspective. Moreover, most readings of this poem overlook the significance of the specific choice of words in the lines 'this elephant-skin / which I inhabit'. It is the 'skin' that the speaker claims to inhabit, not the body of the elephant. The word 'skin' here signifies a borderline between the outside world and the subjective, inner world of the African elephant's consciousness, and it is that borderline that the speaker claims to inhabit. The speaker thereby problematizes the spatial assumptions behind the distinctions between mind and body, transcendence and immanence, since those assumptions would treat the skin as a mere container for the mind, not as a site from which to speak. In this sense, Miller is wrong to suggest that, since 'the black elephant represents the subject position par excellence' (146), the poem endorses such positioning. Instead, the poem moves toward a more complicated understanding of the spaces occupied by racial and gendered subjects than is possible within the notion of a subject position defined by the body as a container for mind or self or identity.

It is also important to note, however, that the speaker's claim to transcendence enables her to revalue the position of immanence previously represented by the elephant, rather than to put that position behind her. 'Black Earth' ends with a question: 'Will / depth be depth, thick skin be thick, to one who can see no / beautiful element of unreason under it?' (48). In my view, this question sums up the central tension in Moore's representation of racial difference, and that tension takes the form of two possible ways to read these lines, depending on whether the question is understood as rhetorical or not. As a rhetorical question, these lines suggest a defense of the elephant's interiority and the autonomy of that interior self from the power of any observer to impose an external definition of the elephant's identity on it and to forcibly categorize the elephant in terms of an external classification system. The result of such an imposition would be to ignore the elephant's 'otherness' to ourselves, to refuse to see the 'beautiful element of unreason' – that is, those qualities of the elephant which do not make sense within our frame of reference but which point toward the elephant's possession of its own, alternate mode of existence. Most readings of 'Black Earth' implicitly endorse this reading, which is encouraged by Moore's other's poems on the alterity of animals to humans.[22]

This reading assumes that the phrase 'beautiful element of unreason' is to be read in a purely positive way, as a desirable goal, without any irony or self-critique of this desire. It seems equally plausible to read this line as a comment on the exoticizing impulse behind the discourse of racial primitivism in the modernist period, especially since feminist readings of this poem, like Miller's, suggest the way that conventional definitions of beauty are interrogated by the poem. If the elephant is read as a figure for gender difference, the argument that the 'beautiful element of unreason' might be associated with stereotypes about feminine intuition (Miller 117) also implies an ironic and self-critical stance toward the construction of the category of 'unreason' or irrationality. This kind of reading, however, can also be applied to the analysis of the poem's stance toward racial difference, which is often constructed through similar stereotypes about African 'unreason'.

From this perspective, the final question that is posed by 'Black Earth' is not rhetorical at all. In this reading, the 'othering' of the African is accomplished precisely by taking it for granted that 'depth' will be depth. That is, the exoticizing of the African as other assumes that there is unintelligible mystery 'under' the surface; the 'otherness' of racial difference is not explicable in cultural and historical terms, but is inherent in African persons. This reading suggests that Moore is precisely critical of depth models for interpreting otherness, to the extent that a depth model here means the assumption of an interiorized, essential racial self.[23] The assumption that the racial other is essentially unknowable to us is one way of constructing racial others as primitive, not only essentially different but essentially inferior. This critique would imply that the question of whether depth will be depth is an urgent question, which might be paraphrased as 'can we imagine racial difference without relying on a distinction between inside and outside, essence and contingency?' The speaker's claim to inhabit the skin rather than the body of the elephant would support this reading, since that claim is another way of rejecting assumptions about 'depth'.

In 'Black Earth', the 'beautiful element of unreason' can also be read as the elephant's difference from itself, or rather its difference from our representations of it and therefore from what we might rationally expect of such a creature, the same kind of ironic difference that Moore's poem introduces into cultural assumptions about women's relation to their bodies by using an elephant to figure that relation. This reading is similar to Slatin's argument about the general meaning of the words 'black' and 'dark' as synonyms for textual obscurity or indirection, what Jakobson refers to as the way poetry foregrounds the non-identity between sign and object (Slatin 6; Jakobson 175). In this reading, the elephant becomes a tentative image for the double necessity of both inhabiting a gendered body and transcending the limits of the position women are assigned on the basis of the bodies they inhabit: 'the elephant is / black earth preceded by a tendril?' (47).[24] The elephant's trunk represents a capacity to move beyond the limits of a body that the elephant here not only inhabits but 'is'. However, the description of the elephant's trunk as a tendril growing out of the 'black earth' of the elephant's body also emphasizes that the tendril comes first, that it precedes the comparison of the body to fertile soil. This image thereby suggests a causal relationship: women's biological capacity to give birth, confirmed by the emergence of the tendril, causes women to be ideologically represented as the nourishing ground of other people's growth, in an inversion of the more traditional assumption that women give birth because they are essentially nurturing and destined to become mothers. Through the figure of the elephant as first-person voice, Moore exposes the role of patriarchal ideology in the social construction of the female body and reclaims that body as a source of power for women: 'Black / but beautiful, my back / is full of the history of power. Of power? What / is powerful and what is not?' (46).

The reading of the poem as focusing on a kind of difference or otherness within gendered categories is supported by the appearance of the phrase 'Black / but beautiful', which makes it almost impossible to avoid reading the poem in terms of racial difference. This phrase alludes to 'The Song of Solomon', chapter 1, verse 5: 'I am black, but comely'. The use of the word 'but', however, also seems to allude to a racist assumption that black is not beautiful and is in need of defense and justification, at the same time that the poem seems to be rejecting such stereotypes (Miller, *Marianne Moore* 275, note 25).

I am particularly interested in the way that the speaker finally abandons the position of an 'I' that can call itself 'Black / but beautiful', or rather refer to its body, its back, with that phrase. This shift away from the use of first-person voice to refer to the elephant is already implicit in the use of the phrase 'Black / but beautiful' to modify the word 'back' rather than the word 'I'. This shift suggests a self-consciousness about the cultural imperialism involved in any appropriation of images of blackness to represent the oppressive effects of how our culture constructs femininity and the female body. It is as if Moore's speaker suddenly realizes that she has no right to describe herself as 'Black', at least not in comparison to actual Africans and African-Americans and especially in comparison to women of color who are discriminated against because they inhabit bodies that are intelligible as both black and female. The shift in poetic voice that characterizes 'Black Earth' marks not only Moore's ethical refusal to appropriate the rhetoric of racial difference for feminist purposes. This characteristic instability of poetic voice in Moore's poems is grounded in the challenge that modern feminism poses to the traditional definition of the category 'woman'.[25] The shift away from the elephant's 'I' to a more expansive or transcendent voice retains within itself an acknowledgment of continuing limitations that circumscribe the female speaking subject, just as the first-person voice is shown to contain the possibility of its own self-transcendence.

4 Tour guides

Moore's poem 'The Hero' makes more explicit the implications of combining a gendered and a racial reading of 'Black Earth'. Miller's excellent reading of 'The Hero' stresses its 'doubled vision of race, one of a black man and other of a (presumably) white woman' (*Marianne Moore* 153).[26] These two characters encounter one another during the white woman's visit to Mount Vernon, where she asks after Martha Washington's grave. The poem's 'decorous frock-coated Negro', Miller suggests, is there as a 'tour guide' (153). Though the poem focuses on this black man as its central character, the poem is organized around a series of contrasts, including not only black/white and male/female, but also the contrast between the white woman as tourist and the black man as local expert; between the white woman as 'financially indigent but independent' and 'footloose' (that is, public) and the black man as 'lower-class' and 'employed'; and between the white woman as aggressive, 'persistently questioning', and therefore 'gender-crossing' and the black man as 'maternally lenient' (he is described in the poem as 'looking upon a fellow creature's error with the / feelings of a mother – a / woman or a cat') (Miller, *Marianne Moore* 154–5). In other words, the white woman is encoded as mobile, both in terms of geographical movement (tourism) and in terms of conventional gender categories, in contrast to the 'decorous', conventional, and place-bound figure of the black man.[27] Ironically, the feminine qualities attributed to the black man signify not mobility but how he defers to others and 'knows his place', on the one hand, and refuses to judge others or impose his own values on them, on the other (depending on whether this quality of lenience and restraint is read negatively or positively). While both these figures cross gender boundaries, then, paradoxically only the woman is associated with freedom of movement, in Miller's reading.

The easiest way to explain the organization of the poem around this contrast is as Miller does, in terms of 'a self-portrait' of the white woman 'that is both ironic and revealing in the boundaries it obscures and crosses' (153) – that is, to read the poem as a comment on the white woman's relative privilege in terms of race. At the same time,

Miller brilliantly argues, with reference to the title, that 'The Hero' also offers a defense of the white woman, who comes off seeming as unlikeable as any stereotypical tourist. For Miller, the poem implies that both the white woman and the black man might embody a form of heroism, the point being that 'you may, in fact, define heroism in a number of ways according to your circumstances or those of the observed subject' (154). This reading argues that the differences in the behavior of the black man and the white woman are justified as responses to the different histories they have experienced: domestic confinement as opposed to forced exile and diaspora.

This is a powerful reading of the poem, but it emphasizes the fundamental discontinuity in the historical backgrounds of these two figures. I would like to offer an alternative reading of the relationship between the white woman and the black man in this poem, which takes these two as linked rather than opposed, despite the obvious contrasts between them and the undeniable differences in their historical situations. Specifically, I would like to argue that both the white woman tourist's social mobility and the figure of the working-class black man represent alternate historical experiences foreclosed on for women by domestic ideology, which canonized a particular form of white, middle-class experience and identified that historical experience with femininity in general. Both the mobile and 'persistently questioning' white woman and the maternal black man embody qualities and potentialities that could be recognized as 'feminine', in a critique of reductive definitions of the domestic sphere and its proper representatives. At the same time, such a recognition would require a pluralized definition of gender. In this reading, the poem runs the risk of reproducing a stereotype of African-American men as feminized, by white, middle-class standards, though I believe the poem's goal is to challenge its readers' tendencies *either* to separate race and gender, as if they represented distinct points of location, *or* to analogize race and gender in a way that assimilates racial difference to gender difference. Like the final lines of 'Silence', 'The Hero' leaves readers with an interpretive choice, with the aim of dramatizing readers' investments in binary categories: either race and gender are distinct or they are the same. The poem attempts to forestall this misreading through its endorsement of the black man's local knowledge and attachment to place, which indirectly signifies the specificity of his racial identity. The poem, in other words, refuses to simply endorse 'homelessness' over 'home' and vice-versa. The encounter between these two figures, then, suggests the multiple referents that Moore believes terms like 'woman' and 'feminine' should have. The fact that these referents cannot simply be included under the heading of those categories, however, points toward the difficulty of this redefinition of gender; Moore implies here that to engage with race as a feminist is to confront issues that are not reducible to gender, that are not directly women's issues, but which may require contact with people of color in general. In this reading, the white woman in this poem encounters the black man not just as someone whose experiences are foreign to her own, but as someone whose differences are internally relevant to her own project of feminist transformation.

The fact that Moore begins 'Silence' by situating her speaker within the boundaries of both the father's discourse and the father's house highlights the point that Moore is not claiming to transcend gender altogether in her poems, despite the fact that she identifies the 'I' of 'Poetry' with a set of values and a position of judgment that are often encoded as masculine. Instead, Moore's position as a gendered speaking subject is marked precisely by the instability and indeterminacy that her poems introduce within the oppositional structure on which gender categories are based. At the same time, her claim to a place within language destabilizes cultural assumptions about 'woman's' proper 'place' within the home and about the possibility of grounding a unified feminine identity in women's shared experiences of domesticity. By utilizing spatial metaphors for the construction of subjectivity and for women's relation to language, Moore's poetry attempts to claim a place for the female subject while simultaneously de-esentializing women's supposedly natural relationship to domestic space. The categories of 'author' and 'experience' traditionally function as prelinguistic bases for the stability of textual meaning, and Moore's resistance to those categories develops as a direct consequence of her attempt to reimagine women's relation to both language and domesticity as positions that women continually claim and reconstruct in a variety of ways.

5

The Grounding of Modern Women's Fiction: Emily Holmes Coleman's *The Shutter of Snow*

> During these years there was no war and if there was it was not any war of mine. But of course there was history, and there were novels historical novels and so there was in a way war all the time.
>
> Gertrude Stein, *Wars I Have Seen* (1945)

1 Gendered space and the historicity of novelistic discourse

The poets I examined in the previous chapters restage and mimic domestic ideologies as 'enunciative modalities' in the construction of their poetic voices, and thereby both reproduce and interrogate traditional constructions of feminine subjectivity in language. It was therefore possible to locate a concern with the historical construction of 'home' as a feminine space in poems that often do not thematize that history in an explicit way. Turning to the genre of the novel, the opposite problem appears. It is much easier to read domestic themes in fiction than to locate the way that domestic ideologies are incorporated into novelistic form. Feminist critics, however, have shown how novelistic form assumes that historicity, the assumptions or preconditions that make historical representation possible, has been structured by the gendered mapping of public and private spaces. Modernist women's writing in the genre of the novel, I argue, is distinguished by its attempts to reimagine these founding assumptions. My focus in the chapters that follow will be on novels that attempt to read modernism's general critique of these preconditions for historical representation back into realist traditions; I will therefore turn to women's novels of the 1930s, which both return to the project of direct historical representation and also incorporate a more properly modernist concern with self-consciously exploring the preconditions for any such representations. These novels represent, then, the first moment in a post-modernist reaction to earlier innovations in literary form.

In relation specifically to the genre of the novel, modernist representations of twentieth-century life as a condition of metaphorical 'homelessness' can be traced back to Lukacs's description of the novel as a formal 'expression of ... transcendental homelessness' (*Theory of the Novel* 41). As J.M. Bernstein has shown in his book on Lukacs's 'philosophy of the novel', Lukacs's famous characterization of the novel's 'transcendental homelessness' encodes the antinomies or dualisms of bourgeois thought, since novelistic form for Lukacs presupposes the isolation of the individual from the social world. The fact that for women during the nineteenth century this isolation resulted from confinement to a newly privatized concept of 'home' explains why this literary form of 'transcendental homelessness' might also be figured by women writers as a form of all-too-familiar homeliness, as Gilbert and Gubar suggest in their account of how women writers can be 'shut up in prose' (*Madwoman* 107). As Bernstein paraphrases Lukacs's account of the 'inner form' of the novel, novelistic form implies that 'unless we are able normatively or ethically to narrate our experience we are unable to say who we are. Conversely, the world as the novel finds it, the world prior to the novel's ethical figuration or constitution of it, the world where freedom is exiled into subjectivity, is a world we cannot narrate (except fictionally), a world in which we are unable to say who we are' (Bernstein xix). It is in this way that the novel takes for granted the philosophical and epistemological opposition between the privatized inner world of individual subjectivity and the public world of shared social meanings.[1]

Vincent Pecora analyzes how this dualism begins to break down in the modernist period. The explicit emergence of the problematic of selfhood and its relation to the external world in modernist fiction is represented by modernism's famous turn toward subjectivity or 'introversion' (Fletcher and Bradbury). In Pecora's view, what might appear to be an inward or psychologizing turn (Lukacs's accusation against modernism) actually results from 'the external rationalization of self as social mechanism' and 'the progressive dissolution of subjectivity by the social apparatus – from economic manipulation to legal codification to the objectification achieved by the psychologist's gaze' (260).[2] This 'dissolution' of subjectivity then defines the mediated effects of what Lefebvre calls the inherent capitalist tendency toward the abstraction of space and away from fixed or 'absolute' spaces.[3]

For Pecora, 'modern narrative's crisis of faith in its organizing spirit', the notion of self as opposed to world, reproduces the logic of this larger social 'dissolution of subjectivity', but only on the level of form. Pecora can therefore claim that modernist techniques for the representation of subjective 'flows' or 'streams of consciousness' that are not necessarily under the control of a coherent individual subject only reflect 'the machinery of an administered society' that has taken over what could previously be regarded as the autonomous, internal space of the private self (Pecora 6). The problem here is that both readings of stream of consciousness narration, the one that celebrates it as a more inclusive representation of psychic processes and Pecora's critique of it as an exteriorizing process that makes psychic processes accessible and therefore vulnerable to social control, remain locked into an opposition between internal and external worlds. In Pecora's reading, the disappearance of private, internal spaces makes all space external (that is, social).[4] But what if the modernist challenge to the interiorization of subjectivity undoes that very distinction and therefore destabilizes the ground of social control as well as the subject's ability to withdraw from it into an individualized critical distance?

Pecora ends up arguing that resistance lies only in reconstituting the 'ideal bourgeois self', as 'the last source of *opposition*' to capitalism's 'totalizing process of reification' (261; my emphasis). But as Lora Romero reminds us, the model for a 'generalized oppositionality' is not just the individual's difference from society but the domestic sphere's difference from the public, so that to reconstitute that opposition is likely to seem much more problematic for women than for men (100). Both Myra Jehlen and Nancy Armstrong have shown how the development of the basic problem of novelistic form Lukacs defines is tied to ideology of separate gender spheres, in ways that make the breakdown of such dualisms seem potentially more liberating for women than Pecora allows. By 'taking woman as metaphor for the interior life ... and – far from suppressing her – expanding hers almost to the exclusion of any other life', Jehlen argues, the novel claimed as its dominant subject matter a 'territory' of subjective experience defined as 'interior, individualistic', and 'alienated' from the external, social world. At the same time, novelistic form places 'the limits of that territory within the structure of the middle-class world it serves' (Jehlen 213). Similarly, Nancy Armstrong argues that treatises on domestic economy, like the one by Catherine Beecher discussed in chapter 1, 'made the welfare of the social group depend, before anything else, on the regulation of the individual's desire', and the rise of the novel 'transformed this fantasy of [individualized and interiorized] self-production into procedures designed to produce men and women fit to occupy the institutions of an industrialized society' (164). It is on the basis of this argument that Armstrong claims 'the modern individual was first and foremost a woman' (8). The basis for the ideal bourgeois self Pecora refers to, the self that exists 'prior to any social identity' and therefore in opposition to it, is the separate domestic sphere (Armstrong 164).

In its representation of the conflict between private life and public responsibility, the novel necessarily suggests that the autonomy of the middle-class home in relation to the social world is precarious and always at risk. However, as D.A. Miller points out, 'the existence of that sheltered space ... is unconditionally taken for granted in the novel form, whose unfolding or consumption has not ceased to occur in such a space all along'; the novel assumes its reader's 'leisured withdrawal to the private, domestic sphere', so that 'every novel-reading subject is constituted ... within the categories of the individual, the inward, the domestic' (Miller 81–2). As Miller puts it, even as the autonomy of the private home is called into question by the novel, that autonomy 'has also by the same token been put into place' in the novel itself (99).

This sense that the novel is a double-edged sword for women seeking to represent themselves as historical subjects is exemplified by Gertrude Stein's comments on her exclusion as a woman from world-historical events: 'During these years there was no war and if there was it was not any war of mine'. At the same time, perhaps as a result of this very withdrawal from the public scene, Stein claims to have access to history through the agency of the novel: 'But of course there was history, and there were novels historical novels and so there was in a way war all the time' (*Wars* 7). The question Stein raises here is how the writing of a novel can itself be understood as part of a struggle to make history, as a form of intervention and a vehicle for social change, given the novel's formal implication in the structures of modern industrial society. If the categories of novelistic production and consumption presume the prior existence of oppositions between public and private, inside and outside, that are grounded in the opposition between separate gendered spheres, then the novel cannot contest those oppositions without abolishing or transforming itself. Modernism's critique of realist conventions of representation constitutes just such a project of transformation.

In the sections that follow, I will examine three novels written by women in the 1930s, after the period of high modernism: Emily

Holmes Coleman's *Shutter of Snow* (1930), Virginia Woolf's *The Years* (1937), and Sylvia Townsend Warner's *Summer Will Show* (1936). These novels map out different strategies for interrogating the novel's traditional appropriation of female subjectivity as a metaphor of interiority. They all attempt to reappropriate feminine spaces and to define new chronotopes for women's stories, in Bakhtin's sense of the chronotope as the space through which the time of a narrative passes and as a representation of how preestablished social spaces are practiced and made habitable in everyday life, a process that often involves the subversion of the intended purposes of those spaces.[5] These new chronotopes range from a women's mental hospital to a family party to the new social spaces created during the 1848 revolution in France. Emily Holmes Coleman's *Shutter of Snow* uses a modernist, stream-of-consciousness technique to explore the enclosure of feminine subjectivity, an enclosure that is thematized in the narrative by the protagonist's confinement in a state psychiatric hospital for women. While the novel represents this institution as a potential space of affiliation between women of different races and classes, it ultimately indicates the limitations of its own formal and thematic strategies, since those strategies are predicated on accepting a position of feminine enclosure. In the end, this type of narrative strategy only reproduces oppositions between inside and outside, public and private, despite its attempt to define a concrete, social setting where an alternate form of feminist subjectivity could sustain itself. The experimental form tends to overwhelm the more public themes. In this way, Coleman's novel provides a standard against which to measure Woolf and Warner's.

Woolf's *The Years* uses the form of a family chronicle to chart the emergence of a group of women from the confines of their nineteenth-century, private home and the processes by which they and their younger female relatives develop a variety of political identities. *The Years* also thematizes the historical transformation of domestic ideology in terms of new communications technologies, specifically the telephone. Warner's *Summer Will Show* is the story of a woman who rejects an identity defined by her role as head of a household, and that rejection takes the form of a lesbian relationship and the establishment of an alternative household located in Paris during the 1848 revolution. Both *The Years* and *Summer Will Show* thematize the heterogeneity of women's narratives and enact the interruption of their own narrative authority, in a combination of realist and modernist techniques.

2 'Flying into new spaces': Emily Holmes Coleman's *Shutter of Snow*

A novel that often reads like a source of inspiration for the imagery of the film *The Snake Pit, The Shutter of Snow* (1930) attempts to transform the story of a woman's confinement in a state psychiatric hospital and her gradual recovery into a narrative of how women might appropriate the spaces to which they are assigned by dominant gender ideologies.[6] Marthe Gail's mental 'breakdown' directly thematizes the breakdown of the self as a principle of formal coherence in the modernist novel, and *The Shutter of Snow* also enacts this loss of the novel's traditional ground of intelligibility through its stream-of-consciousness technique and the 'lyric dislocation of its language' (Marcus, 'Of Method' 3).

Marthe's 'delusion' that she is Jesus Christ come back as a woman is represented not as a pathology but as a crisis of faith in the conventions that establish the reality of everyday life, the same crisis that modernist novels like Coleman's pose in their relation to the realist tradition. Marthe's breakdown unsettles the grounding of feminine subjectivity in domestic institutions. Marthe's husband tells her 'you must get rid of all these delusions before you can go home' (47). This lost 'home' is therefore immediately associated in this novel with Marthe's other losses: feminine self-possession, the security of ego-boundaries, and adherence to social conventions of rationality.

The concept of the private self presupposed by novelistic form is here revealed to be problematic. Marthe Gail's breakdown and her enclosure within the asylum are represented as a condition of exile or metaphorical homelessness, which is what must be cured before she can return home and 'become' herself again, as much as any delusions she is suffering from. Her breakdown, then, generates the narrative as a process of seeking or relearning how to produce such a self through the procedures of self-discipline that are forcibly instilled by the psychiatric institution. *The Shutter of Snow* thereby reveals the practices that produce 'home' as the foundation for a normative feminine self. It also indicates the price that women must pay in order to establish and reproduce those autonomous spaces.

Marthe's hospitalization gives her an insight into the institutional basis and the power relations that characterize the supposedly free and autonomous space of the private home and the family. But the women's ward of the state hospital also offers an alternative conception of how 'home' as a feminine space could be redefined as a space of affiliation between women of different races and classes as well as a space where women's voices could be heard and where women could represent themselves as embodied subjects. In this sense, *The Shutter of Snow* attempts to appropriate the female space of the sex-segregated asylum as an alternative to the dichotomies that structure nineteenth-century women's novels, according to Gilbert and Gubar. The novel tries to find a position for its female protagonist that would resist the roles of both 'the lady who submits to male dicta' by accepting her proper place in the middle-class home and the 'madwoman in the attic' who is denied any social space in which to operate and is stripped of all social identity (86). *The Shutter of Snow* locates the subjectivity of its female protagonist in the position of the madwoman and tries to transform that space into the basis for women's emancipation from established, middle-class norms of femininity by treating it as an intersubjective space of relationships between women of different classes and races. In contrast to other feminist representations of female madness, Coleman's novel is uniquely concerned with the asylum as a collective female space.[7]

In its focus on this collective space, the novel also attempts to recover the suppressed history of what Gilbert and Gubar figure as the mad or monstrous woman. Armstrong shows how both nineteenth-century novels and political rhetoric used this figure of 'a female who lacked femininity' to represent the 'promiscuous' nature of collective social movements against middle-class hegemony, in what Armstrong calls 'the habit of Victorian culture ... to render all collective forms of social organization as sexual violations' (183). This promiscuity was exactly the threat that spurred Catherine Beecher to advocate the severing of home and marketplace to form an alternative domestic economy, in her 1842 *Treatise* (40). The result is to relegate 'a whole realm of social practices to the status of disruption and deviance requiring containment and discipline', just as the madwoman must be confined to the attic or the asylum (Armstrong 166). Armstrong argues that the rhetorical sexualization of these alternative class practices when they 'are contained within the body of a deranged woman' made them 'suddenly lose their political meaning' and thereby helped secure bourgeois cultural hegemony by eliminating these alternatives from political discourse (183).

Coleman's novel tries to restore the political meanings contained within the bodies of deranged women like her protagonist and the women she meets, in the attempt to acknowledge class and racial differences among women that have been displaced onto the figure of the madwoman. The novel affirms the transgressive potential of being female and lacking femininity. Nevertheless, in the end *The Shutter of Snow* recontains these alternatives, which cannot be released from either the enclosure thematized by the disciplinary structures of the asylum or from their enclosure within the purely fictional form of the novel. Within the novel itself, the alternative space of the women's asylum cannot be elaborated into a narrative of emancipation that would move beyond its walls or outside the text, even though Marthe Gail desires just such a narrative, in which she as Christ would initiate 'the opening of the graves' and free 'the strange sounds of the dead bodies strapped under the sheets' – the women patients strapped into their beds and the stories they might tell (13, 113).

The circumstances surrounding the writing of Coleman's only published novel help to clarify her attempt to appropriate the asylum as a female space. The novel is an autobiographical fiction based on two months that Coleman spent in an asylum in upstate New York, suffering from puerperal fever (what the doctor in the novel calls 'toxic exhaustive psychosis' [60]) after the birth of her son in 1924.[8] Several contemporary reviews treated the book as a case history, although one reviewer did remark that the novel was more successful in its attempt 'to accomplish something artistic and literary than to interpret the subjective experiences of a sick mind'.[9] In 1925, Coleman became an expatriate when she and her husband moved to Paris, where she worked for the office of the *Chicago Tribune* and later, from 1928–29, served as secretary to Emma Goldman while the famous anarchist was writing her autobiography, *Living My Life*. During this period, Coleman published poetry in the avant-garde journal *Transition* and became notorious for her own unconventional personal style. Peggy Guggenheim wrote that 'Emily, unlike most people who are mad, did not hide it. On the whole it was a pleasant quality because it manifested itself in terrific enthusiasms and beliefs' (95). A number of her poems from this period also assume the persona of the madwoman; in one, the speaker asks for 'quiet hands' as 'asylum for my bewilderment' and in turn offers to 'be a burst of star-dust / to rend the weary curtain / of your monotony' ('Poem' 93). The most famous comment about Coleman is Djuna Barnes's remark that 'she would be marvelous company slightly stunned' (Guggenheim 140).

Coleman wrote *The Shutter of Snow* while helping Goldman with her autobiography. Alice Wexler argues that Coleman not only provided editorial assistance but that Goldman worked out many of her ideas through conversation and arguments with Coleman (134). I would argue that Coleman's novel also demonstrates Goldman's influence, in at least three ways. First, Coleman's direct treatment of the female body and female sexuality can be understood as inspired by Goldman's attempt to assert 'the importance of sexuality in her life while avoiding physical description, and veiling her experience in clichéd language reminiscent of the sentimental novels she had read as an adolescent'; Coleman is more graphic and deals more directly with preestablished linguistic structures as a problem in any attempt to represent specifically feminine experiences that have been culturally repressed (Wexler 146). Second, Coleman's critique of the power relations in the state hospital reflects Goldman's anarchist resistance to the apparatus of the state at all levels including the personal, rather than a Marxist commitment to class struggle. Third, Coleman's revision of women's domestic enclosure through novelistic appropriation of the asylum as a collective space reflects the themes of exile and the desire to establish an alternative home that recur in Goldman's autobiography, especially after she was deported from the US in 1919 (Wexler 145–6). Despite the social critique implicit in *The Shutter of Snow*, Coleman's relationship with Goldman and Goldman's decidedly non-modernist writing seems to have encouraged Coleman to dissociate writing and movements for political change. In 1928, Coleman published a statement in *transition* that reads in part 'I do not believe that people who are occupied with changing the world can be artists... . I am not interested in revolutionary movements, although I know they are healthy and although I am temperamentally on the side of every rebel.'[10] From her side, Goldman wrote that 'my world of ideas was foreign to [Coleman], natural rebel and anarchist though she was' (vi).

Despite Coleman's skepticism about changing the world, she did attempt to realize in her own life the spatial practices her novel depicts. *The Shutter of Snow* was published in England in 1930, and she divorced her husband that same year. In 1932, Coleman, Djuna Barnes and Peggy Guggenheim moved to England and established an alternative female space in the form of Guggenheim's country house, Hayford Hall.[11] The daughter of Antonia White, one of Coleman's friends who often visited Hayford Hall, calls it 'a version of Boccaccio, written for an all-female cast' (Chitty 61). Mary Lynn Broe describes Hayford Hall as a 'new domestic economy' that 'elevated a language of affective support and intellectual exchange to a norm' (59, 61). In *The Shutter of Snow*, Coleman had already prefigured this transformation of the private home into a collective space where relations between women are primary. But such accounts of alternative domestic economies overestimate the modernist break from nineteenth-century domestic reformists, whose treatment of home as repository of anticapitalist values and virtues depended on reproducing capitalism's distinction between home and marketplace.

The Shutter of Snow opens by emphasizing the various institutional barriers that enclose Marthe Gail and establish boundaries between that interior and the exterior space of freedom: 'Her lips stood out and were cracked and there was water gushing on the other side of the wall. There was chicken wire up over her door. The window was closed and the bars went up and down on the outside ... . There were six bars to the back of her bed' (1–2). The breakdown that put Marthe in this situation is her response to another confinement, her literal confinement during childbirth and her sense that by giving birth she is now identified with the role once played by her own dead mother: 'And she rustled in and out in a carcass of black silk, that was her mother and her father would never see her again ... . Her mother had rustled in and out of the silk and bars and had whispered into her coffin' (30–1). The conflation of the mother's feminine dress and her female body in the phrase 'carcass of black silk' represents a condition of objectification that conflates sex and gender, biology and the cultural construction of identity. In this context embodiment connotes a presocial or natural state, so that the mother is placed outside language and representation, just as the inmates of the asylum and 'the strange sounds of the dead bodies under the sheets' are confined within supposedly presocial spaces (113).[12] Confinement in the asylum and traditional female roles are metaphorically equated throughout the novel. At one point, Marthe describes the patients as 'deathheads rattling in a Bluebeard closet' (191). The novel presents the family as an institution that produces feminine identity and sexuality as something to be repressed: 'this was he, this more than ever her father, munching apples from the tree and saying come away dont look when the bull was in the pen. That was the part she did not understand and this was the part he gave her to understand' (109).[13] The psychiatric institution in which Marthe finds herself functions in precisely the same way.

However, the scene of enclosure with which the novel opens is also a scene of female voice. The novel's first words are 'There were two voices that were louder than the others. At night when the red light was out in the hall and there was someone sitting in a chair in front of the door clearing her throat at intervals there would be the voices far down the hall mingling with sobs and shouts and the drones of those who were beginning to sleep' (1). The narrator later offers this description of a woman in an argument: 'she drew back and shouted like a round ringed hornet's nest that suddenly had been broken into. Her words went wild and circled round and stung uselessly wherever they lighted' (154). These wordless voices or words gone wild thematize what Kristeva calls the semiotic, 'the irruption within language of the anteriority of language' in the form of a 'rhythmic, meaningless, anterior memory' of a moment prior to the organization of sound into the communicative structures that allow us to construct a shared social reality (Kristeva, 'Ethics' 32). The women's asylum is the space of such an 'upheaval of present place and meaning', the refusal of subjection to any preestablished structures of meaning or identity (32).[14]

In *The Shutter of Snow*, this anteriority may be a presocial space, but it is also the place where differences among women emerge, and it is therefore represented as containing the only hope the novel can find for intervening in constructions of social space. Early in the novel, the narrator tells us how Marthe 'threw out her arms and her voice penetrated the bars and drew out their metal marrow' (23). The disruptive voices of the women when they refuse to signify in terms established by others is here presented as having the capacity to transform the space of their enclosure, their enforced feminine interiority. The image of drawing out the bar's 'metal marrow' implies the possibility of claiming the experiences made possible by that enclosure and transforming them into a source of pleasure and nourishment, of bodily sensation. Marthe's writing as well as her voice are affected by this disruption of meaning. She believes that if she can just 'say it all' and thereby communicate her story then 'she would be free' (3, 20). As soon as she can obtain pencil and paper, therefore, Marthe writes to both her father and her husband: 'there were the words, the words that she was capturing out of the red lights and pinning under her pencil like squirming moths. The moths had yellow tails and pulled desperately away from the pencil' (20). Writing here represents Marthe's attempt to fix meaning, to pin it down, and thereby to stabilize her subjectivity and establish her sanity. The narrative that will follow oscillates between the story of Marthe's progressive resocialization and recovery, which pins down her identity, and her desire to resist that movement out of the asylum and to affirm the disruptive potential of her position as a 'madwoman'. The story Marthe wants to tell is presumably intended to explain her reaction to giving birth, a prototypical story of female experience. During the course of the novel, Marthe learns that this story is not as easy to tell as she assumed because she learns that female experience is not unitary.

The narrative follows Marthe's progress through various wards toward her release as her condition is judged to have improved. When she is first released from close confinement within her own room, where she was often under physical restraint, Marthe is described as 'out and away and flying into new spaces' (33). These new spaces are those occupied by the other patients. The asylum functions not only as a site where women's voices can emerge in their heterogeneity, but also as a site where female embodiment can be redefined. After sharing a bath with other patients, Marthe remembers that 'Mary had been beautiful the night in the bath. Shapes, all of them grotesque, the female body. All of them with breasts that did not fit, and rotting elbows. Toenails and trailing hair' (11). This passage demonstrates Marthe's oscillation between a focus on particularized female bodies and a universalizing rhetoric of 'the female body' that renders the bodies it subsumes grotesque, even as Marthe seems to move toward the acceptance of what does 'not fit'. In contrast to the openness that the women display toward one another, when Marthe tells her husband 'I want your body, I have dreamed it in the night', he replies 'there must not be any of this … . I will not kiss even your hand', presumably following the doctors' instructions (160). At this point, the husband and the doctors work together to reinforce the norms of a middle-class sexuality that Marthe has been unlearning, with the help of the 'other' women with whom she is confined.

With her emergence from her room into the ward, Marthe encounters class differences, not only between herself and other patients but between herself and the working women who make up the nursing staff and the professional women who serve as doctors. The hospital is literally organized into upper and lower classes, since the patients in the upper ward are 'the aristocrats of the place' (84). When her condition improves enough that she is moved upstairs, Marthe is told by another patient that 'they are very vulgar down there. The better ones come up here from there but not many of them' (85). This same patient who claims to be 'refined' and 'well bred' in comparison to the more violently disturbed women downstairs later calls a friend of Marthe's a 'Jewess' and tells her 'you crucified the Lord' (149). One of Marthe's friends downstairs is described as having 'black frizzled hair and thick lips', and she tells Marthe about working in a 'nigger cathouse' with her mother (63).

The institution is set up to reinforce these class and racial conflicts between the women. Marthe is told by a nurse that 'you ought to know better than to act the way you do when youve [*sic*] had a college education ... . You ought to behave better than the rest' (48). However, when Marthe refers to a patient with a reputation for being 'the primmest old maid that ever lived' on the outside, she is told 'they lose some of that when they get in here' (176). The institution also discourages the women from transgressing individual property rights. Early in the novel, Marthe is told to remember 'whats mine is mine and is not yours', and when she gives her toothbrush to a patient who does not have one a nurse asks 'dont you know better than to give away your tooth brush, whoever heard of such a thing' (18, 81). Watching their property and learning to take care of their things is also taken as a sign of mental stability and part of a patient's recovery (148).

Marthe resists these attempts to establish relations of dominance among the women in the asylum on the basis of class or race, although the novel does not minimize those differences. In the novel's first paragraph, when Marthe cries out that she is cold, we are told that 'the woman came in and took a blanket out and warmed it for her', not that the nurse came in (1). When Marthe first arrives at the more 'refined' ward upstairs, she refuses a private room and states her preference for joining the rest of the patients in the collective space of the open ward (82). She later links not only having such a room but desiring 'to be alone' in it with the process of resocialization that is aimed at recovering her position within the middle-class home (165). In the open ward one night, Marthe and another woman insist on stripping before the others while preparing for bed, and Marthe stands 'without embarrassment small and white' (91). When she is reprimanded as having 'no decency at all', she begins to dance (92).

These actions constitute a series of attempts to resist the process of returning home, to resist being 'cured', and instead to appropriate the asylum as an institutional basis for redefining female identity outside middle-class norms of femininity. Marthe's resistance culminates in her refusal to take seriously her 'Conference', the oral exam to determine whether she should leave the asylum. Although she is able to state who and where she is, facts she was uncertain of at the beginning of the novel, she also tells one doctor 'you have too many goodlooking clothes' and another that his socks do not match his tie (156, 158). She ends by reasserting her original claim to be Christ: 'my dear Dr. Armitage she said, when I have risen from the dead and have restored my kingdom upon earth, if I can do anything for you or yours a word from you will be considered of the utmost importance' (159). The humor and impertinence here satirize the conventions that determine what counts as a stable, feminine identity. Marthe could clearly adhere to those conventions if she chose, as the doctors recognize, and her departure is only delayed. Marthe's predicament is exemplified when she succeeds in escaping from her restraints while undergoing hydrotherapy by unraveling what she calls 'the spiral casket' (50). But she has nowhere to go. All she can do is submerge herself and tell the nurse 'I like it better down here' (55).[15] When she deliberately fails her 'Conference', she is telling the doctors the same thing. She likes it better 'down here', in the asylum.

Any alternative practice of female identity that Marthe might find in the asylum similarly remains submerged and contained within the walls of the institution, and therefore is unable to effect change or to maintain the changes it does effect beyond its own borders. The women in the asylum have a relation to language, to the body, and to the construction of social space that the novel would like to elaborate into a narrative of women's emancipation, just as Marthe wishes to raise the dead, the women entombed in the hospital. That desire is apparent when the narrator describes one of the patients as having 'been Russia waiting for the Revolution, and after that she had been Marthe's mother, moaning alone and shut away' (39).[16] But the narrator admits that Marthe 'could not get Mrs. Kemp out of it'. Marthe imagines a time when 'all of us shall dance in the snow' (11), but later we are told that 'it had come to her now that there was to be no release, that this would go on for every morning and that most of the mornings would be gray-risen' (99). The novel ends with Martha learning that there would be release for her, that 'I am going home', but there will be no collective release (218). Despite her imminent release, the final image of the novel, the image that provides its title, expresses Marthe's continuing confinement even outside the walls of the asylum: 'I shall have snow on my glassy fingers she said, and a shutter of snow on my grave tonight' (219). The title image of the shutter of snow involves a double conflation: Marthe's body is conflated with domestic space, and that home is conflated with the natural world, but never with the social world, which constitutes the limit to the novel's deconstruction of inner and outer spaces.

This final image of confinement within the tomb or corpse of domestic femininity can be explained by Marthe's belief that it is necessary for her to perform domestic labor before she can return home. In the same way that Marthe tried to pin down and stabilize her subjectivity by writing her story, she also 'cleaned and sang and cleaned, and ferreted out her life' (171). She thinks of housework as 'a composition. The whole floor became the composition and she was making it. ... She would always clean like this when she got home' (61). This work provides Marthe with a way to appropriate the enclosure she occupies, but it also requires her to internalize an ethic of self-discipline, to police her own subjectivity or ferret out her life. By doing so, she reproduces her confinement within the conventions of domestic femininity. Marthe later thinks that the nurses are discouraging her from this constant cleaning 'to keep me from finding out the truth so I can go home' (177). Her only choices are to submit to society's criteria for establishing the 'truth' of femininity or to remain in the asylum where her own version of that truth will be segregated from the rest of society.

The form of the novel enacts the undisciplined and 'mingling' voices of the women, in the way the novel shifts from third-person narration to the first-person voices of the characters, often without identifying which character is speaking or when one stops and another begins (1). The textual space of the novel therefore presents itself as homologous with the collective space created by the patients who disregard the conventions of femininity. Through its formal strategies for occupying the position of the madwoman, Coleman's novel accepts its isolation from the social world and thereby reproduces the enclosure of its alternative social vision within the confines of its fictional form. While Marthe imagines that 'her voice penetrated the bars and drew out their metal marrow', she later feels compelled to point out to another patient that 'the bars ... dont you see, the bars are not broken down' (23, 167). To the extent that its style dramatizes the assumption that resistance resides within a presocial feminine space, *The Shutter of Snow* undermines and recontains its own imagined transformation of the structures that enclose its characters' lives, in part by the way the style tends to assimilate the class differences between the women patients into a model of women's general symbolic exclusion from public life.

6
'Can't One Live in More Places Than One?': Virginia Woolf's *The Years*

The Years (1937) is Virginia Woolf's most explicit intervention in the traditions of domestic fiction and social realism, in the aftermath of her own modernist experiments with literary form. Perhaps for that very reason, the novel receives as little critical attention as Woolf's earlier, still relatively traditional fiction, written prior to *Jacob's Room*. This lack of attention is especially surprising given that critics have long attended to the ways in which 'rooms and windows play a special role in Virginia Woolf's fiction', as might be expected from the author of *A Room of One's Own* (Naremore, *World* 240).[1] James Naremore also points out the way Woolf uses such domestic figures to represent 'the chief problem for [Woolf] and for her characters': how to 'overcome the space between things' and achieve the 'unity with the world' that is denied by spatial barriers between public and private, masculinized and feminized spaces (*World* 242). Nevertheless, it is still relatively common to find *The Years* left out of books devoted to tracing the progression of Woolf's career.[2] The origin of *The Years* was Woolf's 1931 speech 'Professions for Women', later reimagined as 'an Essay-Novel called *The Pargiters*' (Woolf, *Writer's Diary* 162–3, 183). Many critics seem to take Woolf's retreat from this ambitious hybrid form and the fact that the novel therefore had to be massively edited before publication as evidence that the published novel is at best an interesting but failed experiment.[3]

Woolf also initially thought of *The Years* as 'a sequel to *A Room of One's Own*', focusing on 'the sexual life of women'. At various times, she considered entitling the novel 'Professions for Women', 'The Open Door' or 'Opening the Door', suggesting the extent to which Woolf associated considerations of female sexuality with the historical narrative of transformations in the ideology of separate gender spheres that open the border between public and private (*Writer's Diary* 162–3). The deletion of the essay portions of the book Woolf originally imagined writing (at least some of which ended up in *Three Guineas*) leaves critics faced with the necessity of choosing between two distinct reading strategies. On the one hand, *The Years* can be read textually, as Jane Marcus does in suggesting that the unedited manuscript is the true text (*Virginia Woolf* 52–3). On the other hand, critics can choose to focus on the published text of *The Years* and to situate it primarily in relation to Woolf's other novels and her characteristic themes: the changing status of the individual subject in the modernist period and the possibilities and limits of communicating across the boundaries of a privatized consciousness.[4]

I will argue that these two sets of themes, the historical narrative of transformations in the domestic arrangements of the Pargiter women and the more typically modernist problem of how to overcome experiences of isolation and alienation, are more closely interrelated than has typically been recognized in the commentary on *The Years*. Written immediately after *The Waves*, Woolf's most radical experiment with anti-narrative or 'lyrical' forms of novelistic discourse, *The Years* represents a return on Woolf's part to both a realist tradition, specifically the family chronicle, and to problems of representing shared social experiences rather than the pure interiority and private idiolects of the characters, presented through the series of interior monologues that constitute the text of *The Waves*. In the course of rewriting *The Years* as a more traditional novel rather than a hybrid genre combining fictional and non-fictional discourses, Woolf ended up combining this initial thematics of the private home with Woolf's more generally modernist concerns with the status of the individual subject, the possibility of transgressing the boundaries that define that subject, and the difficulty of escaping those enclosures in order to communicate with others.

As Jane Wheare points out, 'whereas in *The Waves* the reader must infer public utterances from private images, in *The Years*, as in ordinary intercourse, he or she can only guess at private experience from the public language of thought and speech' (132). This problem is thematized in one passage, in which Peggy, one of the second generation of Pargiter women, reflects that she and her aunt Eleanor 'were two living people, driving across London; two sparks of life enclosed in two separate bodies; and those sparks of life enclosed in two separate bodies are at this moment, she thought, driving past a picture palace. But what is this moment; and what are we?' (334).[5]

The questioning of supposedly self-evident enclosures and boundaries in this passage can be taken as paradigmatic of the novel's interests in philosophical questions about identity and the problem of solipsism. I would point out, in addition, the typical move to problematize individual alienation by moving from categories of space that are relatively static to categories of time that are relatively mobile; the question 'What is this moment?' seems to make it possible to ask the question 'What are we?' As Rachel Bowlby notes in a commentary on this passage, 'the view of the picture palace occurs as part of what is itself already a sequence of images seen from the car, and so extends the hall of screens and windows which might be seen to characterize modern life as a spectacle perpetually in motion, without a firm point of rest or origin' (125). In other words, this passage evokes the modernist decentering of subjectivity and associates it with the becoming-temporal of spatial fixities. In a similar later passage, Eleanor's niece Peggy, in the privacy of her own bedroom, feels 'as if things were moving past her as she lay stretched on the bed under the single sheet. But it's not the landscape any longer, she thought; it's people's lives, their changing lives' (211). In contrast to the earlier passage in the taxi, the relocating of temporalized experiences of space from the public street to the private home is especially significant, as is the rejection of fixed concepts of space such as 'landscape' and the distinction between character and setting, foreground and background, implicit in the category of landscape. This passage also clearly evokes the modernist figure of the *flaneur*, and is associated with the experience of displacement or homelessness within the modern city, but breaks down the distinction between male *flaneur* and domestic woman, in ways that are reinforced later in the novel by the thematics of the telephone.[6] Woolf refuses to simply abandon 'home' and the concept of location, as the *flaneur* might be understood to do; instead, Woolf's novel redefines that figure.

This passage also exemplifies two other motifs in *The Years*, the private home as a material enclosure for women and the individual body or self as enclosure for subjects in general. In *The Years*, the boundaries of individual subjectivity are often figured in terms of domestic imagery. In a much later passage, Peggy imagines how her aunt's mind works: 'some gust blew open a door; one of the many millions in Eleanor's seventy-odd years; out came a painful thought' (329). A further example comes when another of the main characters, Eleanor Pargiter's sister Rose, is questioned by her younger female relatives, who are surprised to find that Rose did not live only at

Abercorn Terrace, the childhood home where she and her sister resided with their father and the novel's main example of middle-class domesticity. 'Feeling vaguely annoyed', Rose replies 'Can't one live in more places than one?' (166). The pun on the two meanings of the word 'one' is typical of the systematic interconnection in *The Years* between the material mapping of public and private spaces and the interrogation of spatial metaphors for subjectivity. Rose's question literally refers to the possibility of living in multiple places, and one of the novel's questions is whether that can only occur sequentially, or whether one can live in more than one place at the same time. This possibility occurs a few pages later, when a minor character is described as having an 'odd look on his face as if he were in two worlds at once and had to draw them together' (185). Rose's question, however, also suggests the possibility of living as more than just 'one' person – that is, to the possibility of moving beyond the limits of the individual as traditionally understood in terms of a private, inner self modeled on domesticity's supposed separation from the public sphere.

As Rose notes in the passage above, the form that the family chronicle takes in *The Years* is the scattering of the late Victorian Pargiter daughters and the subsequent generations of their family into separate dwelling-places. This break-up of the family unit is represented primarily in terms of the scattering of domestic heirlooms and objects, originally located at Abercorn Terrace, across a variety of apartments and homes. As Bowlby points out, for both characters and readers these objects are charged with meaning as signifiers of 'home' and represent the reemergence and perpetuation of 'home' in a now dispersed form (119–20). This technique is one of the ways in which the novel combines 'home' and 'homelessness' rather than simply buying into either a modernist celebration of 'life as a spectacle perpetually in motion' (Bowlby 125) or a reactionary critique of such mobility that seeks to reinstate fixed spatial categories. Both of these alternatives depend upon distinctions between public and private, stasis and mobility. Instead, the novel attempts to imagine these categories as mutually implicated and as redefining one another. In this way, the novel attempts to mediate between the contradictory tendencies that Karen Kaivola locates in Woolf's fiction, between 'Woolf's acute awareness of her own internalized boundaries, her sense of what she felt she – as a woman – could not or should not represent' in her fiction (21) and the desire expressed in Woolf's more 'lyrical' novels, to 'dissolve all individuality' and all distinctions between self and other, which in *The Waves* results in the death of the character Rhoda.[7]

This dispersal of the private home on the level of imagery is accompanied and reinforced by a dispersal of the novel's language across the boundaries of individual subjectivities. As Wheare argues, specific ideas and phrases migrate from one character to the next, in a series of echoes (144).[8] It is in this way that the form of the novel attempts to answer the question posed by one of its characters: 'what would the world be ... without "I" in it?' (242). It is also in this way that *The Years* acknowledges the conventionality of its own language, in contrast to the attempt to capture the private languages of each character in *The Waves*. As Wheare puts it, 'in *The Years* ... Woolf concentrates on the idea that experience only becomes recognisable and, therefore, communicable when it is expressed in the terms of an already existing language' (140).[9] One of the characters in the novel acknowledges 'they all had lines cut; phrases ready-made' (309). This technique reaches its high point in the final section of the novel, entitled 'Present Day, during a party scene which reconstitutes the domestic as a site of contact across the boundaries of individual subjectivity. This final scene renders the spaces of both home and self internally heterogeneous. As one of the characters puts it, 'What could be more ordinary? ... A large family, living in a large house' (168). The goal of *The Years* is to see how large that house can become and to chart the limits of spatial and familial metaphors to represent the changes that result from this enlargement. Though this trope of largeness echoes the nineteenth-century rhetoric of projecting 'woman's sphere' onto the social world, Woolf's novel demonstrates a greater awareness of the problem of cultural imperialism built into this expansive project and tries to foreground the internal conflicts that result, in order to avoid subsuming social differences under a middle-class model.

1 'Talking of the other world': rewriting domesticity

In its version of family chronicle, *The Years* is directly concerned with the relation of social change and domestic ideology. In an early draft, one of the Pargiter family's younger cousins (Sara Pargiter in the published version) refers to 'an interminable and wonderful procession, from one end of time to the other, The Pargiters' (quoted in Squier, 'Track' 203). The novel raises the question of how much this continuity has been interrupted by changes in modern social existence and how that discontinuity alters or reproduces traditional representations of femininity. In Edward Said's terms, the novel applies to women's domestic lives the typical modernist attitude of refusing to take for granted the 'mere natural continuity between generations'; in this way, modernism makes possible a transition from narratives of generational filiation to narratives of collective affiliation (Said, *World* 16).[10] In its most general outline, the narrative structure of *The Years* traces the progressive breakdown of the domestic ideology exemplified by Colonel Pargiter's articulation of the cliché that 'a girl's place was the home' (*Pargiters* 28). *The Years* is especially important as an intervention in domestic fiction precisely because it does not simply reject such clichés out of hand, in typical modernist fashion, but instead remains willing to reflect on the power such banal formulations continue to wield, often in unexpected ways.

The plot of the novel and the fate of the women of the Pargiter family can therefore be summed up as a movement 'from the protected prison of the Victorian home to the freedom of the modern city streets, there to struggle with men for their rightful public place' (Squier, *Virginia Woolf* 141). But if the novel charts a narrative of liberation from middle-class gender norms, it also represents this movement into the public sphere as a dilemma for the 'daughters of educated men' like the Pargiter sisters, who find themselves

> between the devil and the deep sea. Behind us lies the patriarchal system; the private house, with its nullity, its immorality, its hypocrisy, its servility. Before us lies the public world, the professional system, with its possessiveness, its jealousy, its pugnacity, its greed. The one shuts us up like slaves in a harem; the other forces us to circle, like caterpillars head to tail, round the mulberry tree, the sacred tree of property (Woolf, *Three Guineas* 74).

This quotation measures Woolf's divergence from nineteenth-century domestic reformers who turned to 'the private house' as a site of alternative, anticapitalist values. Woolf here moves toward an understanding of how domestic individualism and possessive individualism, 'the sacred tree of property', mirror one another.[11] In this view, domestic confinement actually prepares women to enter the public sphere in a way that does not disrupt the worship of property and which breaks down the division of public/private spaces without altering the structure of individuation and alienation that was grounded in that division. By problematizing this co-implication of public and private in capitalist ideology, *The Years* also problematizes the structure of gender opposition grounded in the ideology of separate spheres.

In its attempt to challenge the structure of gender opposition underlying the construction of modern subjectivity, the narrative of women's access to the public sphere in *The Years* opens onto the problem of contact between persons of not only different genders, but different generations, classes, races, nationalities and sexualities, differences that cut across gender lines. From this perspective, *The Years* can be divided into three main sections. The first section consists of the '1880' chapter, which depicts the barriers of social convention that confine the four Pargiter sisters and Kitty Malone to the oppressive shelter of the private home. The second section consists of several chapters in which these characters variously attempt to escape the 'abominable system' represented by their family home: the conventional route of marriage for Milly; political involvement and social service for her sisters Rose and Eleanor; and an attempt to combine political work and married life for Delia and Kitty Malone (*Years* 222).

The early sections of the novel thematize the limits of nineteenth-century projects of expanding 'woman's sphere', which the novel links to the rhetoric of civilizing mission that poses people located outside the middle-class home as exoticized others. Beginning with a general image of 'virgins and spinsters with hands that had staunched the sores of Bermondsey and Hoxton' taking tea at home (4), the novel moves on to explicitly associate the young Eleanor with the project of social housekeeping. Eleanor is initially characterized by her 'Grove days', when she visits the Levys, a poor Jewish family, condescendingly referred to within the Pargiter home as 'the dear old Levys' (13). Inverting this condescension into envy, Eleanor is moved to blurt out 'the poor enjoy themselves more than we do', and one of her sisters comments 'I believe you'd like to go and live there if you had your way', begging the question of whether Eleanor would be able to live any differently there, or if she would continue to see it as her job to help the Levys live more like she does (30–1). Similarly, after a visit to a working-class family, another woman character feels 'a sudden rush of self-pity. ... If she had been the daughter of people like the Robsons, she thought; if she had lived in the north....' (73). The way this temptation to become working class in order to escape feminine confinement within the middle-class home only reproduces classist and racist stereotypes is implied when Eleanor goes on to comment that 'they do love finery – Jews' (31). At the same time, however, Eleanor also dislikes 'talking about "the poor" as if they were people in a book' (30–1). Eleanor, whose father calls her 'housekeeper' (92), goes on to become involved in urban reform and thinks of 'Peter Street where she had built houses' that are now in need of repair, indicating her continuing investment in forms of social housekeeping (95). The meetings of Eleanor's urban reform committee represent just another way of 'talking about "the poor" as if they were people in a book'. After her father's death, however, in the '1911' chapter, Eleanor begins to move beyond such transpositions and enlargements of domesticity to a more basic interrogation and redefinition of it (195). This chapter ends with Eleanor's decision to start a new life by refusing 'to take another house, not another house' (213).

The rest of the novel dramatizes this struggle to avoid confinement within just 'another house' – that is, to avoid simply reproducing the structure of the interiorized self, a self that can be possessed, grounded in the Pargiter women's middle-class experience of home. It is this struggle that underlies the third section of the novel, which takes the form of a series of encounters between the older Pargiters, especially Eleanor, Rose and their brother Martin, and their younger relatives, especially their cousins Sara and Maggie Pargiter, Maggie's husband Renny, and their friend Nicholas but also including Eleanor's niece Peggy and her nephew North Pargiter in the final 'Present Day' section. These encounters lead to the conclusion shared at least partially by several of the characters, that 'to live differently' and 'to form – new combinations' requires them to remain attentive to 'far-away sounds, the suggestion they brought in of other worlds, ... of people toiling, grinding, ... in the depths of night' (422, 296, 388). These passages should be read in relation to the dissatisfaction with self-enclosure that Peggy expresses on the cab ride with her aunt, when she wonders 'Where does she begin, and where do I end?' and imagines the two of them as 'two sparks of life enclosed in two separate bodies' (334).[12] *The Years* traces not only a narrative of women's entry onto the public scene, but also the Pargiter women's 'drift' across class boundaries, 'from family life in the upper-middle-class districts of Victorian London and Oxford to independent life in the working-class districts of modern London' (Squier, *Virginia Woolf* 141).

2 'Was there some other?': the telephone, compulsory contact, and the limits of the self

The significance of the urban setting of *The Years* is best defined by Georg Simmel, for whom the modern city is a site of 'obligatory association' between individuals who do not perceive themselves as belonging to the same group, a place where it is not possible to avoid encountering what Simmel calls 'the stranger', a person who is both 'near and far *at the same time*' (327; 144; 148).[13] The result of such encounters is to call into question the spatial metaphors that establish identity by establishing an inside and an outside. Woolf's comments on *The Years* suggest a deliberate attempt to formally capture the experience of being both inside and outside, near and far, that Simmel defines. While Woolf begins by opposing the 'externality' of the book that would become *The Years* to the subjective focus of *The Waves*, she later writes that 'I want to give the whole of the present society – nothing less: facts as well as the vision. And to combine them both. I mean, *The Waves* going on simultaneously with *Night and Day*', Woolf's early realist novel (*Writer's Diary* 191). In other words, she wants both 'externality' and 'internality' at once.

Jane Marcus has analyzed the representation of working-class or homeless women in Woolf's novels, such as *Mrs. Dalloway*, where they are often posed as figures for the presocial negativity of the Kristevan semiotic, the refusal of all preestablished social structures and therefore all meaning, like the voices of the madwomen in Coleman's *The Shutter of Snow* (Marcus, *Virginia Woolf* 12–13). *The Years* reworks Woolf's own earlier writing and points to the necessity for redefining social space so that these women are not excluded from representation or romanticized as a position of resistance entirely outside the structures her middle-class characters inhabit, a representation that reproduces an exclusively middle-class perspective. The novel's problem is how to represent a character like Eleanor Pargiter 'talking of the other world', like the world of another class that Peggy hears in 'the far-away sounds ... of people toiling, grinding' (387–8). Talk of 'the other world' can objectify the other and confirm the hierarchies of self and other, inside and outside, when it means that 'we' are talking *about* the other. But the awareness of that otherness can also interrupt 'our' assumptions about our 'world', when we acknowledge that the other has its own discourse, its own subjectivity. *The Years* continually thematizes and affirms such interruptions within both the social space and the discourses of its characters, in the form of frequent ellipses and incomplete sentences.[14] It is in this way that Woolf infuses 'the modern communication situation with some of its historical ramifications'; her interruptions signify 'what is truly other about the other', the 'strangers' to whom we find ourselves linked by the 'obligatory associations' of modern, urban society (Armstrong 243).[15]

In *The Years*, one of the main ways these linkages are forged is through the new technology of the telephone, which also figures 'the modern communication situation' and its uncertainties, especially the absence of direct physical proximity. In this novel, the phone dramatizes a situation of simultaneous connection to, and detachment from, another person, which is presented as a model for the interruption of the process of defining the limits of the self through its difference from the other, a precondition for acknowledging genuine otherness rather than turning the other into a negative image of the self. The novel is fascinated by the difference between the spatiality of the phone line and the 'generalized oppositionality' of the ideology of separate spheres. Phone conversations at times act as narrative pivots, with the focus of the narration shifting along the phone line from the character on one end of the line to the other, as Bowlby points out, with the result that 'the physical "room" is no longer identifiable as a separate scene' (126). These scenes literalize Woolf's stream-of-consciousness technique in novels like *Mrs. Dalloway*, where the point of view can shift from one character to another as a result of their random encounters, as if they were linked by phone lines visible only to the reader. In this sense, the telephone 'makes explicit the structure' of simultaneous connection and separation 'that operates in any attempt at making connections between what are thought to be two separate, self-contained "people"' (Bowlby 126). In other words, the telephone does not so much interrupt or replace 'ordinary' communication; instead, it reveals the structure of dispersed enunciation and reception implicit in any speech act, and by doing so figures a new experience of space, in which social presence is not completely localized or bounded.

For example, in one scene from the novel, a young man, North, watches Sara, one of the younger generation of Pargiter women, speaking on the telephone: 'she was kneeling at the telephone talking; but there was nobody there' (312). 'There was nobody there' is grammatically parallel to Rose Pargiter's question 'can't one live in more places than one?', which repeats and puns on the word 'one' in the same way that this sentence repeats puns on the word 'there'. The first use of this term is as a shifter, an 'empty' word whose function in the sentence is performative, in the sense of referring to the time and place of the discourse situation in which it appears, so that its meaning shifts every time it is used. In this sense, 'there' means the shared time and place that the utterance creates between the speaker and his or her audience (Benveniste 218–19). But the second time it is used in this sentence, 'there' refers to a specific, material place, or rather it would refer to such a place (like the apartment) if it existed. The point of the statement is that the lack of face-to-face proximity makes it impossible for Sara and the person on the other end of the phone line to share space in the way that our habits of language assume we create a shared space when we speak to others. The point of dramatizing these two different functions of the word 'there' is to make explicit the analogy between language and place; the meaning of the phone metaphor as Woolf elaborates it is that this analogy is breaking down. Both the boundaries of the places we inhabit and the positions we are used to occupying in language are becoming unstable.

Sara's phone conversation in this scene is with a man who has just met her visitor, North, and she goes on to have a brief conversation about North. North then imagines that, as Sara looks at him, 'it was as if she were trying to put two different versions of him together; the one on the telephone perhaps and the one on the chair. Or was there some other? This half knowing people, this half being known, ... how uncomfortable it was, he thought; but inevitable, after all these years' (313). The phone conversation figures a kind of bilocation that for Woolf literalizes the experience of participating in language, as both subject and object of discourse. The phone offers another way of living in more places than one, and locates that condition in the experience of language itself as a performed discursive event rather than merely the reproduction of a set of preestablished structures.

If, as Bowlby points out, the telephone represents a specific mode of connection between people, a connection not directly tied to the physical or visual presence of the other person, it has not been recognized how the use of the telephone to figure this type of connection functions as a counterpoint to another major symbol in *The Years*, from the '1880' chapter which opens the novel. I'm referring specifically to the 'pillar-box' or mailbox. The image of the pillar-box has received a great deal of attention from feminist critics, most notably Susan Squier. The pillar-box first makes its appearance when Rose Pargiter, while still a young child, sneaks out of the house one evening, pretending to be carrying a 'secret message' intended for a British general through 'the enemy's country' (28). Just as she passes a pillar-box, a man emerges who leers at her and attempts to catch her (28). When she returns on her way home, he exposes himself: 'he did not stretch his hands out at her; they were unbuttoning his clothes' (29).

Squier points out the implications of associating the pillar-box with what Woolf calls 'street love', in one of the unpublished essay portions of the original manuscript (Squier 168; Woolf, *Pargiters* 35–8).[16] As a repository for letters, the pillar-box also represents access to the world of writing and public discourse more generally, and Rose's childish attempt to participate in the public life of the British empire leaves her vulnerable to sexual attack. The result is to reinforce the need for the securely bounded private space of 'home' as a form of protection for women. In many ways, the rest of the novel tells the story of the Pargiter women's various attempts to unlearn the desire for protection, including Rose's becoming a militant suffragette. This process of unlearning protection is paralleled by the way that the telephone disrupts the association of communications media with phallic power established in this scene, when posting a letter becomes equated with publicly exhibiting the phallus.

The pillar-box and the telephone are clearly linked as emblems for the public circulation of signs. In addition, they function as historical guideposts to the changes that communications media undergo during the course of the period represented in the novel, from 1880 to the present, presumably the mid-1930s. This process is one of increasing virtualization, as the telephone permits real-time social interaction at a distance. But the telephone is also located domestically, in contrast to the pillar-box. So where the pillar-box functions as a marker of the boundary between public and private and a reminder of the dangers to women of crossing over, the telephone renders that boundary permeable. In this sense, access to the circulation of letters, both literally and figuratively, would be more closely associated with the promenade of the *flaneur*, while the telephone locates the experience of mobility and displacement within the boundaries of the home, in a way that calls into question the spatial distinctions that define those boundaries. As Ronell reminds us, the culture of the telephone 'can barely abide an outside' (94).

One of the consequences of the replacement of the pillar-box by the telephone is that both 'home' and women are increasingly implicated in the larger social world. The private home no longer provides protection against that external world, and that shift means new opportunities and greater exposure to old dangers and forms of sexual violence. While the agency of the phone gives the women characters greater access to the circulation of signs and social meanings in the outside world with less risk to their physical persons, the cost of this increased access is that the women must themselves circulate as signs for others, to some extent. *The Years* presents this increased availability of the women characters not only as a function of how new communications technologies tend to break down clear distinctions between inside and outside, but also as an opportunity for communication across differences – that is, the transformation of home into a site of coalition, a contact zone.

This motif in the novel is first introduced immediately after the scene in which North watches Sara having a phone conversation with someone else. As she turns to him, he reflects that she is looking at him 'as if she were trying to put two different versions of him together; the one on the telephone perhaps and the one on the chair' (313). At this point, as Bowlby suggests, the novel thematizes the telephone as a form of what Allucquere Rosanne Stone calls a location technology, a mechanism for linking a discursive and a physical space, or a social persona and a physical body (Stone 40). But the telephone also functions as a visible reminder of the artificial or prosthetic nature of such linkages. The effect of being confronted with such a reminder is suggested when North is inspired by the spectacle of Sara using the telephone to go on to consider the general experience of 'half knowing people, this half being known, this feeling of the eye on the flesh, like a fly crawling – how uncomfortable it was' (313). Note the oddity of this description of being watched. On the one hand, it suggests the disorganization of the body's unity when mediated through the epistemological structure here represented by communications technologies, and perhaps by language itself. The eye takes on a life separate from its owner and operates independently, like a fly. On the other hand, this same process results in the merging of formerly distinct individuals, as one person's eye is relocated 'on' another person's body. Sight becomes tactile, and seeing is no longer clearly structured by the division between subject and object, viewer and spectacle.

While Bowlby tends to emphasize the way this passage distinguishes phone conversations from physical interaction, where the other person is visible, it seems to me that the passage is ambiguous enough to suggest that the experience of 'half knowing people' or 'half being known' by being viewed from the outside is also being compared by North with the experience of knowing someone only through phone conversation. In both cases, knowledge of the other is incomplete. The suggestion is that persons circulate socially through the medium of the telephone, as signs for others to interpret, in the same way that bodies circulate socially in the streets of the city as visible images for others to interpret. What North is beginning to reflect on here is the emergence of a kind of virtual community, which is not entirely distinct from material physical interactions; rather, these two modes of social interaction, the virtual and the physical, are complexly intertwined and often function as models for how to conceptualize or reconceptualize one another.

This reading of the telephone scene between North and Sara implies that the telephone does not offer an escape from the constraints that dealing with other people places on us. The telephone becomes what Stone, in her book on virtual systems theory, calls a new 'locus of sociality', where social interaction increasingly takes place in a space where the grounding of social presence in a physical body seems less important or relevant (Stone 43). *The Years* imagines the emergence of this new 'locus of sociality' as facilitating contact with strangers, across embodied differences of gender, sexuality, race or ethnicity. The telephone in fact begins to transform the private home into such a locus of sociality, with the results that Bonnie Honig defines, when she argues that 'to resignify home as a coalitional arrangement and to accept the impossibility of the conventional home's promised safety from conflict, dilemmas, and difference is not to reject home but to recover it for the sake of an alternative, future practice of politics. The recovery does, however, admit and embrace a vulnerability that may *look like* homelessness' (270–1). It is this vulnerability that North experiences in the passage above, as he is viewed by Sara.

Sara's vulnerability is defined in a later passage, when North overhears the sound of the water running in the adjacent bathroom. Sara tells him that it's 'the Jew having a bath', and 'tomorrow there'll be a line of grease' around the tub (339). She then launches into a story about how she rushed out of the house in a rage after discovering that she would have to share the tub, ending up at a newspaper office, where she tells one of the workers that 'the Jew's in my bath' (342). This passage deliberately thematizes the virulently anti-Semitic attitudes of the time and Sara's difficulties in working through those attitudes. Her reference to 'my bath' suggests the extent to which she and other characters may remain caught up in the conceptual framework of the private home, in this case reflecting the Pargiters' class and ethnic privilege. Like Eleanor's relationship with the Levy family at the beginning of the novel, Sara is tempted to reassert a model of domestic individualism, in which securing the boundaries of identity is synonymous with a kind of metaphorical housekeeping – in this case, the elimination of the grease stain Sara imagines being produced by the Jewish man's use of their shared bathtub. Like Eleanor's dislike of the phrase 'the poor' at the beginning of the novel, Sara's use of the phrase 'the Jew' still indicates a desire to pose an 'other' as conceptually separate entity, reflecting a logic of spatial segregation at the very moment when that literal separation was being breached.

At the same time, it seems to me that this passage deliberately rewrites Rose's trauma at the pillar-box, with the possibility of such encounters now relocated within Sara's residence, not in the public sphere. This passage also indicates, though, that gender is not the only and not always the primary structure of dominance. This understanding is not just liberating for the middle-class Pargiter women, as part of a general resistance to the ideology of separate gender spheres; it also poses new challenges and responsibilities for them. While women are at risk in specific ways in public spaces, so too is 'the Jew' vulnerable to Sara's stereotypical response, and so are 'the unemployed' that North hears 'singing hymns' under Sara's window as she tells this story (340). What Woolf attempts to imagine is a situation in which this mutual vulnerability becomes the basis for reimagining social space as coalitional. The party scene that concludes *The Years* dramatizes this transformation, by attempting to imagine how the alternative spatiality associated with the telephone could be generalized to other forms of social interactions, between people who are present in the same place. At the same time, this scene invites comparison to Coleman's figure of the women's mental hospital as a transformation of domesticity, in *The Shutter of Snow*. Does Woolf avoid the trap of allowing such alternatives to be recontained that we saw in Coleman's novel?

3 'Living in a large house'

The final chapter, 'Present Day', uses Rose and Eleanor Pargiter's sister Delia's party as a vehicle to redefine the space of the family as it was initially represented by the women's oppressive confinement within the Pargiter family home at Abercorn Terrace. Where that home functioned as a mechanism of exclusion, establishing a sheltered interior and a dangerous exterior (at least for the women), the party is much more inclusive. Delia describes how at the party 'all the generations in our family are so mixed; cousins and aunts, uncles and brothers – but perhaps it's a good thing' (364). Delia's aim is precisely 'to mix people; to do away with the absurd conventions of English life. And she had done it tonight, she thought. There were nobles and commoners; people dressed and people not dressed; people drinking out of mugs, and people waiting with their soup getting cold for a spoon to be brought to them' (398). The final, long party scene thereby attempts to negotiate between the desire to escape an oppressive private sphere and the desire to avoid capitulating to the values of an equally oppressive public sphere, in a rewriting of Woolf's own earlier fiction, specifically the famous party scene in *Mrs. Dalloway*, which through the motif of the hostess dramatizes and attempts to revalue women's unpaid psychological labor in maintaining social relations. As one character puts it, the problem is how to 'down barriers' without making the world 'all one jelly, one mass, ... a rice pudding world, a white counterpane world' (410).

Kitty Lasswade's more conventional and homogeneous party is described as a process of 'talking, as they had talked for the past fifty years. ... They were all talking. They had all settled in to add another sentence to the story that was just ending, or in the middle, or about to begin' (260–1). In contrast, Delia's party demonstrates 'the erratic desire of a hostess always to interrupt' (378–9); it is narrated as a process of continuous discontinuity and reconstruction that involves negotiating differences and not affirming identity or continuity: 'Directly something got together, it broke. ... And then you have to pick up the pieces, and make something new, something different, she thought, and crossed the room, and joined the foreigner' (392). Peggy's desire to make something new echoes Eleanor's conviction that 'there must be another life.... Not in dreams; but here and now, in this room, with living people' (427).

The party ends with a reminder of how difficult is this process of acknowledging the simultaneous proximity and difference of other people. One of the younger Pargiter men questions the limits of Delia's ambition to mix people across social barriers and her 'pride in her promiscuity', commenting that the partygoers 'were all the same sort. Public school and university. ... But where are the Sweeps and the Sewer-men, the Seamstresses and the Stevedores?'; he sees only 'Dons and Duchesses' (404). The answer to this question comes when two working-class children are brought into the party, given cake, and invited to 'sing a song for sixpence' (428–9). When they do sing, 'not a word was recognizable', although the distorted sounds rose and sank as if they followed a tune' (429). In a final recognition of the necessity to redefine shared social reality as a space of heterogeneous meaning, Eleanor turns to Maggie and says '"Beautiful?" ... with a note of interrogation' (431). Maggie replies 'extraordinarily', but 'Eleanor was not sure that they were thinking of the same thing'.[17]

This famous and puzzling interruption of the party might be read in Kristeva's terms, as the intrusion of the anarchy of the semiotic into the rule-governed system of symbolic language. But it seems to me that it might be more useful to read this moment as thematizing the limits of the sense of connection that Eleanor enjoys at the party, thereby returning the model of communication being developed from one of face-to-face interaction to the more limited communicational situation figured by the telephone, which only permits characters to be 'half known' to one another. As one of the characters notes, 'people talked nonsense at parties', and one goal of the party scene seems to be to make that nonsensical element of middle-class discourse visible, not to ghettoize the working-class children as agents of disruption who do the middle-class partygoers a service by allowing them to reimagine themselves and their language (385).

At the same time, the appearance of this incomprehensible younger generation provides a comment on the traditional status of the home as a site for both literal biological reproduction and the reproduction or transmission of culture. What the children's song suggests is that the Pargiter household remains a space of reproduction, but what is reproduced is difference rather than sameness. The risk of openness or vulnerability to resignification and to allowing oneself to be interpreted by another is the risk of less than perfect communication.

In this way, *The Years* attempts to resist what North thinks of as the family 'conspiracy ... the steam roller that smooths, obliterates; rounds into identity; rolls into balls .... [T]hey're not interested in other people's children .... Only in their own; their own property; their own flesh and blood' (378). The other main way in which the novel resists this concept of family and domesticity is by introducing into the space of the family 'the far-away sounds, the suggestion they brought in of other worlds, indifferent to this world, of people toiling, grinding, in the heart of darkness, in the depths of night' (388). The co-implication of 'home' and the social world results not only in the introduction of difference into the cultural space of the family, as suggested by the children's song, but it also raises the question one of the other characters poses to himself: 'Is it "the" world?' (254). 'Home' as a space of contact between different peoples is accompanied by the pluralization of the outside world, as the spatial distinctions that provide the illusion of two homogeneous spaces, inside and outside, public and private, are called into question. This possibility of a collective subject imaged by the party emerges from the unavoidable necessity of contact between individuals located in the same social space.[18] Woolf suggests that this possibility can be realized only through the breakdown of the private home as a separate sphere.

7
'Dream Made Flesh': Sexual Difference and Narratives of Revolution in Sylvia Townsend Warner's *Summer Will Show*

> [The epic poet] must be centered in the normal, he must measure the crooked by the straight, he must exemplify that sanity which has been claimed for true genius. No pronounced homosexual, for instance, could succeed in the epic, not so much for being one as for what his being cuts him off from.
>
> E.M.W. Tillyard, 'The Nature of the Epic' (48)[1]

> Every action, every translation of a collision into deeds requires a certain common territory between the opponents, even if this 'community' is one of sworn social enmity. Exploiter and exploited, oppressor and oppressed may have this territory for their struggle; *sexual abnormality*, however, has no such battleground in its collision with society. Such a passion also lacks the relative, subjective justification either of being rooted in the social order of the past, or of anticipating the future. The struggle of successive systems of love, marriage, family etc., thus has nothing to do with the 'problematic' of this [historical] drama.
>
> Georg Lukacs, *The Historical Novel* (113; my emphasis)

> [T]he particular form of elsewhereness pertaining to the Modernist left-wing writer ... is defined by the way she deconstructs a norm of socialist realism.
>
> Jane Marcus, 'Alibis and Legends' (285)

> In so far as [lesbian fiction] documents a world in which men are 'between women' rather than vice versa, it is an insult to

> the conventional geometries of fictional eros. It dismantles the real, as it were, in a search for the not-yet-real, something unpredicted and unpredictable. As a consequence, it often looks odd, fantastical, implausible, 'not there' – utopian in aspiration if not design.
>
> Terry Castle, 'Sylvia Townsend Warner and the Counterplot of Lesbian Fiction' (231)

> Marxist political practice can succeed only through the attempt to renarrativize experience, to construct a narrative whose narrating would be the production of a narratable world.
>
> J.M. Bernstein, *The Philosophy of the Novel* (266)

1 'Dream made flesh': narratable worlds and lesbian fictions

By locating the story of a lesbian couple within the context of the 1848 revolution in Paris, Sylvia Townsend Warner's novel *Summer Will Show* (1936) launches a double critique. The novel attempts to intervene both in the Marxist tradition of historical narrative and in the modernist novel's turn away from narrative to 'lyrical' or 'introspective' forms (Fletcher and Bradbury). By incorporating modernist assumptions, *Summer Will Show* resists the totalizing tendency of Marxist historical narratives, while at the same time it insists upon historical representation as a precondition for (re)narrativizing same-sex relationships. The novel therefore also resists assertions like the one made by Marxist theorist Georg Lukacs, when he argues that the experience of 'sexual abnormality' has no narrative structure because it has no temporal structure, being neither 'rooted in the social order of the past' nor 'anticipating the future' (*Historical Novel* 113).

At the same time, 'sexual abnormality' produces no significant historical effects because there is no social space, no 'common territory', where these 'abnormalities' could come into conflict with heterosexual norms and enter into a historical dialectic with them. Without the possibility of such a dialectic, 'sexual abnormality' can never become the 'motor of history'. This assertion is only possible if Lukacs assumes homosexuality to be located firmly within the private sphere of 'love, marriage, family, etc.' and therefore clearly distinguishable from class relations. In other words, for Lukacs 'sexual abnormality' is always only a theme for domestic fiction, not the historical novel with its focus on *real* social enmities. This statement of Lukacs's, then, defines how distinctions between public and private spheres might need to be disrupted or rethought as the precondition for producing a lesbian historical novel. Warner's *Summer Will Show* thematizes this rethinking of spatial assumptions in the form of the alternative household established by the two main women characters, during the 1848 revolution in Paris. But that rethinking also structures the novel on a more formal level.

Summer Will Show applies to narratives of both lesbian sexuality and class struggle the point that J.M. Bernstein makes in his reading of Lukacs's theory of class consciousness as a theory of narrative.[2] By focusing on the centrality of narrative in Lukacs's thought, Bernstein locates an anti-foundational tendency within Lukacs's Marxism. For example, Bernstein concludes that:

> the premise of praxial action, of a collective narrating of experience, need not presuppose the actual existence of a collective consciousness. It does, of course, presuppose that there are spaces where such narratives can begin to be told; and further that there are potentialities for a telling, that the present contains grounds of shared interest and possibilities whose realisation depend on their being collectively recognized (264).

Warner's narrative of a lesbian couple's involvement in the 1848 revolution locates precisely such spaces, potentialities, and shared interests, as the basis for producing collective narrations of alternative sexual experiences as an irreducible element of any collective movement. But the novel also shows how it is necessary to reimagine the concept of 'space' that such narratives presuppose, rather than taking that concept for granted.

One reviewer of the 1987 reprint of *Summer Will Show* noted that the novel 'is a virtual catalogue of devices for pre-liberation lesbian narratives' – that is, devices for evading the representation of same-sex desire (Abraham 389). I would argue, however, that Warner's awareness of the politics of representation should also be understood in terms of the novel's 'incredulity toward metanarratives' (Lyotard xxiv). *Summer Will Show*'s deliberate intervention in Marxist representations of emergent social subjects suggests that the refusal to include a sex scene between its main characters is less an act of closeted self-censorship than a recognition of the 'value in the sustained tension of an undefined and unlocated term, not as an indeterminacy that reiterates a cultural paradigm, but as one that plays within and beyond such paradigms' (Roof 64).

It is this form of value that Minna, one of the main women characters in Warner's novel, invokes when she reflects on her seemingly inappropriate response to the materialization of her revolutionary dreams. Minna's comments to her soon-to-be lover Sophia are occasioned by the initial outbreak, in February 1848, of a revolution by the unified middle and working classes against the aristocracy. Her comments, however, apply equally to the erotic relationship that develops between the two women:

> You think I am not very enthusiastic? ... Perhaps you think I am not very sincere. But if you have ever longed for a thing, longed with your whole heart, with year after year of your life, longed for it with all that is noblest in you and worked for it with all that is most base and most calculating, you would understand with what desolation of spirit one beholds the dream made flesh (*Summer* 146).

This passage almost seems to anticipate and forestall contemporary readers' responses to the novel's reticence in representing lesbian sexual practices. By locating the leftist slogan of the revolution as a 'dream made flesh' in the first face-to-face meeting between the two women characters, the novel gives a more literal meaning to this phrase, and the way that Minna's longed-for and deferred 'thing' can be understood as both revolutionary social change and non-normative sexuality is one of the unrecognized accomplishments of Warner's novel.[3]

But this passage also defines Minna's investment in what Terry Castle calls the 'not-yet real' of lesbian fiction and desire. Castle's description of lesbian fiction suggests that it might anticipate the kind of political practice Bernstein calls for, where social change is understood as a renarrativizing of experience in which the act of narration has to produce the material conditions of existence for the narrative, where the narration itself 'would be the production of a narratable world' (266). In its temporality, this model corresponds to Lyotard's definition of the postmodern as structured by the future perfect tense: 'the artist and writer, then, are working without rules in order to formulate the rules of what *will have been done*' (81).[4]

The double movement of Warner's text, the way that modernist and Marxist assumptions about narrative interrupt one another, can then be understood as producing a postmodern narrative form. This double movement is achieved primarily through the novel's attempt to represent a lesbian couple as historically typical at the moment of the 1848 revolution, where the term 'typical' should be understood within the framework of Georg Lukacs's theory of the historical novel, whose goal is 'to *invent* popular figures to represent the people and their predominant trends' (317). *Summer Will Show* raises the question of whether a lesbian couple can or should be invented as a popular figure in Lukacs's sense – that is, as embodying the central contradictions or 'trends' of the historical process. The novel attempts to show that the 'destiny' of a lesbian couple can be represented as 'inwardly connected with the great, typical questions of popular life', as Lukacs argues must occur in the historical novel, while at the same time it challenges Lukacs's assumption that the varied interests of 'the people' can be embodied by any single narrative standpoint (284).

The setting of *Summer Will Show* in Paris during the 1848 revolution is central to this reading of the novel, since Flaubert's novel of 1848, *Sentimental Education,* is identified by Lukacs as the turning point where the historical novel begins to transform itself into the modernist novel. In Lukacs's reading, Flaubert's novel exemplifies how the modern novel is structured by a condition of alienation from both the collective forms of social life and the past, so that meaning resides only in the story of an individual, not in the historical events surrounding that story.[5] It is precisely this alienation from collective story-telling that must be overcome in order to produce what Bernstein calls a 'narratable world'. For Lukacs, 1848 therefore provides a crucial test of the historicity of novelistic representation. From this perspective, Warner's novel raises the question of whether its focus on the story of a lesbian couple during 1848 reproduces this alienation or overcomes it, since it is highly unlikely that Lukacs would regard the story of Sophia and Minna as having any more of an essential connection to the events of 1848 than does Frédéric Moreau's story, in *Sentimental Education.* Lukacs is no more willing to attribute the status of historical type to a lesbian couple than E.M.W. Tillyard is willing to acknowledge that a homosexual could aspire to the status of the epic poet who tells the collective story or 'tale of the tribe'. For both critics, 'the crooked' is indeed measured by 'the straight' (Tillyard 48).

The focus on a lesbian couple in Warner's novel does not just rewrite Flaubert and the tradition of the historical novel which Flaubert's *Sentimental Education* begins to transform, according to Lukacs. *Summer Will Show* also rewrites Jane Austen, who was important enough to Warner that she wrote a critical monograph about Austen's novels. *Summer Will Show* writes beyond the ending of Austen's *Sense and Sensibility,* and in Warner's reemplotment the two sisters outlive their husbands, run off with each other (thereby abdicating the property rights secured by marriage), and finally end up becoming revolutionaries in France. Warner's lesbian couple, Sophia and Minna, also embody the categories of sense and sensibility respectively, although in Warner's novel Austen's distinction between these two forms of feminine subjectivity is displaced onto Engels's distinction between scientific and utopian or romantic socialism. Through the two sets of intertextual relations represented by Austen on the one hand and Flaubert on the other, *Summer Will Show* programmatically disrupts the boundary between domestic or sentimental fiction and the historical novel, a gendered distinction that Lukacs implicitly upholds and which allows him to privatize 'sexual abnormality' as a potential historiographic and novelistic theme.[6] The breakdown of these gender and genre categories enables the narrativizing of other forms of social difference, including not only alternative sexualities but also race and class differences.

2 'Rich and poor can breed alike': class sexualities and lesbian narration

Summer Will Show tells the story of how Sophia Willoughby, an English woman of the property-owning classes, escapes the confinement of her family home and the patriarchal ideology that structures her relation to it. After the death of her children in a smallpox epidemic, Sophia goes to Paris to find her estranged husband and become pregnant again. Instead, she falls in love and moves in with her husband's mistress. It is in this sense that the novel plots 'against what Eve Sedgwick has called the "plot of male homosociality"' and instead 'documents a world in which men are "between women" rather than vice-versa' (Castle 230–1). However, Sophia's lover, Minna Lemuel, is also a Jewish socialist, and the two meet in Paris on the eve of the 1848 revolution. *Summer Will Show* therefore tells three main, related stories, a feminist narrative of Sophia's struggle for emancipation from 'woman's place' as defined by the organization of both class and gender in nineteenth-century Britain, the lesbian counterplot against male homosociality which replaces and supplements the initial narrative of gender emancipation, and a socialist narrative of class struggle which begins with the overthrow of the aristocracy and culminates in a working-class rebellion against its former middle-class allies.

In traditional Marxist analysis, the emergence of conflicts of interest between the middle and the working classes initiates the transformation of the bourgeoisie from a progressive force for social change into an exploitative ruling class, with these conflicts henceforth constituting the dialectical motor of history. For Lukacs, this transformation in the status of the middle class corresponds to the transition from the classic realism of the historical novel to modernism's psychological realism, which Lukacs famously interprets as a withdrawal from the imperatives of collective, historical representation and a retreat to isolated consciousness as the preeminent material of the modern novel in order to facilitate the middle-class's disavowal of its own bad faith toward the working class.

Written on the eve of Warner's own decision to join the British Communist Party in 1935, *Summer Will Show* constitutes a reflection on the problematic relation between women's stories and Marxist traditions of historical analysis.[7] The novel refuses to allow either the women's stories or the historical narrative of the revolution to subsume one another. None of the novel's narrative strands are presented as adequately capturing the totality of the contradictions and antagonisms the novel depicts, and none of these strands can be subordinated to any other, though at times they are also clearly interdependent on one another. The novel thereby implies that neither Marxist nor feminist nor lesbian narratives of emancipation are sufficient to represent the totality of social life, a representation that Lukacs sees as the necessary goal of a historical novel. Instead, the narratives interrupt one another and prevent any achievement of final closure within the novel.[8] In this sense, *Summer Will Show* remains modernist in its historical assumptions and its challenge to realist representational claims, even as it moves beyond the limits of high modernism in its willingness to return to and redefine historical narrative.

In a note on *Summer Will Show* written during the 1960s and included in the published edition of Warner's *Letters*, Warner remembers that as early as 1920 or 1921 she had 'invented a person' named Sophia Willoughby, 'an early Victorian young lady of means with a secret passion for pugilism; she attended prize-fights dressed as a man and kept a punching-ball under lock and key in her dressing-room' (39). Warner also claims that 'a year or so later and equally out of the blue I saw Minna telling about the pogrom in a Paris drawing-room', alluding to the passage in the novel when Sophia Willoughby first meets Minna Lemuel, a notorious Jewish revolutionary living in exile in Paris. In 1930, Warner and Valentine Ackland began to live together, the start of a relationship that would last until Ackland's death in 1969 and one that has obvious parallels with the relation between Sophia and Minna (Harman 149).[9]

In 1932, the two women visited Paris, and 'in the rue Mouffetard, outside a grocer's shop, I found that I wanted to write a novel about 1848. And Sophie and Minna started up and rushed into it' (*Letters* 39–40).

As Warner presents it, Sophia and Minna find a place for themselves in the idea of a novel about 1848. This story of the novel's origins then implicitly allegorizes its main thematic concerns: first, the place that women and the story of women's liberation from patriarchal confinements occupy in relation to the Marxist narrative of revolution and class struggle; and second, how to find a place within the tradition of the novel to represent lesbian existence, when that tradition 'canonizes the subject of male homosociality' and poses women as objects of exchange through which relations between men are established (Castle 216).[10] As Warner's note on *Summer Will Show* implies, for her, Paris during the events of 1848, provides just such a space of lesbian narration, where her dream of the two characters can become flesh. However, the lesbian story necessarily exists in a problematic tension with the story of the revolution. Warner therefore rejects her own earlier attempt, in her first novel *Lolly Willowes*, to 'envision a wilderness of one's own, away from family control of domestic space and male control of public space' (Marcus, 'Wilderness' 136). In *Summer Will Show*, this alternative space of women's autonomy emerges only through revolutionary struggle to restructure, rather than to step outside, either the public sphere and the private home, institutions grounded in a set of 'ordering principles' and spatial practices whose oppositional structure is 'derived from an acceptance of absolute property' (Fox-Genovese and Genovese 318). As an intervention in the conventions of 'social representation' that the novel shares with the 'ordering principles' of domestic economy, *Summer Will Show* tells the story of how its lesbian protagonists are both implicated in and affected by the disruption of those principles during the 1848 revolution.

Warner's original conception of Sophia as an 'early Victorian young lady of means with a secret passion for pugilism', a woman who 'dressed as a man', is altered almost beyond recognition in the novel. All that remains is Sophia's comment after her children catch smallpox from a worker who holds them over a kiln to breathe the fumes as a cure for coughing. The narrator tells us that the event confirms Sophia's belief that 'God was not an honest English pugilist' (56). While, throughout the novel, Sophia is associated with the qualities of practicality and good sense, conventionally gendered as masculine, in fact her gender identity is ambiguous in ways that she initially evades.

The novel opens with Sophia thinking that 'it was a pity ... that she was not a man,' but only because she would then be able to raise her son 'with more assurance' (6). The 'assurance' she seeks is not only a psychological connection but also a legal assurance that she will be able to pass on her inheritance to her son in the absence of her husband. She is proud not only of being 'a mother, and a landowner', but also of her good fortune in no longer needing 'to be counted among the wives' since she is separated from her husband and lives alone on the estate she inherited from her parents (20). Sophia thinks 'I go to my house ... alone. I rule and order it alone. And no one doubts my sufficiency, no one questions my right to live as I do. I am far safer than if I were a widow' (22). 'Both to wine and the love of man' Sophia 'opposed an immovably good head' (77). The 'love of man' here signifies participation both in the social activities appropriate to her class and in heterosexuality; it points to Sophia's eventual failure to operate within the structure of marital relations and property rights.

The narrator underscores this point by parenthetically adding 'for many reasons it was a pity' that Sophia 'was not a man', a comment that parodically invokes the sexological discourse of homosexual desire as 'inversion'. As the first section of the novel proceeds, Sophia begins to realize how her middle-class autonomy over her house and land only reinforces her subordinate position as a woman: 'It was boring to be a woman, nothing that one did had any meat in it. And her peculiar freedom, well-incomed, dis-husbanded, seemed now only to increase the impotence of her life' (53). At this point, Sophia questions her 'peculiar freedom' through metaphors of male sexual dysfunction, impotence, which mark the failure of her performance of masculinity at the same time that she is cut off, 'dis-husbanded', from her culture's sources of feminine authority. Sophia's 'peculiar freedom' marks the instability of the social space she wishes to inhabit, which tends to collapse either into public masculinity or private femininity. Sophia comes to realize that this space will never be legitimated as a *social* space within her cultural context. If she departs from convention, 'the deed would only be granted to her on the terms that it was a woman's whim, a nonsense to be tidied up as soon as possible by the responsible part of the world' (53). The starkest formulation of this evacuation of alternatives to the gendered spheres of middle-class culture comes when Sophia states 'she could do nothing out of doors, a woman's sphere was the home' (53). Sophia's initial optimism about her possibilities for stepping outside gender structure, of being 'no longer counted among the wives', is revealed to be an illusion generated by class privilege. She has 'been brought up to feel at home' in the world of the land-owning class with its 'mud-walled cottages, tithe barn, and one great house', not in what she regards as 'the new world' of the emergent middle class (89). But Sophia begins to ask 'what difference, save a larger den ... between [the middle-class women's] lot and the lot designed for her' (91).

Sophia only succeeds in breaking with convention when she decides to imitate the sexual practices of working-class women by going to the man who tends her kiln and whom she regards as responsible for infecting her children with smallpox, thinking since 'he robbed me of my children, he shall give me others' (94). He only tells her 'rich and poor can breed alike' (97). This contact represents the first time Sophia ever 'heard a speech that was not respectful' from a worker. But this statement of class resistance also indicates the complex interaction between class, gender and sexuality in the novel. This worker deploys the discourse of essential heteronormativity in order to critique the construction of essential class differences; breeding provides the basis for a metanarrative that eradicates class distinctions. To the extent that this remark can be rewritten as 'rich and poor *women* can breed alike', it also invokes an essentializing, middle-class discourse on gender that identifies femininity with motherhood.

Sophia's response is to take this worker at his word. She decides to go to Paris and persuade her estranged husband Frederick to replace the children she has lost. For Sophia, this decision represents an identification with the different class sexuality of 'other women', as indicated by her reference to herself in the third person: 'as other women could trudge up to the lime-kiln, Mrs. Willoughby might go to Paris' (99). This cross-class performance of sexual desire begins the novel's break with novelistic convention, the implausibility that Castle emphasizes in her reading. This decision is the first example of a kind of 'nonsense' that cannot easily 'be tidied up ... by the responsible part of the world' – that is, by men operating within a middle-class frame of reference strictly divided into gender hierarchies (53). For male readers like myself, this passage defines precisely our responsibility to Warner's text, which we must learn to read as other than nonsense but without tidying it up.

Sophia's initial decision to model her sexuality on that of working-class women culminates in Sophia's involvement with Minna and their mutual marginalization of the man in their lives. By the end of the novel, she is conceptualizing 'The Institution of Labour' as a prison within which workers are forced to 'kick their heels, and starve, and *breed* on', until the revolution breaks down the walls and frees them from those imperatives (365; my emphasis).

3 'We must be practical': displacements of desire

Even before her decision to go to France, the novel already begins to reverse the system of male homosociality that Sedgwick describes, in which 'normative man uses a woman as a "conduit of a relationship" in which the true *partner* is a man' (26). Instead, when Frederick returns to England for the children's funeral, Sophia sees him as a medium through which Minna's presence communicates itself to her: 'in everything he has said or done he had borne witness to Minna, trailed her invisible portrait through the house. Every alteration in him made up a portrait of her' (86). In effect, Frederick becomes a text in which Sophia can read nothing but Minna. This rewriting of Frederick's masculinity elicits Sophia's desire for Minna, triangulated through Frederick, as much as for her former lover.

In Paris, Sophia goes immediately to Minna's apartment to find Frederick. As Sophia enters, Minna begins a story about her childhood and the pogrom that killed her parents. During this story, the February revolution breaks out, and Sophia is unable to return to her hotel. In her embarrassment at being forced to witness Frederick's infidelity and at having given up her own pretense of independence from all men by being reduced to asking him to impregnate her again, she feels 'for the first time in my life, I am in his power' (143). But she also realizes that 'if Frederick were jealous of any one, it was of her ... . No doubt it would be a painful sight to any man to see even the smallest attention ... bestowed by the mistress upon the wife' (143).

Sophia ends up spending the night with Minna. The next day, she feels 'the weight of her whole life throbbing to be recounted', and as she tells her story to Minna Sophia forgets Frederick's 'existence, save as a character in her narrative' (158). The triangular relationship between the women mediated by Frederick collapses into one that excludes Frederick and objectifies him as only a minor figure in the women's stories. Sophia finds a new standpoint from which to produce her experience as narratable. Castle concludes that the implication of Warner's novel for lesbian fiction is that 'in every lesbian relationship there is a man who has been sacrificed' (225). The novel, however, complicates this conclusion, since that exclusion cannot be maintained in relation to the concurrent storyline of the 1848 revolution, which cannot be represented as a story taking place exclusively 'between women'.

Castle's conclusion is further complicated by the fact that Sophia and Minna's sexual relationship is only indirectly implied, though the sexual overtones are clear from the beginning. After Sophia tells Minna her story, the two go out to a restaurant where Sophia asks 'Am I as good as Frederick?' Minna replies 'You are much better' (161). The narrator comments that 'for an answer to an outrageous, to an unprovoked, insult, it was dexterous. It was more; for the words were spoken with a composure and candour that seemed, in that stroke of speech, to dismiss for ever any need to insult or to be insulted' (161). What Minna dismisses, of course, is Frederick and the assumption that the two women's relationship to this man should take priority over their relationship with one another. Sophia figuratively compares herself to Minna's lover in order to reassert her own status as the wronged wife, as Frederick's proper lover, precisely the role she felt put her in Frederick's power the night before. Minna's 'stroke of speech' consists of literalizing this figure of the two women as lovers and taking Sophia seriously.

The passage implies that for Sophia at this point the possibility of a lesbian relationship is implausible and consigned to the status of a metaphor or a fiction. Minna's response, however, implies a critique of the cultural conventions of plausibility that Sophia invokes and on which the realist novel is founded. In effect, Minna reverses the insult and transforms it into 'an insult to the conventional geometries of fictional eros' (Castle 231). Sophia's reaction, as paraphrased by the narrator, suggests that Minna's literalizing of Sophia's insult transforms Sophia's understanding of the 'geometries' of desire, so that an 'insult' in one frame of reference indicates the possibility of an alternative framing of desire. Minna's comment demonstrates the 'profoundly attenuated relationship with what we think of ... as narrative verisimilitude ... or "truth to life"' that Castle attributes to lesbian fiction in general. As Sophia realizes, Minna is 'capable of staring facts in the face and denying their existence', a capacity that aligns her both with the category of sensibility rather than sense and with the utopian strand of socialist thought (227).

After spending the night with Minna, Sophia thinks of herself as a 'fallen woman', a change in status that provides her with the freedom she had earlier sought: 'she could do anything, go anywhere, if she could spend a day in such passionate amity with her husband's mistress. Hers was the liberty of a fallen woman now' (156). At the same time, Sophia's sleeping with Minna changes the response to the revolution that Sophia might have had when she still identified with her father the land-owner: 'the day had passed, and the February dusk had fallen, and Sophia had not once bethought her that death might wait upon a revolution' (155).

After this first night and day, Sophia goes back to stay with her aunt Leocadie, who tries to maneuver a reconciliation between Sophia and Frederick. When Sophia becomes concerned about Minna's welfare and returns to look after the other woman, Frederick asserts his legal right as Sophia's husband to take control of her finances, and he cuts her off. Minna urges Sophia to remain with her 'if only to gall' Frederick. Sophia replies that she will stay if Minna wishes it and thinks 'it seemed to her that the words fell cold and glum as ice-pellets. Only beneath that crust of thought did her being assent as by right to that flush of pleasure, that triumphant cry' (274). The novel's next words are '"But of course", said Minna a few hours later, thoughtfully licking the last oyster shell, "we must be practical"' (274). The novel leaves it up to the reader to bridge this break in narrative continuity, but the surrounding passages, with the reference to 'that flush of pleasure' and the suggestive image of 'licking the last oyster shell', clearly favor a sexual reading, as Castle points out (222). A reader's willingness or reluctance to accept this possibility is perhaps intended to measure our capacity to join the novel in departing from the cultural conventions of verisimilitude, figured by the imperative to 'be practical' that Minna reasserts after this break in the narrative. As Castle argues, *Summer Will Show* calls into question novelistic conventions by representing Sophia and Minna's sexual relation as 'a perfectly natural elaboration of the wife–mistress situation' that deserves no particular comment, as if acceptance of their relationship could simply be assumed between narrator and reader (221). It is in this sense that the novel, while seemingly a realistic account, also stands as a type of fantasy that is 'utopian in aspiration if not in design' (Castle 231). The temporality implicit in the narrative's representation of sexuality anticipates what it might be like when lesbian existence is an established and legitimated social practice; Minna and Sophia's relationship is written in the future perfect tense, as what will have been.

The narrative can avoid more direct sexual references in part because they are displaced onto an earlier scene between Sophia and the wife of a doctor, Mrs. Hervey. Sophia refuses to write Frederick about the children's smallpox, and the doctor takes it upon himself to do so. Mrs. Hervey steals the letter and brings it to Sophia one night, because she thinks it is outrageous for her husband to assume that Sophia 'needed a man' (72). Sophia had earlier thought that Mrs. Hervey 'might be in love with me' (58). When she appears with the letter, Sophia thinks the letter itself has 'no real part in this to-do. Some other motive, violent and unexperienced as the emotions of youth, trembled undeclared between them' (72). The narrator goes on to say 'there was something to be done, if [Sophia] could but remember what, something practical, proper and immediate' (72). The language of this passage deliberately confuses the reference of the word 'something', which might refer either to the ostensible, and socially acceptable, reason for the other woman's visit or might refer to the realization of the desire they experience for one another, imagined as both proper and practical and improper and impractical.

The passion that is not yet declared between the two women in this earlier passage is assumed to have been declared between Sophia and Minna, structurally encoding the temporality of the future perfect which transforms the present into both past and future at once. After Mrs. Hervey leaves, Sophia reflects on how this transgression of the 'practical' and 'proper' constitutes both a violation of 'sexual decorum' and a transformation of the middle-class home and the gender identity it represents for women. Sophia thinks that Mrs. Hervey's 'declaring on one's behalf that one didn't' need a husband is something that 'in the lowest class' of women could be said 'without offense', since 'down there ... sexual decorum could be kilted out of the way like an impeding petticoat' (74). In contrast, she goes on to describe how 'in this room, the serene demonstration of how a lady of the upper classes spends her leisure amid flowers and books and arts, words had been spoken such as these walls had never heard before' (75). Sophia imagines the transformation of her room into a space of both lesbian desire and the narration of that desire. In other words, she imagines lesbian desire as 'a narrative whose narrating would be the production of a narratable world' or at least a narratable room (Bernstein 231). This passage, however, is a better description of the transformation of Minna's apartment in Paris than of Sophia's home in England, where whatever material effects Mrs. Hervey's words might have are foreclosed upon. Those effects are displaced onto the setting of the 1848 revolution.

4 'From the ante-room into the room beyond': lesbian desire in a revolutionary frame

When Sophia goes to Minna's apartment for the first time looking for Frederick, she walks into a story, a textual space, where Minna narrates her experience of the pogrom in Lithuania in which her parents died. This story explains how she learned the meaning of 'the wintry words of my race, such words as exile, and captivity, and bondage' and how she learned to desire freedom (123). Sophia describes the gathering she encounters as 'the party to which she had not been invited' (113). This 'party' figures both the freedom of Minna and Frederick's sexual relationship and Minna's revolutionary entourage as Sophia imagines it, and Sophia thinks of herself as unwelcome to participate in either Minna's socialist politics or her sexual politics. As she stands in an 'ante-room', she at first thinks that all the guests are of her own class, and it is only gradually that she notices 'the extraordinary mixture of people present' (114). When Minna starts to speak, Sophia moves to look 'from the ante-room into the room beyond' where she sees Minna sitting. At this point, the first section of the novel ends, there is a blank page, and the next section starts in Minna's voice: 'But the first thing I can remember is the lighting of a candle.' There follows a description of a Sabbath ceremony (119). The image of the 'ante-room' conflates the temporal and spatial dimensions of Sophia's tentative movement beyond the confinements of her middle-class home and gender identity into 'the room beyond'. But Sophia is still caught in the waiting room, the non-space outside legitimate social intercourse. As Wendy Mulford argues, the placement of Minna's narrative in the novel 'pitches the reader as well as the salon audience out of the world of bourgeois gentility, ... and creates a world of unattached possibility', a 'space of artistic freedom in which the two women can reach each other – a space which would otherwise be closed, positioned as they are each in relation to one man' (114). The space of this story is also retrospectively thematized as one in which 'women could address themselves to women' (de Lauretis 115), when Minna later asks Sophia 'did you not know that I was speaking to you?' (140).

Because of the chapter break, Minna's story formally interrupts the story that we have been reading, of Sophia's desire to recuperate the family she has lost and to reconstitute her middle-class home, by asking Frederick to impregnate her. Minna's story also interrupts Sophia's because it is not specifically a woman's story in the sense that Sophia's is. Minna's narrative is about anti-Semitism and the experience of exile, not a desire for home. However, Minna's story is itself interrupted by the outbreak of the revolution, and one of the first things Sophia says to her is 'I wish you had not been interrupted' (140). In *Summer Will Show*, no one story is allowed to achieve either completion or complete authority; no narrative perspective is privileged over all others.[11] These disruptions of narrative sequence mark the convergence of distinct structures of domination and resistances to them.

When 'Sophia and Minna started up and rushed into' Warner's idea for a novel about 1848, Warner had found a place where she could represent the kind of life she had with Valentine Ackland. *Summer Will Show* is the only novel of Warner's that thematizes a lesbian relationship. Sophia and Minna set up their own alternative household during the February revolution that deposed Louis Philippe and created the republic, but that household survives only during the period between the February revolution and the June days, when a workers' uprising is brutally repressed by the republic which represents the workers as the enemies of 'property, family, religion, order', as Marx puts it in his narrative of 1848 (25). Marx's comment suggests how the February revolution released desires for emancipation that European society was not ready to fulfill or at least created a social space where these desires could be expressed, and for Warner that social space includes lesbian desire. In *Summer Will Show*, 'love that cannot speak its name', which 'trembled undeclared', is part of a revolution in which 'the content goes beyond the phrase', as Marx describes the first specifically proletarian revolution against the bourgeoisie in Europe (Marx 18).

In *Summer Will Show*, the private home functions as a material and representational structure that produces the boundaries establishing gender difference, heterosexuality and class identity. Armstrong emphasizes how the domestic novel and its construction of separate gender spheres had the historical function of ideologically recontaining class conflicts by representing them as a battle of the sexes (253), but that same subsumption of all differences under the mark of gender has just as strong an effect on the representation of alternative sexualities. In contrast to the tradition of domestic fiction as Armstrong defines it, the household that Sophia and Minna create during the 1848 uprising transforms the gendered space of the home and the oppositions that define it.[12] The first night that Sophia sleeps with Minna, she thinks of her dead parents who still maintain 'their rightful ownership' of the family estate 'from their double-bedded grave' (256). She contrasts that conflation of separate gender spheres and property rights with her own situation, lying on the floor with 'her body fostering this enigmatical sleeper, her mind wandering excited and tentative through this newly begun riff-raff existence, as one wanders through a new house, where everything is still uncertain or unknown, where none of the furniture has been unpacked' (256). As the final phrase suggests, this is a home without property, a space of transience rather than confinement. As Frederick tells Sophia, 'go with Minna Lemuel if you please. But you go without what you please to call your property' (264).

Both the novel's lesbian plot and the space in which it takes place, the household that the two women establish in Minna's apartment, are equally precarious in their relation to the events of the revolution that surround them. However, the novel presents this instability as a function of Sophia's liberation from the confines of her middle-class home. The third section of the novel begins after Sophia has returned to Minna's apartment for good, and it opens with Sophia turning from the window to comment 'how odd it is to see houses, and be on land. For I feel exactly as though I had run away and gone to sea, like a bad youth in a Sunday School story-book' (217). Minna replies that 'I've encouraged a quantity of people to run away, but I have never seen any one so decisively escaped as you.' While this conversation is going on Minna has 'dusters tied on her feet' and is simultaneously skating over the floor and polishing it, with what the narrator describes as 'the majestic unconvincingness of a gifted tragedy actress playing the part of a servant' (217). To Sophia's question 'what have I run away from?', Minna replies 'from sitting bored among the tyrants. From Sunday Schools, and cold-hearted respectability, and hypocrisy, and prison.' She then steps out of her dusters and adds 'and domesticity' (217). The point of the whole scene is that the women have not escaped domesticity but redefined it as a game or performance rather than a 'prison', and this transformation of middle-class norms for femininity also involves contact across class boundaries. The narrator comments that 'one of the main reasons why [Sophia] was so intensely happy' was because 'the life she was now leading released her so thoroughly into a low way of living' (286). While 'she had been brought up (and had brought up her own children) to consider the chiefest part of mankind as an inferior race, people to be addressed in a selected tone of voice and with a selected brand of language', now 'in addition to singing in the street "for money" she shopped in the street also' (286–7). While the novel encourages readers to ask whether the two women are only 'playing the part of a servant', playing at being outside the middle class and thereby doubly displacing working-class women, this later passage implies that the women's story is not analogous to that of the revolution but instead structurally implicated in that 'other' story.

Sophia, however, initially fights to keep the 'revolution ... going on outside'; she wishes to maintain precisely the opposition between this 'outside' where history takes place and the sheltered, interior space where the story of her transformed domestic life with Minna unfolds (157). Sophia represents the precarious nature of life during the period between the February revolution and the June uprising with another spatial image. She finds Minna's circle of revolutionaries make 'very unsettling company' because they give the impression 'of being somehow perched temporarily, like a large family stranded for a night in a waiting-room', reminiscent of the image of Sophia listening to Minna's story from her ante-room (280). Minna's fellow travellers find themselves on the verge of a new society. Sophia later applies this same image to the space she shares with Minna, when she describes how she attempts to ward off intrusions from the 'outside'. Sophia thinks of domesticity, 'habit, method, the facets of a daily routine', as a defense 'against the menace of that day when everything would fall to pieces, when the roof of the waiting-room would fall in' (346). Sophia's attempt to define her life with Minna as an interior space protected against this menace is described as an act of building a house around them. She wants to transform the waiting room into a middle-class home. Sophia tries 'to build up that routine of coffee-cups and clock-setting, fastening these cobweb exactitudes round Minna like a first scaffolding of something that time ... might stiffen into a defence' (347). However, Sophia's relationship with Minna is inherently opposed to the type of distinction she wishes to preserve. In this relationship, Sophia is simultaneously inside and outside her proper place; she sees herself 'simultaneously as a figure ludicrously inappropriate, and as something exactly fitted into its right station on the face of the globe' (226). Warner's lesbian narrative resists the reification of lesbian narration into a metanarrative of emancipation and identity formation, a resistance figured in terms of resistance to domestic enclosure and private property – that is, by implicating the lesbian plot in another metanarrative.

The novel suggests that the lesbian plot and the story of the revolution are not mutually exclusive by associating the revolution with the very transformation of domestic life that Sophia wishes to preserve from historical events. When the barricades first go up, the people in the street are described as 'rearranging the confusion of boughs and bedsteads, like demented furniture-removers' (140–1). The next morning, Sophia observes how 'some tin coffee-pots, long wands of gold bread, a sausage in a paper chemise, gave a domesticated appearance to the barricade, as though the objects had arrived of their own good will in order to assure the beds and tables that there was nothing, after all, so particularly odd or discreditable in having spent a night in the street' (152–3). In fact, it is Sophia who is provided with an assurance that there is 'nothing, after all, so particularly odd or discreditable' in her having spent a night with her husband's mistress, relative to the upheaval taking place all around her.

5 'Symptoms of capitalistic anxiety': rereading Marx, rewriting revolution

While domestic plots tend to subsume class issues in the tradition of domestic fiction that Armstrong analyzes, in the Marxist tradition represented by Lukacs both gender and sexuality are subordinated to class analysis. The implausibility and apparent inappropriateness of Warner's lesbian plot in relation to the story of the revolution can be read as a comment on the limitations of the Marxist tradition that Warner invokes by writing about 1848, at the same time that she invokes the modernist tradition of Flaubert and comments on its limitations through her return to the form of the historical novel.[13] In the Marxist tradition, 1848 represents the 'first great battle for power between the proletariat and the bourgeoisie', the moment when the central historical contradiction between these two classes emerged as such and became the motor of history (Engels 654). By focusing on the women's story, Warner's novel attempts to restore some of the ambiguity of historical process and revolutionary agency that is lost beneath such formulations. Warner thereby attempts to 'give revolutionary democracy new, higher, more advanced, more general, more democratic, and more social contents' by showing how 'a real popular revolution never breaks out as a result of a single, isolated social contradiction' (Lukacs, *History* 344, 98).

The risk that the women's story will be subsumed by the revolution's story is articulated by one of Minna's revolutionary friends, a communist named Ingelbrecht, who is based on Engels (Warner, *Letters* 40). When Sophia returns after learning that the husband she has left for Minna has taken control of her finances, Ingelbrecht comments 'A lock-out .... Very natural. It is a symptom of capitalistic anxiety' (266). This interpretation might appear as a sympathetic feminist elaboration of a Marxist analysis, which seems to be Ingelbrecht's intent. But at the same time, through the trope of analogy, his interpretation translates women's experience into the terms of working-class experience, so that gender as an asymmetrical power relation becomes only 'a symptom of capitalistic anxiety' whose motivation, the punishment of same-sex desire between women, is elided entirely. To what extent is capitalistic anxiety produced by institutional homophobia? How accurate is it to understand the pathologizing of homosexuality as a function of capitalist social organization? These are the questions that the novel poses at this point, and those questions are only obscured by the presentation of class, gender and sexuality as analogous to one another. As Minna asks Ingelbrecht when she learns that he is writing a book on types of revolutionaries that is reminiscent of Engels's *Socialism: Scientific and Utopian*, the question is 'Am *I* in your book?,' and for Warner this question is not just rhetorical (277). I have argued that, if Sophia and Minna's story is 'inwardly connected with the great, typical questions of popular life' (Lukacs, *Historical Novel* 284), it is through their relation to the ideology of private property and its imbrication with the ideology of separate gender spheres.

When the June uprising of workers against the bourgeois Republic breaks out, Sophia joins Minna and their neighbors on the barricades. At this point Sophia thinks 'I have no place here', implying that she sees the story of her life with Minna and the story of the revolution as mutually exclusive (376). The difficulty of bringing the two stories into relation is reinforced when Sophia experiences an impulse to laugh at the sight of Minna on the barricades holding a gun (375). But the novel refuses to endorse this perception of the women's participation as inappropriate. Sophia experiences her 'first moment of identification with those around her' when the barricades become a public site of domestic life, during the first meal she shares there with her neighbors (377). This connection between women's experience and revolutionary experience continues when the fighting starts. After the ammunition runs low, Sophia remembers the communists' motto 'bread or lead' and thinks 'this was how one felt when one's children were starving, when there was no more bread in the cupboard, no more milk in the breast' (381).

On the barricades, a subplot unfolds that returns the story of the women's participation in revolutionary struggle to the story of the women's lesbian relationship and its consequences. Earlier in the novel, a slaveholding uncle of Sophia's living in the West Indies foists off onto Sophia one of his illegitimate children, a mixed-race boy named Caspar. Against Minna's advice, Sophia refuses to play the role of mother within this colonial schema and sends the boy to boarding school. Despite this fact, Caspar idolizes her and treats Minna as a rival at whom he directs anti-Semitic epithets which he learns from the women's landlady. After Sophia moves in with Minna, Sophia's husband arranges for Caspar to enlist in the Gardes Mobiles, so that he can pocket the money that Sophia's uncle puts into her account to pay for Caspar's care. The Gardes Mobiles were a special force recruited from the unemployed and the *lumpenproletariat* and exploited for counterrevolutionary purposes during the June uprising.[14] In a plot twist that strains the novel's plausibility at least as much as the formation of a lesbian relationship between Frederick's wife and his mistress, and with what the narrator calls 'the certainty of a bad dream', Caspar appears among the members of the Gardes Mobiles who overrun Sophia's and Minna's barricade. He recognizes Sophia, and 'for an instant his face wore a look of sheepish devotion' (382). The next instant Minna says 'Why, it's Caspar.' The boy turns and immediately drives his bayonet 'into Minna's breast', with cries of 'Drab' and 'Jewess'. Sophia then shoots Caspar in the head at pointblank range.

Within what Marxist commentators typically describe as the first 'pure' example of class antagonism, the novel embeds conflicts between a lesbian who has chosen not to reproduce and the social forces that demand that she assume the role of mother. At this point in the novel, its main narratives interrupt one another, thereby calling into question the authority of either of those narratives, the revolution's or Sophia and Minna's, to typify the totality of social life. This same moment of interruption also points to the existence of narratives organized around other social antagonisms, between a member of an English colonial family and a West Indian mulatto, between a Jewish emigrant and a child indoctrinated with nationalist and anti-Semitic propaganda.[15] Less obvious, perhaps, is the fact that it is only the breakdown of a privatized, middle-class model of domestic femininity which allows this different narrative to emerge.

After the June revolution is suppressed, Sophia returns to the apartment she had shared with Minna. There, she fears that without Minna she will be subsumed by the class conventions that define her as a 'lady' and that she will feel 'exactly as she had felt before she loved Minna' (405). At this point, Sophia picks up a copy of the leaflets that the communists had earlier recruited her to distribute, and she begins to read the opening paragraphs of *The Communist Manifesto*, reprinted verbatim. The final words of the novel stop quoting Marx and depict how Sophia 'seated herself; and leaning her elbows on the table, and sinking her head in her hand, went on reading, obdurately attentive and by degrees absorbed' (406). The word 'absorbed' carries a double meaning, in light of the demonstrated tendency for class struggle to subsume women's issues.[16] But given the narrative's intertextuality with Marx's *Eighteenth Brumaire*, the reader, if not Sophia, is now positioned to *re*read the texts of the Marxist tradition, with the knowledge of oppositional elements in the culture which that tradition has tended to ignore or minimize. The novel therefore points beyond its own fictional boundaries to implicate the reader, 'to continue the story of the novel in another domain, in another form of storytelling' (Bernstein 267).

Summer Will Show therefore suggests the possibility of feminist intervention around issues of sexuality and pleasure in the Marxist narrative of revolution, while at the same time it demonstrates the need for women's stories of liberation and narratives of same-sex desire to come into contact with narratives of class, race and colonialism, beyond their own borders. *Summer Will Show* thereby demonstrates, perhaps more fully than any text I have examined so far, the implications of rejecting an idealized version of domestic femininity, along with the privilege that the model of femininity accorded white, middle-class women. If Lukacs, using Hegel, argues that the goal of the historical novel is to bring 'the past to life as the prehistory of the present' so that 'we ... may find ourselves at home therein, and not be obliged to halt before it, as before some alien and unintelligible world' (53), *Summer Will Show* conforms to that definition, while at the same time it opens the question of who Lukacs's 'we' might include. The novel implies that the revolutionary 'production of a narratable world' is a goal in which lesbian fiction might participate. At the same time, the novel demonstrates that the production of such 'worlds' also requires a rethinking of that spatial metaphor of 'world', usually defined in opposition to 'home'.

8
From Domestic Grounding to Domestic Play: Problems of Reproduction and Subversion in Gertrude Stein and Zora Neale Hurston

> The ground of modernism is both the absence of a ground and the explicit normative rejection by modernism of a ground, even if there were one.
>
> Theodor Adorno, *Aesthetic Theory* (34)

> In the midst of writing there is merriment.
>
> Gertrude Stein, 'Lifting Belly' (54)

In the preceding chapters, I have traced several different forms that the project of redefining domesticity took in the work of different modernist women writers, where the historical gendering of the opposition between public and domestic spheres represented the limits of women's social authority to either produce public discourse or to act as historical agents more generally. In this concluding chapter, I want to foreground two main points or defining tensions that have emerged over the course of this analysis: the tension between realistic representation and avant-garde experimentation, and the question of the extent to which modernist transformations of domesticity constitute a process of unlearning or undoing the forms of racial and class privilege that are presupposed by the model of domestic womanhood inherited from the nineteenth century.

In terms of the tension between realism and experimentation, my readings of poetry and fiction taken together suggest that women's modernist traditions go beyond the usual definition of the modernist project as making it new, defamiliarizing the linguistic conventions that provide the basis for our sense that we occupy a shared social space. For these women writers, this project of defamiliarization is inextricable from a project of social representation, and more specifically the representation of domesticity, the most banal and unremarkable aspects of day-to-day life, the very paradigm of the familiar and, for male modernists, the very paradigm of the kind of conventionality that they thought they had to reject in order to define themselves as modernists. 'Home' and 'homelessness', familiarity and defamiliarization, social representation and the critique of the assumptions and conventions that inform our ideas of the social and of representation itself, are tightly imbricated in this feminist version of literary modernism. In poetry, this imbrication takes the form of incorporating domestic imagery and social commentary on it into the formal and linguistic innovation that distinguishes their work and the representation of the speaking subject, the lyric 'I', that is typical of poetry more generally. Similarly, the novelists introduce such innovations into the novel's framework of social representation and its originary narrative of individual alienation.

Gertrude Stein's *Tender Buttons*, a sequence of prose poems written between 1911–14, dramatizes the juxtaposition of these two seemingly incompatible literary projects within the same text.[1] An example of the desire to make everything 'simply different' and 'to make words write without sense', these prose poems exemplify one of the most extreme experimental styles of the period (Stein, *Selected Writings*, 519; *Primer* 18). At the same time, *Tender Buttons* is one of the first texts in which Stein began to affirm domesticity, since it was written around the time that Stein's brother Leo moved out and her lover Alice B. Toklas moved in.[2] This change in the arrangement of Stein's domestic life extends beyond the personal, however, to a more basic shift in the concept of space that underlies the idea of home. Ultimately, I read these prose poems as an attempt to exemplify the difference that redefining domesticity makes. They stand as one of the most rigorous attempts to imagine what women's linguistic acts would be like, if they were based on an alternate concept of the position or location of the female 'speaker' rather than a concept grounded in the opposition between inner thoughts and public speech generalized from the ideology of separate spheres.

The second main point that has emerged throughout the previous chapters has to do with the social and political consequences of the transformations of domesticity that white middle-class modernist women imagine might take place as a result of reimagining the concept of space. These transformations constitute the precondition for a self-critique of the relative privilege such women enjoyed, given that the transformation of domesticity and the critique of the spatial rhetoric of 'separate spheres' also implies a critique of how 'woman's sphere' provided nineteenth and early twentieth-century women with the illusion of a 'circumstantial unity' of gender identity (Cott, *Grounding* 7). The way in which modernist women writers challenge the spatial metaphor implicit in the 'circumstantial unity' of the domestic sphere then opens up the possibility of reimagining feminist politics as coalition by making it possible to acknowledge differences among women. But the danger of subsuming such differences under a domestic umbrella appears in the appropriation of racial imagery, especially darkness, to represent the separation of the domestic sphere from the public world that these writers wish to transform. In *Tender Buttons*, we see such imagery used to define both the style and content of the poems, with Stein claiming that both the difficult language and domestic activities have to 'shine in the darkness necessarily' (*Selected Writings* 468).[3] In the work of H.D. and Moore, especially, there are attempts to work through such metaphors, and in the fiction of Coleman, Woolf and Stead there are similar attempts to engage with class differences. I want to emphasize, however, that participation in the critique of the spatial assumptions informing womanhood's domestic 'unity' by no means inevitably translates into a political project of relativizing the position of white, middle-class women. There is a tendency for critiques of domesticity to reassert the universalization of that position precisely as a result of the breakdown of middle-class women's ideological association with the private home, if that critique leads to a rejection of the domestic as a representation of the partial or situated character of white, middle-class perspectives. These two impulses, toward self-critique and toward re-universalization of race and class privilege exist in an uneasy tension throughout the women's modernist tradition I have defined. I will end this chapter, therefore, by turning to a novel from the African-American tradition, Zora Neale Hurston's *Their Eyes Were Watching God* (1937). Hurston's novel both borrows from the literary techniques modernist women devised for transforming domestic ideology and comments critically on that modernist tradition, by recontextualizing its conventions within the framework of a project of black feminist representation. In doing so, Hurston defines the relevance of domesticity as an element of class formation for African-American women and therefore the partial relevance of the kinds of self-critiques white women underwent in this period, in their efforts to redefine their relation to the institution of the private home. At the same time, Hurston offers an implicit criticism of the failure of many women authors in the modernist period to fully develop the implications of these efforts to rethink the spatial logic of domestic womanhood by developing a more sustained engagement with issues of racial and class difference. While I have argued that more attention needs to be paid to the cultural work modernist women's writing performs in transforming domestic ideology and that such work constitutes a significant contribution to feminism, it is also true that too often the implications of these critiques remain merely implicit, merely theoretical.

1 'In every space there is a hint of more': Stein's *Tender Buttons*

The prose poem is an especially apt genre for combining a focus on domestic commonplaces with a project of literary defamiliarization. In *Tender Buttons,* prose represents both those elements of social existence that usually receive little attention, the prosaic, and also what Jonathan Monroe calls 'the intractable medium of ... history, that "experience of necessity" which imposes inexorable limits on individual as well as collective praxis' (21). In contrast, 'poetry represents the desire to transcend such limits and achieve a more authentic integration of the individual and the collective', an integration suggested by the name 'prose poem' itself (Monroe 22). In relation to the lyric tradition, 'the prose poem's incorporation of marginalized prosaic discourse' provides a social and political context for 'the "sovereign" lyrical subject' in its claims to self-transcendence and reveals 'the extent to which the lyrical self is always already inscribed' in such a context (24, 27). In relation to the tradition of the realist novel, 'the prose poem's deliberate formal fragmentation' provides a critical perspective on the novel's claims to map out the totality of social relations and historical process (19). This reading of the implications of the prose poem, or at least Stein's version, sums up the way modernist women writers more generally intervene in and hybridize the genres of lyric poetry and the realist novel.

In *Tender Buttons,* domestic space is posed as a possible site for alternative representational practices that refuse subjection to preestablished discursive or linguistic structures and the subject positions established within them. In particular, home becomes the very place where women's position within the structure of gender relations can be redefined, where the structures that name or categorize women can be changed because the spaces that women occupy are shown to contain 'a hint of more' (*Selected Writings* 504–5). Stein appropriates home as the site where activities that our culture recognizes as specifically feminine are typically located, but her purpose is both to transform cultural assumptions about what counts as significant historical action and to denaturalize women's supposedly unique relation to domesticity through her refusal to accept that relation as normative or compulsory. Rather than accepting the home as a space of feminine autonomy and thereby confirming the limitations that the conflation of femininity and domesticity imposes on women's lives, the representational practice that *Tender Buttons* locates within domestic boundaries dramatizes a breakdown in the shared social reality that is both presupposed and produced by the act of communication.

This breakdown makes it possible to imagine new structures of intelligibility for defining female subjectivity linguistically. As Stein later commented about the period during which she wrote *Tender Buttons,* 'I made innumerable efforts to make words write without sense and found it impossible. Any human being putting down words had to make sense out of them' (*Primer* 18). Monroe similarly points out that the experimental style of *Tender Buttons* confronts 'the impossibility of a private language or of any wholly private sphere or object freed and/or cut off from its sociolinguistic context' (180). Stein points to domesticity as the specific context invoked in *Tender Buttons* when she describes herself as trying to create 'portraits of things and enclosures that is rooms and places', in the attempt 'to include what is seen with hearing and listening' (*Lectures* 189) – that is, to transpose domesticity's spatial 'enclosures' into the temporal flow of language (what Ellen Berry calls Stein's 'textual wandering'; 153–5).

Stein's appropriation of the private home as a recognized feminine space in which to speak and act has the effect of calling into question the very boundaries between public and private, inside and outside, that define domestic space as feminine. In *Tender Buttons,* Stein's version of the figure of homelessness at home appears in the claim that 'if there is no place to hold there is no place to spread' (479). The negative formulation of this hypothesis is qualified by the way Stein's text begins by asserting 'the difference is spreading' (461). The transformation of domestic space into a site of flows across boundaries, of 'spreading', only makes sense in the context of 'holding' to that space, of combining 'home' and 'homelessness'. For Stein, the act of holding to domesticity is also an act of transforming it, just as she manages to transform conventions of linguistic usage even as she ends up having to 'make sense'. Judy Grahn defines the way in which this transformation challenges the 'circumstantial unity' of womanhood when she poses the rhetorical question 'can I enter her ... writing only if I already recognize myself and my own past experiences in it?' (6). Arguing that the answer is no, Grahn suggests that the precondition for reading Stein at all is 'agreeing with myself to keep reading even when I can't find a way to recognize myself' (6). This analysis astutely defines the nature of Stein's redefinition of domesticity, which no longer provides women readers with a spatial locus of identification, at the same time that it continues to be a significant if bewildering place to 'enter', a place of signification.[4]

DeKoven's argument that 'the presence of anterior thematic content', such as domestic work, in experimental writing like *Tender Buttons* 'is generally irrelevant' should not be taken as evidence to ignore domestic imagery in the prose poems (*Different* 11). Instead, we need to understand Stein's project in this text as one of transforming domesticity from a normative ground for the 'circumstantial unity' of domestic womanhood into an open-ended, performative process of the production of new meanings.[5] Stein makes a similar point in an account of her development from her early repetitive style (in *The Making of Americans* and her early portraits) to the project of making everything 'simply different' in *Tender Buttons*. In writing these later prose poems, Stein wanted to include 'looking' in the act of composition, but 'looking was not to mix itself up with remembering': 'I made portraits of rooms and food and everything because there I could avoid this difficulty of suggesting remembering' (*Lectures* 189, 188). Stein's resistance to 'remembering' and her shift to an aesthetic of 'looking' defines her resistance to the typical modernist thematics of temporality and stream of consciousness, associated with interiorized subjectivity; in Stein, such a focus is replaced by a concern with space and with surfaces, but reconceptualized as open to the kind of flows normally associated with the passage of time. At the same time, 'remembering' is also clearly rejected as a form of dependence on preestablished and inherited structures of meaning.[6] Stein associated Toklas's presence in their home together with the emergence of possibilities for movement and flows of exchange within domesticity, as in this short poem: 'She is. / She is the best way. / She is the best way from here to there' (Stimpson, 'Transposition' 3; Stein, *Bee* 221).[7] Reimagining domestic space as a site of travel across the distance separating herself and Toklas, and language as the means of transport, is how Stein defines 'the hint of more' that inhabits 'every space', the architectural become intersubjective (*Selected Writings* 504–5).

Tender Buttons begins with a focus on feminine enclosures in the initial poems of the 'Objects' section, an emphasis apparent even in the titles of poems like 'A Substance in a Cushion', 'A Box' (used twice), 'A Method of a Cloak', and 'A Long Dress'. But a poem called 'A Long Dress' uses the metaphor of electricity to define the ways in which the home is mediated by external, ideological forces and the 'necessary' norms of gender that are culturally 'current': 'What is the current that makes machinery, that makes it crackle, what is the current that presents a long line and a necessary waist. What is this current' (467). Despite this rather ominous depiction of domestic work, by the beginning of the final section, 'Rooms', the speaker can answer her own question 'Is there pleasure when there is a passage?' with the assertion 'there is when every room is open' (*Selected Writings* 500).

This redefinition of domesticity as a space of pleasurable possibility is dramatized in the short poem 'Nothing Elegant': 'A charm a single charm is doubtful. If the red is rose and there is a gate surrounding it, if inside is let in and there places change then certainly something is upright' (464). Despite the way Stein's style deliberately leaves itself open to multiple interpretations, it seems worthwhile to read this poem as an inscription of Stein's relationship with Toklas. The passage narrates and enacts the consequences of letting 'inside' in, a doubling of the categories of 'inside' and 'outside' that in itself causes 'places' to 'change', given the impossibility within a spatial logic of 'inside' ever being 'outside' to begin with. This passage therefore simultaneously retains and problematizes those spatial categories and the boundaries between 'inside' and 'outside'. But that same phrase also evokes a condition of no longer being doubtfully 'single', but having a lover move in, evoking the narrative of Stein's altered living arrangements and suggesting that 'inside' might also evoke femininity and the history of the privatization of femininity within a separate, domestic sphere. This change leaves 'something upright', but perhaps not that history.

Stein applies this same imagery of self-enclosure to herself when she writes that 'the author of all that is in there behind the door' (499). If 'all that' refers to the poems of *Tender Buttons*, then Stein both locates herself within a domestic enclosure and redefines that enclosure as a site of significant literary production. However, 'all that' might also refer to the various objects and rooms that provide Stein with many of her titles, in which case Toklas, the housekeeper, would be the metaphorical 'author' of the two women's living arrangements. In support of this second reading, *Tender Buttons* contains two other representations of domestic space or domestic activities as compositions, specifically paintings. At the beginning of the 'Rooms' section, the speaker states that 'a whole centre and a border make hanging a way of dressing', and later in the same section asks 'looking into a place that was hanging and was visible looking into this place and seeing a chair did that mean relief' (498, 504). The first sentence compares a style of clothing to a painting that can be hung, while the second compares the arrangement of furniture in a room to a painter's composition, so that the room becomes 'a place that was hanging'. These same images suggest that Stein and Toklas's relationship did not so much reproduce middle-class heterosexual conventions as frame them in such a way as to reveal their arbitrary nature, recalling Butler's argument that 'the replication of heterosexual constructs in non-heterosexual frames brings into relief the utterly constructed status of the so-called heterosexual original' ('Imitation' 31).

The opening of *Tender Buttons* foregrounds the problematic referent of the word 'that', in phrases like 'A Carafe, That is a Blind Glass' and 'the change in that is that red weakens an hour' (461).[8] Neil Schmitz describes such references to the present act of discourse as 'vexing absences where there should be presences' (the pronoun's reference), though these absences also offer 'openings through which one glimpses the quotidian [domestic] world, bizarre as a New Guinea rain forest, coalescing in Gertrude Stein's consciousness' ('Gertrude Stein' 1209–10). From this perspective, 'In the midst of writing "there" is merriment' ('Lifting Belly' 54), because words like 'there' open a potential space of freedom within preestablished linguistic structures, to the extent that such demonstratives or shifters mark the necessity to establish a consensus about their contextual reference that can be taken for granted by all parties involved (Rommetveit 40–51). In *Tender Buttons*, however, Stein's demonstratives point specifically to the domestic environment in which she locates her acts of composition, her instances of discourse, and they mark the necessity of performing that space as a site of meanings that are shared in the sense of being irresolvably multiple, and therefore open-ended and indeterminate. As Maria Damon puts it, 'for Stein 'there'-ness is a suspect category' (500).

Written in 1913, one year after Stein completed *Tender Buttons*, her short piece 'Thank You' dramatizes the political implications of Stein's skepticism toward 'there-ness' and specifically toward any assumption of consensus about the meaning of spatial references and terms. The text of 'Thank You' consists entirely of the words 'Thank you thank you thank you I'll be there. Thank you. I'll be there. Thank you. Thank you. A good time in knee grows hands' (*Bee* 43). Virgil Thomson's note identifies this fragment as an allusion to Sylvia Pankhurst, the British suffragette, 'who when released from arrest on her promise to reappear for trial had said to the magistrate, "Thank you, I'll be there."' After she failed to appear as promised, she explained that 'The word "there" had not, in her mind, as she said it, meant the courtroom' (*Bee* 43).[9] In other words, Pankhurst mimed the performative act of making a promise and therefore prevented the language from doing what it was supposed to do, in an example of what J.L. Austin calls an 'abuse' as opposed to a 'misfire' (16). This abuse is enacted stylistically by the shift from familiar phrases to the seemingly unintelligible sentence 'a good time in knee grows hands'.

The pun on 'knee grows', however, suggests that the 'other place' Pankhurst is supposed to have in mind was the place of the other, the position of marginalized groups who are excluded from existing systems of legal, political and discursive representation on the basis of race or class as well as gender. The analogy between such a position and the eruption of nonsense language in Stein's text characterizes such a position of otherness not just as subversive but as fundamentally different, thereby reproducing racist stereotypes, like the idea that people of African descent necessarily speak poor English. Stein's affirmation of that position of exclusion only doubly displaces the people of color whose supposed speech patterns the phrase 'knee grows' seems designed to imitate, as Michael North has argued. This text then shows the limits of Stein's ability to think through the implication of her own critique of domesticity and its function in establishing middle-class femininity's false universality.[10] To develop this point, I will now turn to Hurston's novel.

2 'Yuh can't beat uh woman': Zora Neale Hurston's *Their Eyes Were Watching God*

Their Eyes Were Watching God has rightly been praised as a narrative of a black woman's development as both a sexual and a speaking subject.[11] Not only does the main character, Janie, move through two unsatisfactory marriages, by doing so she rejects her spatial confinement on the basis of either race or gender. That confinement is figured by the two early scenes of simultaneous self-recognition and self-alienation, the first racial and the second sexual and gendered. In the first scene, Janie cannot recognize herself in the photograph of a 'dark chile' until the other children point her out, at which point she realizes 'aw, aw! Ah'm colored!' (9). The second scene immediately follows this one, in a famous moment when Janie recognizes her own sexuality in a blossoming pear tree (10), only to be instructed in the necessity for black women of disciplining their sexuality to avoid being exploited (12). The narrator describes Janie's response as 'she extended herself outside of her dream and went inside of the house' (12). The narrative separation of race and female sexuality into these two distinct moments dramatizes the problem of articulating multiple forms of social positioning: in both, Janie has to acknowledge the power of preexisting social structures to categorize or contain her, but that acknowledgement is presented as if she can only be defined in one of these ways at a time. However, as Houston A. Baker, Jr., argues, Janie's subsequent development represents a rejection of the fixity of reference inherent in such socially mediated scenes of self-recognition. Instead, the novel offers a narrative of 'the motion of Afro-American woman's self-making' as a temporal process of becoming (*Workings* 166–7). I would add that the very separation of these two moments might also be read as a challenge to the stability that focusing on a single axis of difference (race or gender) provides, precisely through the doubling and narrative separation of these primal scenes of (mis)recognition; Janie learns to occupy the space between these two structures of identity and difference.

The passage that most directly supports a reading of Hurston's novel in relation to white modernist women's critique of domesticity and its conflation with female subjectivity comes in a lyrical reflection on Janie's disillusionment with her second husband, Joe Starks or Jody, the mayor of an all-black township. After he slaps her for the first time,

> she stood there until something fell off the shelf inside her. Then she went inside there to see what it was. It was her image of Jody tumbled down and shattered ... . She found that she had a host of thoughts she had never expressed to him, and numerous emotions she had never let Jody know about. Things packed up and put away in parts of her heart where he could never find them. She was saving up feelings for some man she had never seen. She had an inside and an outside now and suddenly she knew how not to mix them (68).

Both Henry Louis Gates, Jr., and Barbara Johnson take this passage as a key to mapping Janie's development in terms of Hurston's use of shifting inside/outside distinctions. This learning how not to mix inside and outside is taken by Johnson to mark a recognition that it is not necessary to 'blend or merge them into one unified identity' and also to mean that Janie 'has stepped irrevocably into the necessity of figurative language, where inside and outside', tenor and vehicle, 'are never the same' (163). For Johnson, then, 'Janie's acquisition of voice', when she talks back to Jody later in the novel, 'grows not out of her identity but out of her division into inside and outside' (163). Similarly, Gates concludes that 'Janie's quest for consciousness ... always remains that for the consciousness of her own division', which comprises 'the modernism of this text' (*Signifying* 208). In other words, Hurston's text demonstrates a self-consciousness, if not skepticism, about the founding categories of an expressive epistemology in a way that at least complicates the reading of *Their Eyes Were Watching God* as being about a process of acquiring voice.[12] The accession to voice through this internal splitting is also a form of silencing and alienation. In this context, however, it is also possible to read Janie's subsequent development, especially her third major relationship with a character named Tea Cake, as a search for an alternate basis for achieving voice, another kind of spatial metaphor that would not be organized around an absolute distinction between insides and outsides. It is this search that links Hurston's novel to Stein's *Tender Buttons*, as different as these texts seem otherwise. What distinguishes Hurston from Stein is that Hurston is much more aware of the possibility that breaking down these spatial distinctions might have the effect of eliminating difference entirely, within the subject and between different social groups.

If Janie's division into inside and outside is inescapable for any speaking subject, it is equally true that those categories and the boundaries that separate them are not fixed but shifting and resisted throughout the novel, as Gates himself suggests when he points out that 'Hurston's use of free indirect discourse' is 'the rhetorical analogue to the text's metaphors of inside and outside, so fundamental to the depiction of Janie's quest for consciousness, her very quest to become a speaking black subject' (181). Free indirect discourse represents the blurring of boundaries between the language of the characters and the language of the narrator, as the narrator speaks for and in the voice of the characters. In Hurston's novel, Gates argues, this distinction corresponds to the difference between standard or literary English and the black dialects, which also start to 'mix' across the boundaries of inside and outside. In the novel itself, Janie's learning not to mix inside and outside is presented as both providing her a much-needed refuge from Jody's abuse but also as representing and reinforcing an alienation from her community, as in the funeral scene for Jody, when Janie 'did not reach outside for anything, nor did the things of death reach inside to disturb her calm. She sent her face to Joe's funeral, and herself went rollicking with the springtime across the world' (84–5). The narrator here seems to be at least ambivalent about the value of dividing Janie into a public 'face' and a private, 'rollicking' self. It is the appearance of her third lover, Tea Cake, that allows Janie to mix this desire for inner freedom with her public life.

The thematics of play that Tea Cake introduces into Janie's life is another famous motif in *Their Eyes Were Watching God*, one that is generally read in a positive light, a reading the novel certainly seems to justify.[13] When Tea Cake offers to teach Janie to play checkers, for example, the narrator paraphrases her thoughts (through free indirect discourse) as 'somebody wanted her to play. Somebody thought it natural for her to play' (91–2). Tea Cake's actions here are intended to contrast with Jody's desire to discipline Janie and to force her into the mold of a middle-class white woman, thereby making her fit to be wife of the mayor. This enforced and internalized self-discipline takes such forms as requiring Janie to wear her hair covered and to stay inside the store they run together, rather than to participate in the communal storytelling that takes place on the front porch of the store. As Janie puts it, 'Jody classed me off' (107), by putting her on the pedestal of 'true womanhood'. This confinement within a home explicitly modeled on those of white, middle-class families provides the literal referent for the metaphorical process of interiorization that Johnson and Gates emphasize and which the novel presents as encouraging Janie to class herself off. It is precisely this process of being 'classed off' by taking a particular, oppositional notion of domesticity as the basis for feminine identity that white modernist women also try to critique.

In contrast, Tea Cake allows her 'tuh utilize mahself all over' rather than divide herself into a clear inside and outside (107). It is significant that the metaphors of inside and outside used in Hurston's novel are all articulated through analogies to domestic and public spaces, beginning with the presentation of Janie's dreams of freedom and mobility being contrasted to the space of the home that she enters upon exiting her dream, and continuing through the representation of Janie's private self as a parlor. Janie's 'classing off' takes the form of grounding her femininity in a domestic space and conforming to a falsely universalized, white, middle-class model of womanhood. In this sense, Hurston's novel recapitulates the critiques of domestic ideology and individualism that I have traced in white women's modernist writing (6).

Maria Tai Wolff argues that Janie's grandmother and her first two husbands all presented her with 'a ready-made text, a definition of her role' to which she was expected to conform. In contrast, Tea Cake offers her 'an invitation to live a text, to formulate a role' as they go (Gates and Appiah 224). In other words, Tea Cake's emphasis on play encourages Janie to take a more performative attitude toward her own life, in an equivalent of Stein's rejection of preestablished themes in favor of a process of (self)composition that 'makes it as it is made' (Stein, *Selected Writings* 514).[14] The particular form that this invitation takes is a narrative of immersion in black folk life, to use Robert Stepto's phrase, in which Janie and Tea Cake move down to the 'muck' to join a temporary community of migrant workers. On the one hand, this community is represented as a site where 'all night now the jooks clanged and clamored. Pianos living three lifetimes in one. Blues made and used right on the spot. Dancing, fighting, singing, crying, laughing, winning and losing love every hour' (125). Such representations extend the metaphor of play and the association of play with fulfillment and vitality, in the early scenes between Tea Cake and Janie, and this representation of black community is foreshadowed by the scenes of storytelling and verbal play associated with the social space of the porch of Joe Starks's store, from which Janie is initially excluded by Joe but where she begins to emerge as a speaking subject. On the other hand, this same passage about the muck also represents working-class life as composed of 'people ugly from ignorance and broken from being poor' (125).

One way to read such juxtapositions is as reminders of Janie's relatively privileged and potentially judgmental position with respect to these people, a position which has already been thematized at the beginning of the novel in the frame-tale, in which Janie returns not only to the black township, but to her own private home, presumably inherited after Jody's death. Janie takes a serious risk by going with Tea Cake, both in terms of damage to her reputation and in the way she makes herself vulnerable to exploitation, as demonstrated in the chapter just before the trip to the muck, when Janie fears that Tea Cake has run off with her money (114–15). This second kind of risk is clearly gendered and invokes the difficulties involved for black women at this time in articulating their sexuality publicly. These risks and vulnerabilities underscore the extent to which Janie commits herself to becoming part of the working-class black community she joins. Nevertheless, the thematics of play associated with that community also lend themselves to a reading of role-playing, in both a positive and a negative sense: positive, in that Janie is able to actively compose her own life and self, but negative in that she might still make a distinction between her true (middle-class) self and the role she plays as Tea Cake's 'woman' on the muck. This latter possibility is what Baker refers to as the 'capitalistic enabling conditions' that allow Janie to travel to the muck (Blues 58–9). Janie has options that the other people in this community do not have; her presence there is relatively voluntary. However, I want to argue that the novel does not privilege Janie's middle-class prerogatives as her true self. Instead, the point of the novel is that Janie is divided between a middle-class model of domestic womanhood and an alternative to it; the juxtapositioning of these two lifestyles is intended to create a gap, a space of possibility, within the conflation of domesticity and a falsely universalized femininity. A continuing relationship to middle-class norms, then, is necessary in order to elaborate this critique of how domestic femininity classes women off, so that Janie is presented as engaging a self-critique of class privilege, a refusal to be idealized and spatially segregated as a domestic woman on the white, middle-class model. Janie's racial solidarity with Tea Cake and the migrant workers allows her a line of flight, an access to the world beyond the walls of the private home, that is harder to establish for the white modernist writers who engage in a similar critique of how domesticity taught women to distinguish interior and exterior spaces and keep them from mixing; it is clear in the novel, however, that racial solidarity across classes is by no means a given, but has to be achieved through work and struggle.

The moment in which the performativity of Janie's life on the muck with Tea Cake becomes most apparent is the disturbing chapter in which Tea Cake feels it necessary to beat Janie. This passage is staged in the novel with a great deal of self-consciousness, both thematically in the beating scene itself and formally, since the passage invokes an earlier statement by Tea Cake after playing checkers with Janie: Tea Cake says 'Yuh can't beat uh woman. Dey jes won't stand fuh it' (92). On the muck, however, Tea Cake can beat Janie. This act is a jealous response to a neighbor who thinks the light-skinned Janie is too good for Tea Cake and who tries to fix Janie up with her brother, thereby revealing the internal differences that ultimately fracture the community on the muck (140). By 'being able to whip' Janie, Tea Cake is 'reassured ... in possession' (140).[15] The public response to this action, however, is particularly telling, and the novel makes a particular point of emphasizing the public reception of the beating, which gives it a symbolic significance, rather than its private and more literal significance to Janie, a traumatic experience intended to limit her agency and assert her subordination to Tea Cake as a man. Tea Cake and Janie's fellow day-laborers explicitly interpret the beating as a performance rather than a serious threat of violence against women:

> He just slapped her around a bit to show he was boss. Everybody talked about it next day in the fields. It aroused a sort of envy in both men and women. The way he petted and pampered her as if those two or three face slaps had nearly killed her made the women see visions and the helpless way she hung on him made men dream dreams (140).

The phrase 'as if' is especially important here, since it marks the difficult distinction this interpretive community tries to make between an actual beating and its mimicry. In fact, in the novel this distinction can only be supported by recourse to the class difference between Janie and the other women, figured by her lighter skin color, so that it is at this point that Janie's attempt to cross that class boundary breaks down and her different class relation to domesticity and private property is reasserted, in a way that seems to undermine her claim to be a fellow traveler in the wider world. Immediately after the description of the community's reaction to the beating, Tea Cake brags to another man: 'mah Janie is uh high time woman and useter things. Ah didn't git her outa de middle uh de road. Ah got her outa uh big fine house. Right now she got money enough in de bank tuh buy up dese ziggaboos and give 'em away' (141). Janie is here restored to, or at least reminded of, her domestic location as a class position. However, far from delegitimating Janie's story as a narrative of liberation, this passage should be understood in its intertextual relation to the tradition of white feminist modernism that I have defined in this book. On the one hand, the passage stands as a rebuke to the idea that a middle-class person, of either race, can simply escape the implications of that positioning by traveling to a working-class community; on the other hand, the novel also contextualizes that rebuke by suggesting that awareness of this continuing implication in structures of class differentiation and privilege opens up critical possibilities that are missed by the fantasy of declassing oneself.

The beating scene also represents an ironic and critical presentation of the possibility of distinguishing performance from actuality. Despite the way that the novel depicts Tea Cake's justifications for this domestic violence, in terms of the lack of outlets available to him to fight back against racism and color prejudice, it is also clear in this passage that domestic violence against women is naturalized and reproduced as a normal feature of gender relations precisely through self-conscious performances of such violence, like Tea Cake's.[16] Moreover, this later passage is ironized by the way in which it inverts and literalizes Tea Cake's earlier claim that 'yuh can't beat uh woman. Dey jes won't stand fuh it'. Even as the novel moves between playful and metaphorical 'beatings' and literal and violent ones, it also challenges that distinction itself, as the categories of figurative and literal, performance and actuality, tend to collapse into one another.

In this way, *Their Eyes Were Watching God* demonstrates that performativity can reproduce social norms at least as often as it subverts them. Tea Cake's beating of Janie is 'denaturalized' and defamiliarized in good modernist form; the characters and their community are explicitly presented as recognizing this action as 'artificial' in the sense of not being what Tea Cake really meant. But that denaturalization changes absolutely nothing. The gendered relations of dominance and subordination that are installed and reproduced by such actions are not only shown to remain in place but are even reinforced more strongly than if Tea Cake *had* meant to hurt Janie. The effect of this self-conscious performance of domestic violence is both to indicate the limits of individual good intentions to change either communal expectations or structural relationships of power, and also to rule out other possible, alternative performances of gender relations.

This passage therefore constitutes the novel's sharpest critique of modernism generally and of women's modernist traditions more specifically. Janie and Tea Cake are shown to transform the domestic from a secure foundation or grounding for feminine subjectivity into a site where domesticity can be performed differently, just as much as Stein's *Tender Buttons* transforms domestic life into a site of performativity, temporal process, constructed meaning, and subversive iteration of cultural norms. But *Their Eyes Were Watching God* also implies that this performative redefinition in itself is not enough to produce social change, since power relations can be reproduced performatively, in a denaturalized or defamiliarized form, as easily as they can be reproduced by naturalizing social relations. As Hurston's narrator puts it, in a description of the source of Joe Starks's hold over the town that he rules as mayor, 'they bowed down to him ... because he was all of these things, and then again he was all of these things because the town bowed down' (47). However, the instability and vulnerability of power conceptualized in this performative manner is also dramatized by the novel, in the famous scene in which Janie's talking back to Joe and returning an insult is presented as precipitating his decline and ultimate death. This scene is complicated by the fact that Janie's accession to voice is based on her insistence that Joe's verbal attack should be part of an exchange of insults and therefore constitutes a kind of game of playing the dozens, in which she can participate. To allow the insults to go unanswered would be to assent to the truth value of Joe's deprecation of her and thereby to naturalize the unequal power relations his statements try to produce. The irony of the passage is that when Janie refuses to take Joe's insult literally, Joe ends up responding literally and physically to Janie's insult; Joe is unable to accept that his relationship with Janie is capable of becoming mutual or that relations of power can be exchangeable. Joe must die in order to preserve his own belief that there must be an absolute distinction between empowerment and victimization, that society is a zero-sum game and that to win is to cause someone else to lose. The scene then dramatizes the self-destructiveness of this concept of power and social relations.

I have analyzed a series of critiques by modernist women writers of domestic space and the discourse of domestic economy as providing the 'circumstantial unity' for a model of femininity that falsely universalized white, middle-class femininity. This reading of *Their Eyes Were Watching God* implies that these self-critiques by white women modernists are only a first step. To realize the potential opened by these critiques, it is necessary to make connections across boundaries of race, sexuality, and nationality, which never occurs in a text like Stein's *Tender Buttons*, though there are suggestions of this movement in many of the other women writers I have discussed. The limitation of this tradition, dramatized by Stein, is its failure to fully break down the dichotomy between formal experimentation and the exploration of social consequences.

On the other hand, Hurston's novel does use the same imagery of homelessness at home found in the work of these other white women writers, and *Their Eyes Were Watching God* participates in the same interrogation of the categories that map public and private spaces, though in Hurston's case this imagery undoubtedly arises from a different historical experience, including the history of violence against captive women during slavery. In Hurston's novel, it is that history of home invasion and sexual violence that explains why Janie's grandmother insists marriage and domesticity represent much-needed 'protection', even though that protection turns out more often to be a trap for Janie (14).[17]

The ending of Hurston's novel presents her version of the figure of homelessness at home; the narrator tells us that, as memories of Tea Cake 'made pictures of love and light against the wall' of her home, Janie 'pulled in her horizon like a great fish-net. Pulled it from around the waist of the world and draped it over her shoulder. So much of life in its meshes!' (184). The larger world is collapsed into the domestic, at the same moment that the domestic is shown to contain what is supposed to contain it. It is at this moment that the novel rewrites the gendered categories of home and horizon that famously begin the novel, with its description of how 'ships at a distance have every man's wish on board', while women domesticate their experiences by forgetting 'all those things they don't want to remember' and accepting 'the dream' as 'the truth', so that they are able to 'act and do things' in conformity with a social situation that they accept as given (1).[18]

Carla Kaplan argues that when Janie defines her relationship to her friend Phoeby with the words 'mah tongue is in mah friend's mouf' (6), Hurston deliberately emphasizes her intimacy with Phoeby as ideal audience to such an extent that she is likely to 'discomfort' most of Hurston's readers, especially white or male readers who may already feel distant from these black women characters (Kaplan, *Erotics of Talk* 119).[19] In other words, this moment in the novel is intended to remind many potential readers of our own limited perspectives, the ways in which we cannot claim this same relation to Janie and her story. For Kaplan, our discomfort as readers results from our desire to identify with characters who are different from us. On the other hand, it is also possible that we are being encouraged to experience such intimacy, that Phoeby is a model for what the audience should try to be, even if we cannot entirely succeed, a prospect likely to be equally discomforting to many readers; this discomfort stems from our desire to remain different from these characters, to imagine that we speak with entirely different 'tongues'. This ambiguity is precisely what I have argued that modernist women writers try to produce by challenging distinctions between home and world, private and public, self and other, whether they realized it at the time or not. Hurston's novel demonstrates the logical extension of the critiques of domesticity launched by white, middle-class women in the modernist period. In doing so, she both comments on the limitations of that tradition and acknowledges its potential value to women black and white, working and middle-class.

Notes

1 What Comes after the Ideology of Separate Spheres? Women Writers and Modernism.

1 Such influential works as Gilbert and Gubar's *No Man's Land* and Friedman's early work on H.D. in *Psyche Reborn* follow modernist tradition in emphasizing the First World War as a historical rupture with the nineteenth century. In contrast, Clark's turn to the sentimental and Ardis's to the figure of the 'new woman' both provide alternative nineteenth-century cultural contexts for women's modernist writing, while Caren Kaplan offers one of the few readings of modernism's continuities with postmodernism, specifically the value that they both place on travel and mobility.

2 Key works of the postmodern geography movement include Lefebvre, Soja and Harvey; the feminist interventions of Massey and Rose; and essay collections edited by Sibley, Duncan, Watson and Gibson, Keith and Pile, and Crang and Thrift. *See* Philo for a reading of Foucault's contribution to this movement, and Vidler and Wigley for a parallel tendency within architectural theory.

3 Massey makes a similar point in her critique of Harvey and Soja (235).

4 Geographer Linda McDowell argues that a 'spatialized' feminist politics that wishes to avoid the problem of essentialism must reimagine both space and gender as 'a network of relations, unbounded and unstable' (36). McDowell specifically defines this reimagining of space as a problem for feminist standpoint epistemologies and cites Haraway's intervention in standpoint theories, in Haraway's essay on 'Situated Knowledges' (McDowell 35–6; Haraway 195–6).

5 *See* Ezra Pound's attacks on romantic sentimentality (*Literary Essays of Ezra Pound* 11–12); Zach analyses Pound's gendered metaphors of 'soft' romanticism vs. 'hard' modernism (235, 238). Clark argues that this break with romanticism is more complicated for women writers, as a result of the ways in which romanticism was gendered by male modernists. DeKoven's 'Gendered Doubleness' theorizes women's modernism in terms of this ambivalent relation to the general modernist project and its self-authorizing strategies.

6 Wallace Stevens's poem 'Notes toward a Supreme Fiction' is one of the best literary examples of how male modernists treated the figure of 'home'; in part 1, canto 8, the speaker suggests that it is anachronistic and self-deluding to imagine that 'we' can still construct a securely interiorized domestic space or 'castle-fortress-home' (386). For commentators who associate either processes of social and political modernization or modernist culture and aesthetics with a condition of metaphorical or metaphysical homelessness, *see* Berger, *et al.* (82); Lukacs (*Theory of the Novel* 41); Marshall Berman (5); Steiner; Bradbury; Levin; Cowley. *See also* Benstock ('Expatriate') and Caren

Kaplan's feminist critiques of the tendency to privilege homelessness in definitions of modernism (36–9, 41–9).

7 Romero and Gillian Brown's books offer the fullest examples of what Romero calls this 'third wave' of feminist reinterpretations of domesticity (Brown 4), but *see also* Higonnet (4). Cherniavsky offers a similar reinterpretation of American sentimental culture more generally. Among historians, *see* Isenberg (xvi, 44) and Cott's *The Grounding of Modern Feminism* (1987), which revises her classic work on the ideology of separate spheres, *The Bonds of Womanhood* (1977), by arguing that modern feminism redefines the spatial 'unity' of the domestic sphere as merely 'circumstantial' (*Grounding* 7). Fox-Genovese and Genovese offer an important analysis of domestic economy's role in constructing a binary logic of spatial relations (318). *See* Nicholson for an argument about the necessary failure of industrialization to ever completely sever production from reproduction, marketplace from home (29).

8 *See also* Tompkins on Catherine Beecher's 1842 *Treatise on Domestic Economy* (144); Cott (*Bonds* 62); Fox-Genovese ('Placing' 25–6); and Dorothy Smith. Both Davidoff and Hayden offer excellent histories of feminist attempts to 'rationalize' and modernize domestic labor.

9 One difference in the British and American critical contexts is the relatively greater resistance among British feminists to the idea that domesticity represents any genuine alternative to capitalism, certainly not one based on the premise of domestic work's total exclusion from capitalist economic networks. *See* Poovey (3); Newton (168); Rowbotham's *Woman's Consciousness* (chs 4 and 5; and Barrett (chs 5 and 6). Romero (31) cites Poovey as a model for bringing more of this skepticism into the American tradition.

10 Modernism can be defined philosophically through its rejection of such a stable ontological or epistemological 'ground', as Adorno argues (*Aesthetic Theory* 34). Cott interprets the semantic shift from the nineteenth-century 'woman's movement' to 'feminism' as implying a modernist rejection of these types of spatial metaphors, with the shift in terminology creating a 'semantic claim' to a female modernism (*Grounding* 7, 15). For an idiosyncratic challenge to the category of 'woman' in the modernist period, *see* Laura (Riding) Jackson.

Standpoint epistemologies depend on a dialectical model (adapted from Marxism) for the formation of resistant consciousness on the basis of social antagonisms and antitheses; *see* Hartsock, Mackinnon and Harding for examples of key texts in this tradition, and Hekman for a more recent reassessment. *See* Flax (56) and Jaggar (385) for critiques of the spatial assumptions implicit in standpoint epistemologies, particularly the tendency to homogenize gender and the difficulty such models have in articulating race, class and gender as anything but distinct positions, linked only externally, in an additive manner. *See* Jameson for a critique of this same problem in Georg Lukacs's Marxist theory of class consciousness ('*History* '69–70), and Caren Kaplan for a similar critique of Adrienne Rich's 'politics of location' (Kaplan 166–7; Rich, *Blood* 213). For other responses to Rich, *see* Clifford, Smith and Katz, Mohanty, Mani, and Dhareshwar. Friedman's *Mappings* offers another, longer reflection on the feminist use of such spatial metaphors.

11 Carby and Giddings offer African-American critiques of domestic womanhood, while Spivak ('Imperialism'; 'Three Women's Texts'), Grewal, Sanchez-Eppler ('Raising Empires like Children'), and George (6; *see also* chapter 2) do the same from post-colonial perspectives. Chatterjee offers a historical account of how domestic economy was exported to India as a disciplinary apparatus for producing colonial subjects. Romero cites Wexler as an example of how feminist critics of the nineteenth century have responded to these critiques (Romero 3; Wexler 15).

12 *See* Patricia Hill Scott for a historical analysis of one such missionary project, and Baym's argument for recognizing the agency of the women involved in this kind of activism (48); Kelley offers a critique of this feminist revaluation of 'social housekeeping' (222). Working in the British context, Vicinus offers an ambivalent assessment of this project, since she emphasizes the value of domestic rhetorics for the achievement of independence for women but also shows how the rhetoric of enlarging 'woman's sphere' was often articulated through metaphors of the colonization of workers and the unemployed (39–40, 219–21). Note, however, the appropriation of such rhetorics by African-American women to define the project of racial uplift in the late nineteenth century (Giddings 52, 80–3; Tate 133–4; Romero 29).

13 I am here drawing on Foucault's famous argument about the role played by the internalization of disciplinary structures in the formation of the modern self, in *Discipline and Punish*, as does Chatterjee (note 11 above). Armstrong applies Foucault to the discourse of domestic economy, arguing that domestic treatises served as the basis for imagining the modern individual, whose separation from society is modeled on the separation of the domestic from the public sphere (8); *see also* Jehlen (211–12). Romero notes how 'using the home as a metaphor for interiority (in the sense of "selfhood")' was a way 'to redefine woman's value in terms of internal qualities' rather than male-dominated standards of physical beauty (20–1).

14 Commentaries on Reagon's important essay include Martin and Mohanty (192); Foster, 'The Very House of Difference' (29–30); Kaplan (172–5); and Honig (267–70). My analysis of the trope of homelessness at home has been especially influenced by Martin and Mohanty's argument that feminist subjectivity is structured by 'two specific modalities: being home and not being home. "Being home" refers to the place where one lives within familiar, safe, protected boundaries; "not being home" is a matter of realizing that home was an illusion of coherence and safety based on the exclusion of specific histories of oppression and resistance, the repression of differences even within oneself' (195–6).

15 On this point I disagree with Romero's claim that enlarged or social housekeeping 'became conventional enough to make the dichotomy of home and world insufficient' (33); instead such rhetorics preserved the conceptual distinction between home and world even as they detached that distinction from the material architecture of the private home. The result was the recontainment of women's agency rather than a subversion of the frameworks that defined it.

16 Drawing on Ann Douglas's work on 'the feminization of America', Romero also argues that 'home' signified conventional forces of socialization, a

coding of 'home' that underlies (male) modernist practices of expatriation and the privileging of techniques of defamiliarization as a stylistic analogy to exile or homelessness, as Benstock ('Expatriate' 26–7) and Caren Kaplan point out (38).

17 Dickinson's poems using the trope of homelessness at home are poems #624 and 1573, following the numbering system used in Thomas Johnson's standard edition of the poems. I will discuss these poems and this trope at length in the section on Dickinson in the next chapter. *See* Bonnie Kime Scott for an important analysis of modernist women's alternative domestic arrangements (*Refiguring*, vol. 1, 187). I would link such rethinkings of the domestic with the rethinking of the public that Felski argues is implicit in feminist modernism as a 'counter-public sphere', defined by the tension between 'universality and particularity' or public and private (167). Gilbert and Gubar suggest the trope of 'no man's land' as a representation for such ambiguously gendered spaces in the modernist period (*No Man's Land*, vol. 1, 21).

18 Hull comments on these same lines as exemplifying Lorde's 'ceaseless negotiations of a positionality from which she can speak', the 'series of displacements' that maintain Lorde's 'difference-defined, complexly constructed self' precisely because of her 'inability to rest – in place, time, or consciousness' ('Living on the Line' 155–6, 158). I discuss this poem in greater detail elsewhere ('The Very House'). Another contemporary example of this rewriting of the figure of 'home' occurs in Marilynne Robinson's novel *Housekeeping*. My essay on that novel and 'The Very House of Difference' constitute the origins of the present book, which sets out to define the historical resources these contemporary feminist texts draw on.

19 *See* Judith Butler's call for feminist recognition of the 'futural' nature of identity signs, their openness to change and redefinition ('Imitation' 19).

20 The text which most vividly demonstrates the failure of home to constitute a prophylaxis against state power and economic forces is Harriet Jacobs's autobiography, *Incidents in the Life of a Slave Girl*. This aspect of Jacobs's narrative has received a good deal of commentary; for example, *see also* Carby (45–61), Valerie Smith ('Loopholes'), and Cherniavsky, ch. 5.

21 In the US context, New York was the first state to pass legislation permitting married women to retain ownership of property acquired before marriage, in 1848, but it wasn't until 1860 that New York State legalized the right of married women to acquire property after marriage. Most of the rest of the US had passed such legislation by 1890 (Mary Ryan 148, 215). In England, the first step in this process was accomplished by the first Married Women's Property Act, 1882, and women were allowed to control property acquired after marriage by the second such Act, passed in 1893.

22 Domestic ideology is the historical origin for the problem of false universality that Spivak targets when she proposes to 'name as "woman" that disenfranchised woman whom we, strictly, historically, geo-politically *cannot imagine*, as literal referent' ('Feminism' 220). In 'Can the Subaltern Speak?', Spivak articulates this project as one of learning 'to speak to (rather than listen to or speak for) the historically muted subject of the subaltern woman' (295).

23 On the role of postmodern media culture in breaking down distinctions between public and private spheres, *see* Baudrillard and Meyrowitz.

24 *See* Kaplan on this problem in modernism (1), and Harper for a similar critique of how postmodernism generalizes the experience of 'dislocation' or homelessness (*Framing* 193). Marcus specifically warns against treating 'homelessness' as a metaphor, when 'our cities are full of the nonwriting homeless' and urges attention to the 'ethic' of 'elsewhereness' ('Alibis' 275). Deutsche suggests that the responsibility of the critic to the homeless is precisely to demonstrate that there is no representation of 'home' which 'is not *at the same time* a document of homelessness' (Deutsche 5).

25 On this point, *see* the important work by black feminist critics like Christian, Carby, McDowell and Wall, on the ways in which African-American women in the late nineteenth and early twentieth centuries appropriated the conventions of domestic fiction in order to define a role for black women in the project of racial uplift.

26 Since this double bind is a general problem in the modernist period, implicit in this analysis is the idea that modernist women's writing is also relevant to the situation of their male contemporaries. The continuing relevance of this work for male readers like myself becomes apparent when we realize that the general political issue (addressed here in terms of class and racial differences among women) is how to take responsibility for the specificity of one's own 'point of location' within historically unequal social relations (Rich 219), while at the same time still launching a critique of the reductive spatial logic that assumes each point of location is distinct and separate from every other (Kaplan 166–7). This same issue applies to the relation of male readers to women's texts, and I am arguing that modernist women's writing, in particular, speaks beyond its own gender boundaries to address issues relevant to male readers, but through a focus on issues specific to women, such as the fate of domestic ideology. For male critics to ignore such possibilities is to once again reassert the binary logic of separate gender spheres. On the danger of such a reassertion, *see* Romero (106). Friedman warns against the other danger, of denying the specificity of social differences and divergent histories (*Mappings* 26–7), and this is the double bind that modernist women writers negotiate in relation to the figure of 'home'.

27 *See* Colomina for an architect's take on the motives behind the modernist rethinking of the category of space, who argues that early mass media and other technologies cause 'a displacement of the traditional sense of an inside, an enclosed space, established in clear opposition to an outside' (12). *See also* Quinones (158).

28 *See also* Foucault (*Power/Knowledge* 70). Within the modernist period, the source for such a shift from 'dead' space to 'living' time, was of course Henri Bergson. Said offers one of the few contrasting views, in his work on modernism as a crisis in narrative continuity and temporal experience (*Beginnings* 81–8) and especially his argument that modernism involves a general shift from models of 'filiation' and historical genealogy to 'affiliation' or networks of lateral and synchronic relationships (*World* 16). *See also* Bonnie Kime Scott on the metaphor of the web as a way to represent this shift (*Refiguring Modernism*, vol. 1, xvi).

29 One of the central contradictions within this narrative of separate gendered spheres is the way it yields an oversimplified 'reality of (self-)alienated men and (self-)identical women' (Romero 107). While femininity became the very paradigm for a localized and bounded subject position, through the conflation of femininity and domestic space, the association of the public sphere with masculinity also links masculinity with a new fluidity of social identities or what Foucault refers to as the 'dispersion' of subjectivity across a variety of institutional sites and discursive formations (*Archeology* 55). The ideology of separate spheres thereby contains within itself an alternate conception of space, a space of flows across boundaries that stands in contrast to the dominant idea that space can be divided in absolute, binary ways. This contradiction makes it possible to deconstruct the oppositional structure of that ideology.

30 *See* Yoshimoto for an analysis of how the abstraction or 'dissociation of space from place' is inherent in capitalism as Marx defines it (Yoshimoto 115; Marx, ch. 4 of part 2 of *Capital*, vol. 1; for a similar reading, *see* Massumi 200). The ultimate realization of this process of abstraction is virtual reality or cyberspace. In an analysis of computer-mediated communication, Stone argues that it is the increasing mediation and textualization of the relationship between physical location and social identity by discourse in the modernist period that 'eventually produced the subjectivity that could fairly unproblematically inhabit the virtual spaces of the nets' (97). *See* Barthes's claim that 'the metaphor of the Text is ... the *network*' (161), and Kern on how the introduction of the telephone by 1913–14 as a form of distant communication affected the modernist conceptualization of space (Kern 215).

31 Lefebvre therefore offers a theoretical explanation for the contradiction (discussed in note 29 above) between the spatial assumptions underlying the private/public distinction and the spatial assumptions underlying the new fluidity of identity formation possible in the public sphere. On the imbrication of public and private spaces, as one expression of this contradiction, *see* Lefebvre (228) and Habermas (*Structural Transformation* 49).

32 On the centrality of the concept of positionality within contemporary theory, and the problem of defining rhetorics of 'spatiality' that results, *see* Friedman's *Mappings* (19). For critiques of the assumption implicit in the metaphor of subject position that space is defined by clear borders, *see* Kirby (2) and Paul Smith (*Discerning*). Both Kirby (18) and Smith (xxx) also discuss alternative conceptions of space defined by fluidity rather than fixity. The classic text on spatial metaphors is Bachelard's *Poetics of Space*; neither Bachelard, Kirby, nor Smith pay sufficient attention to the historical process by which different conceptions of space were gendered.

33 The two most influential essays initiating this shift are Benveniste's 'Subjectivity in Language', with its discussion of how learning to designate oneself as 'I' also institutes an '"interior/exterior" opposition' that corresponds to the opposition between the positions of 'I' and 'you' in language (225), and Lacan's essay on the mirror stage, especially his famous argument about how language acquisition displaces the 'spatial captation manifested in the mirror stage', a sense of bodily enclosure that is only subsequently displaced by the decentering of the social subject within preexisting linguistic

structures (*Ecrits* 4). Young defines the reasons why such models might be especially problematic for women when she argues that 'feminine body spatiality is such that the woman experiences herself as rooted and enclosed' (153).

34 As Eve Sedgwick has shown, one of the other main modern languages for figuring the inner space of subjectivity is the hetero/homosexuality distinction and the rhetoric of the closet (*Epistemology*).

35 The best known critique of expressive subjectivity Jameson's *Postmodernism* 11, 15. Butler's critique of the essentialization of gender argues that spatialized forms of identity are actually temporally produced, through repetition, imitation, and mimicry, 'a set of repeated acts ... that congeal over time to produce the appearance of substance, of a natural sort of being' (*Gender* 33). Butler therefore tends to privilege the temporality of gender over its spatiality. In contrast, I argue that such a shift away from the 'congealing' of identity can result in a redefinition of the category of space itself.

36 Eliot's 'Tradition and the Individual Talent' is the paradigm for this resistance, in its articulation of the modernist aesthetic of impersonality. *See* Ross for a critique of how this resistance tends to move beyond redefining subjectivity to the impossible goal of eliminating it (*Failure* 25).

37 For similar formulations of this tension, *see* Herrmann on Virginia Woolf (9), and the theoretical dialogue between Nancy K. Miller ('Text's Heroine') and Kamuf.

38 Armstrong analyzes this process in the British context, Fox-Genovese and Genovese in Europe generally (ch. 11, *Fruits of Merchant Capital*, and Brown in the US (3). The fact that Beecher was the American protégée of British educator Hannah More, one of the originators of modern domestic ideology, is another example of the cross-cultural currency of this model of domestic selfhood (Romero 23).

39 For feminist critiques of Foucault, *see* de Lauretis ('Technology') and the Diamond and Quinby collection. Less attention has been given to the question of institutional authorization for feminine discourse, though the essays in that collection by Kathleen Jones and Diamond and Quinby raise some of the same issues I address in adapting and revising Foucault's concept of enunciative modality.

40 For Eliot, 'impersonality' refers to how authors find themselves always already embedded in prior textual networks or traditions, and in that sense impersonality resembles Foucault's dispersed subjectivity.

41 For analyses of how Beecher contextualizes domesticity as a defense against the disorder of democracy, *see* Gillian Brown (3), and on Beecher's rhetoric of 'promiscuity' or social mixing, *see* Isenberg (45–6). On the importance of clear gender distinctions in the nineteenth-century US, *see* Cott (*Bonds* 98–9), Sklar (153) and Hayden (56–8). Isenberg analyzes domestic economy as a way for women to demonstrate qualities of rational self-discipline as the basis for claims about women's fitness for democratic citizenship (41–3); *see* Romero on Beecher's association of domestic hygiene with mental health and self-control (75–6).

42 Woolf is here defining a version of William James's famous metaphor of the stream of consciousness, which 'is nothing jointed; it flows' (James 239). This metaphor is usually read as defining a temporal process, but as James's

term 'jointed' suggests, the stream of consciousness can also be read as a different kind of spatial metaphor, especially since it was intended precisely as an alternative to what he saw as artificial boundaries imposed on experience by discrete linguistic categories.

43 Kristeva appropriates the term thetic from Husserl's phenomenology (*Ideas* 95–6, 136–9); she associates the thetic with 'positionality', the stability of a unitary identity produced by acceptance of the subject's role in simply reproducing linguistic structures that insure rational communication of meaning (*Revolution* 43–5, 9). Romero's discussion of Beecher's rationalization of domestic life suggests the relevance of Kristeva's thetic positionality to domesticity (ch. 4). The 'semiotic' or the signifying process defines an alternative to this spatialization of subjectivity, though Kristeva has been critiqued for locating this alternative in a relation to language that precedes social communication (Butler, *Gender* 81).

44 For excellent analyses of Gilman's general project of modernizing domesticity as the source of her resistance to the public/private distinction, *see* Hayden (182–205) and Allen (16–20).

45 For a fuller account, *see* Habermas's *Structural Transformation of the Public Sphere* (ch. 6).

46 In effect, Gilman transforms the phrase 'hands of woman' from a synechdoche for a naturalized female body to a catachresis. Catachresis is the rhetorical term for a metaphor that has no literal or proper term, such as the face of a coin. *See* Spivak on the political motives for redefining woman as a catachresis, without a proper referent, in order to make that category more inclusive and open to redefinition ('Feminism and Deconstruction' 220).

47 On the temporality of housekeeping, *see* Rowbotham (*Woman's Consciousness* 70–5). Simone de Beauvoir defines how housekeeping is traditionally imagined as a transformation of time into a form of spatial stasis (504). In this context, Butler's argument about contesting the reification of gender categories by revealing them to be 'constituted' through a '*social temporality*' is especially suggestive (*Gender Trouble* 141; *see* note 35 above).

48 For DeKoven, Gertrude Stein is a paradigm for experimental writing in general, because Stein rejects any preexisting thematic 'ground' that is re-presented in her texts (*Different Language*). This experimental aesthetic takes on a political dimension when domesticity is rejected as a preexisting theme, since that rejection implies the refusal of domesticity as the defining ground of feminine identity.

49 For discussion of poetics in terms of the production of speaking subjects, *see* Kristeva ('The Ethics of Linguistics'; Easthope; and Montefiore on feminist poetry more specifically.

50 These novels therefore enact the disappearance of unifying metanarratives that Lyotard associates with postmodernism. In this way, these novels retain the experimental impulse of modernism, within a more realist framework of social and historical representation.

51 *See* Romero on the possibility of 'cultural resistance' that is performed *through* 'domesticity' (Romero 108). I argue treating domesticity as a performative site that has to be continually produced and reproduced rather than as a fixed location implies a qualitative transformation in the concepts of space that

underlie these two different ideas about 'home'; *see* Butler on the way in which subjects are produced only through frameworks such as domesticity, whose terms can neither be 'summarily refused' nor 'followed in strict obedience' (*Bodies* 124).

2 Homelessness at Home: Placing Emily Dickinson in (Women's) History

1 Emily Dickinson, *The Letters of Emily Dickinson*, vol. 1. (211–12); this is letter #94. Martha Nell Smith is the only critic who has even briefly remarked on this letter, in a footnote, where she cites it as an example of Dickinson's consciousness about gender politics (250–1, note 39).

2 One of the passages that Joseph Lyman copied and preserved from Emily Dickinson's letters to him, tentatively dated about 1865, suggests just such a redefinition of experiences of space and time, a redefinition usually associated with the modernist period. Dickinson writes, 'So I concluded that space & time are things of the body & have little or nothing to do with our selves' (Sewall, *Lyman Letters* 71). Sanchez-Eppler begins her chapter on Dickinson by citing this same passage, which she reads as evidence of Dickinson's desire for homelessness and as a rejection of any location, whether embodied, domestic, or national (*Touching* 105–6). For Sanchez-Eppler, such a rejection is part of Dickinson's insistence on privacy and detachment from history. In contrast, I argue that what Dickinson rejects is any *fixed* location, as Sanchez-Eppler herself suggests when she notes that while Dickinson 'employs houses as useful images for the contours of her identity, she does not permit these structures to confine or define the self' (*Touching* 113).

3 This debate begins with F.O. Matthiessen's 'The Private Poet: Emily Dickinson'; for the feminist implications of this reading, *see* Gilbert and Gubar on Dickinson's domestic confinement (*Madwoman* 87–8); Juhasz (1–3); Wendy Martin (127); Pollak (ch. 8, 'The Female Artist as Private Poet'), and Erkkila ('Emily Dickinson' 7). In contrast, Dobson argues that Dickinson's domesticity constitutes a 'culturally sanctioned' form of oppositionality (236); *see also* Leder and Andrea (*The Language of Exclusion* 2) and Diggory (139). Homans suggests that the terms of the debate might more productively be shifted to a consideration of Dickinson's relationship to language itself (*Women Writers and Poetic Identity* 212), a suggestion developed by Cristanne Miller's book on Dickinson and especially by Loeffelholz's analysis of 'the poetics of Emily Dickinson's home space' (116–17).

4 I am alluding to one of Dickinson's more famous poems, which begins 'I dwell in Possibility – / A fairer House than Prose – ' (*P* 657), though I am suggesting that we read the imagery of the house in that poem literally, and not just as a metaphor for poetry. Sanchez-Eppler tends to see the contradiction between the 'domestic and unbounded' in this poem as an example of Dickinson's political limits or incoherence on the topic of domesticity, while I read such confusions as more deliberate, as a function of Dickinson's attempted intervention in the imagined construction of social space itself.

5 This letter then suggests that Dickinson had a more self-critical perspective on her own class privilege than some recent critics have allowed. Erkkila's essay on Dickinson is indicative of a tendency in recent Americanist criticism to qualify the celebration of Dickinson as a feminist icon (*see* Rich's 'Vesuvius') by pointing out how Dickinson's rejection of many of the conventional expectations both for women (marriage) and for poets (publication) is grounded in such privilege (21, 23).

6 How (and whether) to define Dickinson's sexuality is another perennial debate in the criticism. For a discussion of Dickinson's 'emotional and erotic ties' to both women and men, *see* Morris ('Love') and Henneberg. For specific commentaries on Dickinson's relationship with Susan Gilbert and the erotics of Dickinson's other letters to her, *see* Martha Nell Smith (ch. 4) and Farr.

7 See Stimpson on the general significance of the lesbian kiss as literary device ('Zero Degree Deviancy' 246–7), and Bennett on the trope of the 'kiss' in Dickinson's letters, as a metaphor for poetry, among other things. She also notes that Dickinson often included gifts of candy in her letters, which might provide a more literal reference for the 'kiss' in this one ('By a Mouth' 90).

8 This reading of the letter's self-consciousness about who might read it reflects the assumptions about print culture that were typical of seventeenth and eighteenth-century American literature. Michael Warner has analyzed the association of print with the public sphere, and argues that one of the results was that readers incorporated '*into the meaning of the printed object* an awareness of the potentially limitless others who may also be reading' (*Letters* xii). Dickinson's letter to Susan Gilbert blurs the distinction between public and private spheres by applying this understanding of the public dimension of printed texts to supposedly private, personal letters, at the same time that Dickinson also blurs the conventional gendering of the public and the private. Loeffelholz (ch. 4) discusses a similar motif in Dickinson's poems, in which speakers located within the home are able to overhear sounds originating from outside; Loeffelholz takes this motif as an example of how Dickinson's poems present the home as a transgressable border rather than an absolute container (110–11); *see also* Blasing (178).

9 One major topic of debate in recent Dickinson criticism is the importance of returning to the manuscript versions of her poems and her arrangement of them in small groups or 'fascicles', as well as the related question of the extent to which Dickinson's letters should be read along with her poetry, since she often uses the same phrases in both kinds of texts and often included poems in the letters, as a form of limited circulation. *See* Howe, Martha Nell Smith (chs 2 and 3), and Cameron (*Choosing*; Cameron usefully suggests that Dickinson's fascicles should be read in relation to and as an intervention in the norms of print culture generally). On the issue of the letters' relation to the poetry, *see* Farr and Bennett ('By a Mouth'). Nancy Walker is especially useful in analyzing how Dickinson's letters seem intended to function as both private and public discourse and therefore to express her 'uneasy' relationships both with domesticity and with her audience (274–5; 281).

10 I am here suggesting that Dickinson poses the same question to male critics today that she posed to the only literary critic with whom she had contact during her life, Thomas Wentworth Higginson. After visiting Dickinson in Amherst, Higginson wrote his wife that Dickinson asked him 'Could you tell me what home is?' Higginson's letters on this occasion are appended to Dickinson's initial letter of invitation to Higginson, dated 16 August 1870 (*Letters*, vol. 2, 475).

11 On this point, I have been influenced by Herrmann's discussion of women's epistolary forms (ch. 2).

12 For a similar discussion of the double necessity of defining resistance and deconstructing the binary oppositions that produce resistant consciousness, *see* Spivak ('The New Historicism' 283). Both Lerner, in *The Majority Finds Its Past: Placing Women in History*, and Elizabeth Fox-Genovese, in 'Placing Women's History in History', insist that 'placing women in history' cannot mean simply fitting women into the 'empty spaces' in already existing historical narratives; the recognition of women's historical agency poses 'new questions to all of history', questions that cannot be contained within a single conceptual framework (Lerner 158).

13 All poems are quoted from Thomas Johnson's three-volume edition of Dickinson's *Poems*. Individual poems will be identified in the body of the paper according to the numbering system Johnson uses in this edition.

14 I take this phrase from Rich's essay on Dickinson, where she explains Dickinson's reclusiveness in terms of the 'necessary economies' Dickinson had to practice if she was both 'to survive' and 'to use her powers' ('Vesuvius at Home' 160).

15 There is some historical debate about when the power of domestic ideology began to decline. Degler (298–327), Matthews (35–91), and Bennett ('Descent' 593–5) all argue that by the late 1850s, domesticity was already under serious challenge from feminists, in the aftermath of the 1848 Seneca Falls convention. This reading depends upon the idea that 1850 marks a shift from the strong claims of 'high sentimentalism', which took domesticity as a site of qualitatively different forms of feminine knowledge and influence, and 'low sentimentalism', in which sentimentalism claims for women only distinct powers of feeling, not different forms of knowledge or morality ('Descent' 606, note 2; *see also* 594). *See* especially Bennett's discussion of other, much less well-known women poets contemporary with Dickinson who also challenged the ideology of separate spheres, often more directly than Dickinson. Hayden exemplifies the opposing argument, that domesticity was not being rejected but assimilated, appropriated, and transformed in more or less fundamental ways by women writers and activists.

16 Gelpi (*Tenth Muse* 263, 268), Eberwein, and Juhasz (24) all comment on Dickinson's use of domestic imagery as metaphors for what Juhasz calls 'mental space', in a psychological reading of such imagery. More materialist approaches include Dobson (236–7); Gilbert ('Wayward Nun' 30–1, 38); and Phillips (7–10). Loeffelholz combines both these approaches, with a Lacanian reading of Dickinson's spatial metaphors (ch. 3) and a consideration of how Dickinson's 'poetics ... of home space' contrasts with the 'construction of a home' more generally in American literature (ch. 4; 116–17). McNeil explicitly rejects reading Dickinson's domestic themes as purely

metaphorical and contrasts the more complex 'poetics of container and contained' provided by the figure of 'home' in Dickinson's poetry with the 'easy dualism' between inside and outside provided by body imagery (113–15). In a letter, Dickinson once distinguished house from home in a way that suggests her sensitivity to these issues and to the idealization of home by domestic ideology: 'home is not where the heart is but the house and adjacent buildings' (quoted in Rich, 'Vesuvius at Home' 158). *See* Wolff's biography, on the personal history of Dickinson's relationship to her family home and its inheritance, as that history affected her use of the terms 'house' and 'home' (431).

17 In *Emily Dickinson and the Image of Home*, Jean McClure Mudge lists these definitions, which also include the 'dwelling house', the 'seat' or 'place of constant residence', and the 'grave, death; or a future state' (11–12). Mudge draws on the 1844 edition of Webster's dictionary, a copy of which the Dickinson family owned.

18 In a passage with direct relevance to Dickinson's situation, Mary Ryan notes the American legal tradition in which 'discrimination against daughters was equally distinct and explicit' as discrimination against wives, in terms of allowing or forbidding women the right to own property, with some loopholes, such as widowhood (25). While New York State had passed pioneering legislation giving married women property rights by 1860, Ryan warns against overestimating the significance of such legal changes, given the cultural pressure to allow women ownership only of types of property that could be justified in terms of women's supposedly natural roles in organizing and maintaining their family's domestic economy (147–8). While such legal changes may have given middle-class women a more direct stake in the homes they managed, domesticity continued to function as a limit to women's participation in the marketplace.

19 *See* Howe on the association between displacement and poetic identity in Dickinson, what Howe calls her 'freedom to roam poetically' (80); Karl Keller on Dickinson's 'politics of refusal' (7); and Kristeva on experimental writing's 'upheaval of present place and meaning' ('Ethics' 32).

20 It is by focusing on the potential for disruption and crisis that resides within the key categories of capitalist modernity that Dickinson anticipates the modernist project. *See* Bennett on the epistemological crisis and 'ironic awareness' that results from the shift from high to low sentimentalism, qualities typical of the modernist period ('Descent' 594). Short reads Dickinson as a modernist because of her rejection of linear progress and temporality (13). Both Howe (11) and Miller's books on Dickinson define her skeptical relation to linguistic norms as prefigurations of modernist experimentation; Miller, in particular, focuses on Dickinson's critique of the grammar of gender and sexual difference (180–1).

21 Wolff discusses Dickinson's 'proleptic voice' in a number of poems (219–38). *See also* Howe (70) and Gelpi ('Emily Dickinson' 131), who both read death as a metaphor for transcendence of individual will or experience. Bauerley and Short both analyze Dickinson's rhetoric of temporality, with Bauerly focusing on the contrast between linguistic and natural time, and Short arguing that Dickinson rejects linear temporality or progress for more spatialized forms of textuality (13).

22 Dickinson herself expressed just such concern about taking over her own mother's role, in a letter to her sister Lavinia (who was off at school), dated 7 and 17 May 1850, at the beginning of their mother's long illness. Dickinson satirizes the conventional metaphor of women as monarchs reigning over their own domestic sphere, when she writes 'I am yet the Queen of the court, if regalia be dust, and dirt, have three loyal subjects, whom I'd rather releive [*sic*] from service. ... Wouldn't you love to see me in these bonds, looking around my kitchen, and praying for kind deliverance. ... *My* kitchen I think I called it, God forbid that it was, or shall be my own.' *See* Loeffelholz's final chapter on Dickinson's elegiac mode.

23 Both Diggory (135–40) and Gilbert ('American Sexual Poetics') contrast Walt Whitman's trope of the open road with Dickinson's domesticity.

24 Mossberg argues that Dickinson only reproduces these gendered choices by consistently devaluing domestic roles in order to achieve separation from her mother (52–5).

25 Sanchez-Eppler discusses this poem as an example of what she sees as the impasse Dickinson reaches in rejecting both 'body and home' as inadequate signifiers of 'the female self'; Sanchez-Eppler reads this poem as dramatizing the way in which 'it remains equally impossible to adopt any other signs', leaving Dickinson's speaker constituted only as 'a bodiless, postmortem soul' (119). This impasse, however, seems to depend on the idea that both body and home can only function as fixed, spatial containers for the self or soul.

26 Erkkila argues that similar kinds of imagery should be read as indexes of Dickinson's 'aristocratic resistance to the twin forces of democratization and commercialization' (17). In contrast, Dickinson's poetry seems to me fascinated with economics as often as it is disgusted.

27 The theme of 'reticence' and its connection to the figure of 'home' makes this poem a direct precursor to Marianne Moore's 'Silence', discussed in Ch. 4. Gilbert and Gubar read this poem as a confrontation with those forces of decay and mortality that cannot be excluded even from the supposedly secure interior of the home and particularly as an attempt to come to grips with the social stigma of spinsterhood (*Madwoman* 631–2).

28 In particular, there are a group of poems that describe wandering outside and looking in at scenes of abundance, best exemplified by 'I had been hungry, all the Years–' (*P* 579). The poem plays on the ambiguity of which side of a window is the 'outside'. *See* Mossberg (ch. 8) for a reading of the figure of hunger in poems like this one as expressing their speaker's dissatisfaction as a daughter with what motherhood has to offer her.

29 Another recurrent motif in Dickinson's poems is the insect buzzing at a window. In 'It would have starved a Gnat' (*P* 612), the speaker contrasts the brevity of the insect's struggle to escape with her own, since she lacks the 'Art' (of dying) required to 'not begin – again'. In this type of poem, the window specifically signifies a barrier that the insect cannot perceive as such and therefore figures the conceptual distinction between public and private spaces.

30 Erkkila implicitly identifies Dickinson with the attitudes and rhetoric I located (in Ch. 1) in Catherine Beecher's 1842 *Treatise on Domestic Economy*, specifically Beecher's rejection of democracy's 'promiscuous

masses' (Beecher 40). *See* Sanchez-Eppler for a similar reading of how Dickinson rejected the feminist reformers' project of expanding 'woman's sphere' because of her 'fear of the figures they sought to help' (*Touching* 129–30). Isenberg usefully notes the use of public drunkenness as a popular figure for unfit citizenship in antebellum America, and the link made to women who were often represented as similarly unfit for public life because of their lack of self-control (41–2). The best evidence to support Erkkila's thesis are poems that use racial rather than class imagery, such as Dickinson's 'Races – nurtured in the Dark' (*P* 581), in which the speaker appropriates the imagery of racial difference to define women's confinement to the nurturing or maternal space of the private home (in *Touching Liberty*, Sanchez-Eppler offers an important critique of the similar appropriation of slavery as a metaphor by the women's suffrage movement). I read both H.D. and Marianne Moore as directly addressing this limitation of Dickinson's, in the next two chapters. *See* Adelson and Smith on the racist implications of feminist appropriations of blackness to represent women's oppression. Barker traces this appropriation back to Emily Dickinson's 'metaphoric identification with darkness', which is not only 'a politics of refusal to engage in a world dominated by a prosaic, patriarchal and prescriptive sun but also a poetics of acceptance, even assertion, of her position as a woman writer', a position of exclusion represented by the image of blackness (75).

31 *See* Mossberg for a reading of how for Dickinson both poetry and 'Possibility' are associated with a period prior to the assumption of adult female roles that are exclusively domestic and perceived as limiting (99–100).

32 On this point, I disagree with Mossberg, who cites a similar image of a hatching egg in *P* 728 to argue that leaving home for Dickinson would necessarily mean destroying the shell (Mossberg 154).

3 'We Are All Haunted Houses': H.D.'s (Dis)Location

1 *See* Friedman on H.D.'s expatriatism as a rejection of feminine domestication and on 'homelessness' as a precondition to H.D.'s art ('Exile' 92). Kaplan critiques the aestheticization of 'modernist exile' which tends to 'suppress most economic or historically material elements in constructing explanations and legitimations of authorship' (*Questions* 41).

2 H.D.'s own *Notes on Thought and Vision* is the best statement of this mystical desire for transcendence. Friedman devotes the final four chapters of *Psyche Reborn* to discussions of H.D.'s interest in a variety of religious and occult traditions; ch. 9 focuses on H.D.'s use of religious materials in the attempt to transcend traditional ideologies of the feminine. This reading depends upon connecting H.D.'s ideas about spiritual transcendence with the distinction Simone de Beauvoir makes between the association of masculinity with transcendence of embodied particularity and the definition of femininity as trapped within immanence (Beauvoir xxxiii–xxxiv; *see* Friedman, *Psyche* 275, for a similar reading of H.D.'s 'poetics of polarity'). *See* Paul Smith for a critique of H.D.'s desire for de

Beauvoir's type of transcendence (*Pound Revised* 117; 'H.D.'s Flaws' 78–9). *See also* Morris ('Concept' 426), as well as Chisolm (100) on H.D.'s 'fantasy of transcendence'.

3 As I did with Dickinson in the previous chapter, I intend to define a literal, materialist 'dimension' to H.D.'s spatial metaphors that is sometimes lost in more psychologizing readings. H.D. herself uses the term 'fourth-dimensional' in *The Gift*, to describe the 'unwalled province' of psychic space (84). *See* Chisolm's reading of this metaphor in relation to cinematic techniques of montage, where she notes that Eisenstein uses the term 'fourth dimension' to refer to the effects montage creates through juxtaposition of images (97–8). By 1930, H.D. had already become involved in avant-garde cinema, and her essay on the film *Borderline* also appeared in 1930 (Friedman, *Penelope's Web* 15–18). Pound and H.D.'s Imagist poetry had already used a literary version of montage or parataxis to create, as Pound famously put it, 'an intellectual and emotional complex in an instant of time', with the goal of producing precisely an effect of transcendence or 'sense of freedom from time limits and space limits' (Pound, '*Literary Essays*' 4).

All quotations from *The Gift* are from the 1998 complete version of the text.

4 See Friedman for a reading of *The Gift* as both personal and historical or collective analysis (*Penelope's Web* 140, 329–30). Edmunds calls *The Gift* a narrative of 'maternal mourning' (69), and Chisolm argues that this work of mourning '"frees" Hilda from her defensive enclosure, her melancholic frigidity' (128).

5 See similar imagery in 'The Walls Do Not Fall', the first section of H.D.'s long poem *Trilogy*, a response to the Second World War whose composition followed H.D.'s writing of *The Gift*. For commentaries on this spatial imagery in *Trilogy*, *see* Edmunds (22); Gubar ('Echoing' 204–5); and Ostriker, who reads this imagery as 'a set of variations on the armored, hidden, enclosed self of Dickinson' (*Stealing* 51). Part of H.D.'s project in *The Gift* is to use her exploration of her Moravian roots to challenge the demonization of the 'enemy', the Germans, during the Second World War; during the Blitz, at one point H.D. hears planes and cannot say 'whether it's them or whether it's us' (220), dramatizing her refusal to think of the English and Germans in terms of us and them. In the 'Notes' section of *The Gift*, H.D. attributes this willingness to incorporate otherness into the self to her Moravian mother's side of the family with its 'suggestion of racial admixtures and cross-currents' (251).

6 The metaphor of the dark room, as a site where photographic images are developed, can be read as figuring how Imagist poems indirectly imply a subjective processing of images, rather than functioning as simple and supposedly objective descriptions, a typical accusation made against Imagist poetry (*see* Zach). In this sense, the metaphor of the dark room constitutes a process of self-reflection on the kind of poetry H.D. began her career writing.

7 Derrida's analysis of Freud's shift from photographic metaphors, which emphasize interiority, to the metaphor of the 'mystic writing-pad', which emphasizes a more complex relation of coexistence between layers (what

H.D. calls a 'palimpsest') represents Freud's self-critique of his own spatial assumptions. H.D.'s interest in these technological metaphors for psychic processes exemplifies the general modernist interest in the textualization or technologizing of subjectivity (*see* ch. 1, note 30); *see* Chisolm's commentary on H.D.'s adaptation of Freud's photographic metaphor (94).

8 *See also* Benstock, on how women writers experienced nationalism as a form of exclusion from public life and that exclusion functioned as 'an internalized conditon that expatriation allowed to be externalized *through writing*' ('Expatriate Modernism' 28).

9 Paul Smith defines a similar kind of positionality with respect to language, when he discusses the 'different kind of "I am"' that we find in H.D.'s poetry, a statement of identity that 'breaks with the fixed positions that language appears to offer' ('H.D.'s Identity' 332).

10 Quoted in Gelpi (*A Coherent Splendor* 313). Gelpi is citing an unpublished personal essay written in journal form, entitled *Compassionate Friendship* and located in the Beinecke Library, Yale University, pp. 12–13. Compare this metaphor to the image in *The Gift*, of H.D.'s early school lesson on the Egyptians, who 'built little houses to live in when they were dead' (*Gift* 38).

11 The groundbreaking reading of H.D.'s resistance to Freud over the interpretation of bisexuality is found in DuPlessis and Friedman, 'Woman Is Perfect' (418, 423–5); *see also* their reading of H.D.'s poetry in these terms ('I Had Two Loves Separate'); Friedman on bisexuality in H.D.'s autobiographical texts and fiction *(Penelope's Web* 132–5); Laity; and Chisolm on H.D.'s long poem *Helen in Egypt* (Chisolm 185–8, 192–3).

12 In effect, H.D. reads 'the house' and her own sexuality as overdetermined, in a way that reflects Freud's insistence on the multiple meanings implicit in dream imagery, using the metaphor of the 'navel' to define the 'tangle of dream-thoughts which cannot be unravelled' (*Interpretation of Dreams* 564).

13 On H.D.'s use of this trope in other prose texts, *see* Friedman on H.D.'s 'Ghost Stories: (Un)Masking the Self in *Palimpsest* and *Hedylus*' (*Penelope's Web*, ch. 4, part II).

14 Marcus argues that the building of this 'counter-world' is implicit in the idea of establishing 'a room of one's own' in Woolf's own text. This text of Woolf's is obviously an important intervention in spatial metaphors; *see* ch. 6, note 1. On the importance of H.D.'s mother and her Moravian-American ancestry, *see* Gollin and Morris ('A Relay of Power and of Peace').

15 *See* Chisolm (128) on *The Gift* as a recovery of the mother's legacy.

16 The phrase 'dark room' is first introduced in the epigraph to *The Gift*, taken from Camille Flammarion's *Death and its Mystery*: 'the telephone is not the person speaking over it. The dark room is not the photograph.' This quotation therefore emphasizes the technological mediation of subjectivity, and associates such mediation with the unconsciousness, the part of a person which is not a part of them in the sense that it is not assimilable to the structure of the ego. *See* Chisolm on the introduction of the theme of photography in the beginning of *The Gift* in the form of family photos whose reliability as an objective record of the past is deliberately undermined and thereby already associated with the subjectivity of memory (Chisolm 93–4).

17 Compare the effects of this doubling of interior spaces to my analysis, in ch. 2, of Dickinson's similar imagery in the poem 'I heard a Fly buzz – when I died (*P* 465).

18 Chisolm reads H.D.'s trope of the 'dark room' in relation to Freud's writings about memory and Derrida's reading of Freud on this point and comments on both the photographic and cinematic imagery (Chisolm 91–101). I argue that the figure of the dark room should be read in relation to histories of domestic ideology rather than as a site for 'individual and racial prehistory', as Chisolm argues (95). Friedman offers the best biographical discussion of H.D.'s active involvement in film production in the 1930s, which brought her into close contact with African-American expatriate Paul Robeson (*Penelope's Web* 15–18).

19 Compare Freud's use of the photographic negative as a metaphor for the unconscious: in 'A Note on the Unconscious in Psychoanalysis (1912)', Freud writes 'the first stage of the photograph is the "negative"; every photographic picture has to pass through the "negative process", and some of these negatives which have held good in examination are admitted to the "positive process" ending in the picture' (264). However, in *Beyond the Pleasure Principle* (1920), Freud insists that unconscious memory-traces cannot be transposed or translated into conscious thoughts or images without altering those memories through processes like the dream-work. He was led 'to suspect that becoming conscious and leaving behind a memory-trace are processes incompatible with each other within one and the same system' (19); *see also* Freud's self-critique of the photographic metaphor for its implication that the unconscious can be overcome and eliminated ('A Note upon the "Mystic Writing-Pad"' 228); Smith connects the trope of the writing-pad to H.D.'s figure of the palimpsest (*Pound* 122). *See also* Edmunds, on the relevance of Derrida's reading of this essay of Freud's to H.D.'s *Trilogy* (39). Freud's later image of the unconscious as a photographic negative that cannot be fully or accurately developed is used by H.D. as a way of defining the continuing value of the private, domestic sphere and the way in which it cannot simply be abandoned in favor of already existing, public forms of representation.

20 *See* Friedman on H.D.'s use of images of space to represent the unconscious in *Tribute to Freud* (*Psyche* 51–2; H.D., *Tribute* 23). Smith warns against any 'simplistic equating of the unconscious with woman's "natural" state' (*Pound* 125), which in *The Gift* is the state of domesticity, but I believe H.D. is taking this risk precisely in order to put the 'nature' of femininity in question marks herself.

21 This transformation of the home into a stage is also imagined to result in an increased self-consciousness about how everyday life is determined by ideological scripts (*The Gift* 49), resulting in the denaturalization of the idea that there is only one story of family life.

22 *See* the final chapter of Lott's book on blackface minstrelsy for an analysis of the proliferation of these adaptations of Stowe, popularly referred to as 'Tom shows', beginning in the 1850s in the US. H.D.'s description of attending such a Tom show might suggest that she is participating in what Lott calls 'competing attempts to capture the authority of blackface' by

renarrating Stowe's text, as the various theatrical adaptations of Stowe's novel did (Lott 220); the 'authority of blackface' is the power to establish norms of 'blackness' through the deployment of racist stereotypes, and the question is whether H.D. has recourse to such stereotypes in order to reimagine domesticity. Friedman reads this scene from *The Gift* in terms of H.D.'s sympathy for 'the suffering of the black mother and child' depicted in the play and as a basis for H.D.'s later 'identification with all the outcasts of the mainstream' (349–50).

23 Nielsen criticizes H.D. for precisely this kind of appropriation of African-American marginality (*Reading Race* 85–9). *See also* North on the general modernist convention of 'rebellion through racial ventriloquism' (9). North cites a brief passage from H.D.'s autobiographical fiction, *HERmione*, as evidence that H.D. 'envied' black speech 'to the point of mimicry' (North10; H.D., *HERmione* 9–10).

24 Friedman has written about H.D.'s identification with the figure of Paul Robeson in both H.D.'s fiction ('Two Americans') and her poetry ('Red Roses for Bronze'; Friedman, *Penelope's Web* 260; 'Modernism of the Scattered Remnant'). *See*, especially, Friedman's claim that H.D. was 'careful not to collapse the distinction between racial oppression and other forms of alienation' ('Modernism' 108), and Edmunds's reading of cross-racial desire in the first section of H.D.'s poem *Hermetic Definition*, a poem entitled 'Red Roses and a Beggar' (Edmunds 158); Edmunds also comments on a kind of textual blackface in H.D.'s *Helen in Egypt* (Edmunds 120–1, 138–9). The danger is that such identifications will perpetuate what Wiegman calls the 'faulty and politically disabling analogy between "blacks and women"', disturbing in part because it assumes that 'black' and 'woman' represent separate and 'monolithic' social locations and therefore reproduces the simplistic spatial logic of the ideology of separate spheres (Wiegman 7). *See* Gilroy for a theory of diaspora as an alternative spatial logic, one that 'can accommodate non-synchronous, heterocultural modes of social life in close proximity' (197).

25 Friedman comments on this same aspect of H.D.'s narration of the scene from the play (*Penelope's Web* 349). *See also* Chisolm on the significance of Eva's death in the play, as a figure for how H.D. is haunted by memories throughout *The Gift* (Chisolm 99).

26 Lott points out that the 'Tom shows' typically omitted 'the self-conscious trickery' of some of Stowe's black characters (such as Sam and Andy); the result was to erase 'some of the novel's more telling instances of black agency under slavery' (Lott 214). H.D.'s reactions to the play's black stereotypes might be understood, then, as a refusal to accept a one-dimensional representation of anyone, and even as an acknowledgment that she cannot know with any certainty what it is like to be in someone else's position: to what extent is someone else free? Are they 'terrible' or are they 'very good?' H.D. seems willing to allow for contradictory possibilities in others precisely as a way of refusing to project her own stereotypes onto them. This is the main point dramatized in her poem 'Pursuit'.

27 All poems are cited from H.D.'s *Collected Poems, 1912–1944*. Further references will be given by page number in the text.

28 For readings of *Sea Garden* in these terms, *see* Fritz (2, 22); Riddel (447). Martz discusses H.D.'s figure of the 'borderline' in his introduction to H.D.'s *Collected Poems* (xi), as does Friedman ('Modernism' 107–10).

29 Friedman points out that 'the imaginary realm of the poems is not overtly gendered', but the imagined sea garden 'covertly constitutes the poet's womanhood in opposition to the confining social order' ('Exile' 99)

30 Eileen Gregory discusses how the poems in *Sea Garden* anticipate and resist being read in terms of this figure of the poetess (525–7). *See also* Friedman, 'Exile' (100). Ostriker points out that the type of poem that came to be associated with this figure often depicted an 'inspirational world of nature' (*Stealing* 32).

31 Friedman points out that H.D.'s early lyrics 'create an alternate world, a fourth dimension seemingly outside historical time and geographical space' and therefore 'remove her from the social order with its web of obligation' ('Exile' 97). *See also Penelope's Web* (ch. 1, section II, 'The Early H.D.: Lyric Impersonalism').

32 H.D.'s account of how she acquired her signature from Pound is found in H.D.'s *End to Torment* (18). Pondrom argues that Pound's poem 'Ortus' alludes to H.D.; that poem includes the lines 'How have I not laboured / To bring her soul to birth, / To give these elements a name and a centre! / ... I beseech you learn to say "I"' (Pondrom, 'H.D.' 95–6; *Personae* 84). On the 'Dryad' nickname, *see End to Torment* (17). This edition also contains the poems Pound wrote to H.D. during the years 1905–07, including one called 'The Tree' that uses the image of Daphne and Apollo (*End to Torment* 81). *See also* Friedman *(Penelope's Web*, ch. 1, section I) on the issue of naming.

33 *See* Pondrom's reading of how 'Orchard' expresses the speaker's perception that she must choose between 'physical or poetic barrenness' ('H.D.' 85). Homans sees this conflict between literal and figurative creativity as paradigmatic for nineteenth-century women writers (*Bearing the Word* 4–5). Hollenberg analyzes H.D.'s entire body of work in terms of this dilemma.

34 Gelpi points out that 'when H.D. spurns the predatory male's enclosed garden for the open water' in the poems of *Sea Garden*, 'it is not in identification but in contention with the mother sea' (*Coherent Splendor* 164). Friedman argues that H.D. anticipated contemporary feminism by rejecting in her poetry 'the option of becoming "masculinized", adopting the values of hierarchical society' (*Psyche* 265).

35 Kenner fails to recognize the way H.D. not only invokes but rewrites this Greek myth when he comments that 'Hermes of the Ways' is '"about" her taut state of mind, a wried stasis like a sterile homecoming, and a homecoming not to a person but to a mute numinous ikon' (*Pound Era* 176).

36 DuPlessis explicitly compares H.D.'s 'scrutiny of dualisms' (*H.D.* 12) to Homans's reading of Emily Dickinson's poetic practices, in Homans's *Women Writers and Poetic Identity*.

37 Fritz, for example, uses 'Pursuit' as a model for the situation of discontinuity and dislocation that she finds typical of the poems in *Sea Garden* (2, 24).

38 Gelpi suggests that '"Pursuit" might be the words of Apollo on the trail of Daphne' (*Coherent Splendor* 262). Given H.D.'s fascination with the pursuit

of the fugitive slave Eliza across the ice in the theatrical version of *Uncle Tom's Cabin* that she witnesses as a child, as described in *The Gift*, it is intriguing to read 'Pursuit' as an allusion to that famous scene from Stowe's novel. This reading would suggest that 'Pursuit' also allegorizes H.D.'s refusal of the primitivizing impulse that frequently characterizes modernist attitudes toward African-American, since she refuses to either simply identify with or ignore the existence of the racial other she pursues.

4 'A Place for the Genuine': Marianne Moore's 'Poetry'

1 On the relation between Moore and H.D., *see* Ostriker's essay ('What Do Women (Poets) Want?'); Pondrom ('Marianne Moore and H.D.'); and Phelan. H.D. was in part responsible for the publication of Moore's first collection of poems in England. Ostriker discusses Dickinson's importance for later women poets (*Stealing* 4–5, 37–43). Gelpi argues that 'Moore's and H.D.'s public careers dramatize the still-unresolved dilemma at the heart of Dickinson's situation as a female poet' ('Emily Dickinson' 256).

2 Moore's insistence on challenging the determinate boundaries of her poetry's 'place' is perhaps explained by the unusually public and relentless gendering of her poetic style by reviewers and critics, most notably T.S. Eliot's review of her first book as 'feminine' in style (quoted in Tomlinson 51); *see also* the essays on Moore by R.P. Blackmur (Tomlinson 85), Randall Jarrell (Tomlinson 115, 122), and Costello, who reviews this critical history ('"Feminine" Language'). Gilmore points out how such characterizations of Moore's poetry violate Eliot's own modernist aesthetic of impersonality (Gilmore 95). Moore's sensitivity to being 'placed' or categorized is undoubtedly in part a response to having her work gendered in this way. Moore once told an interviewer 'what I write ... could only be called poetry because there is no other category in which to put it' (Tomlinson 27). On Moore's use of, and resistance to, categorical statements and definitions, *see* Cristanne Miller ('Marianne Moore's'); DuPlessis ('No Moore' 7); and Costello ('"Feminine" Language' 222–3). Feminist critics have tended to either take Moore's skepticism toward gender categories as a rejection of gender entirely (Ostriker, *Stealing* 52), or take the absence of an explicitly feminist stance as evidence that Moore accepted traditional concepts of feminine restraint, silence and self-effacement, as Costello does. For critiques of both these approaches, *see* Durham (224–5) and Taffy Martin (119–24).

3 Ostriker offers the best formulation of this problem (*Stealing* 28–30).

4 Kenner points to the image of the 'imaginary garden' in the longer version of 'Poetry' as a spatial metaphor for poetry: 'that's what poetry is, a place; not a deed but a location' (*Homemade* 108). Moore's famous revisions to 'Poetry', especially cutting the original longer version down to three lines, demonstrate her transformation of our assumptions about what such a 'place' or 'location' is, while they also dramatize the attitude of 'contempt' for any fixed ideas about poetry. However, since Moore *Complete Poems* not only publishes this final version but also includes the full text of the poem in a note, the text of 'Poetry' itself exists in two places at once, in an

implicit redefinition of the idea of 'locality' as well as a destabilization of the poetic object. On the effects of this act of revision, *see* Taffy Martin (ix; 92); Peterson (224); Honigsblum; and especially DuPlessis ('No Moore') (9–11).

5 On the importance of this poem in Moore's body of work, *see* Kenner ('Disliking It' in *Homemade*); Costello ('Defining the Genuine' in *Marianne Moore*); and Slatin (40–58).

6 *See* Leverenz on these gender codes and the rhetorical structures of address that are informed by them, in classic American literature (7–41).

7 In a late essay, Moore reiterates 'Of poetry, I once said, "I, too, dislike it"; and say it again of anything mannered, dictatorial, disparaging, or calculated to reduce to the ranks what offends one' (*Complete Prose* 504). I find Slatin illuminating on how 'perfect contempt' is 'not really a feeling' but 'a way of reading – a means by which the reader may "stand outside and laugh"' (42). Kenner reads these lines as exemplifying the populist tendencies of American modernism (111–12); *see also* DuPlessis on how Moore's poetry (in part through strategies of quotation) chooses to disperse 'the capacity to make verbal excellence ... across a wide human field' ('No Moore' 16).

8 Costello (*Imaginary Possessions* 20). Heuving offers an excellent reading of the ambiguities Moore creates in defining what counts as 'the genuine' (92). Slatin and Holley (120–3) are especially attentive to how Moore articulates the problem of poetic identity and first-person voice. *See also* Cristanne Miller for an important reading of Moore's essay 'The Accented Syllable', as a key to Moore's 'rejection of voice-based lyric' and consequent interrogation of the concept of subjectivity (*Marianne Moore* 62); Kenner makes a similar point (*Homemade* 102). Equally important is Miller's analysis of how gender functions on the level of 'structure' rather than 'content' in Moore's poetry, so that Miller argues for a gendered reading of Moore's attempts to create a 'non-gendered voice' (*Marianne Moore* 94). In the previous chapter, I argued for a similar reading of H.D.'s *Sea Garden*. Moore, who served on the usage panel of the *American Heritage Dictionary* for years, might well have known that the words 'gender', 'genre', and 'genuine' all stem from a common root, the Latin *genus* or birth. This root sense of childbearing or the act of generation is embedded in one definition of the word 'genuine': actually produced by or proceeding from the alleged source or author.

9 Montefiore points to a similar gap between language and experience as a problem in contemporary poetry by women who explicitly identify themselves as feminist (178–9).

10 Hotelling offers an important reading of Moore's 'refusal of the stable lyric "I" and the resulting displacement of one's sense of inner and outer' (76, 85).

11 *See* Holley on the 'interplay between determinate and indeterminate elements of language' in Moore's poetry (99). Gilbert and Gubar argue that the women's movement rendered 'the *place* of the woman writer in the twentieth century' indeterminate (*No Man's Land*, vol. 1, 4; my emphasis). Holley cites Moore's emphasis on the importance of feminism and the suffrage movement in her college years (Holley 3); *see also* Elizabeth Bishop's essay on Moore, 'Efforts of Affection' (144), and Cristanne Miller (*Marianne Moore* 97, 100–1).

12 'Silence' is unusual in its relatively limited use of quotation, since Moore often builds the body of her poems out of a collage of quotations from wildly varying sources. This citational strategy has received a great deal of critical attention. *See* Kenner, 111–14; Slatin, 8–11, 86–93, 109–13, 140–8, and 151–5; Martin 105–12; Holley, 14–16, 37–43 and 66–9; and Miller, *Marianne Moore*, ch. 6 (167–203). Homans discusses the importance of citation for women writers in general, as a strategy of feminine self-effacement (*Bearing* 31). Moore's use of citation both in 'Poetry' and in 'Silence' demonstrates her subversion of this strategy.

13 Here I disagree with Durham, who argues that in the final lines '[the father's] words effectively dominate to drown out [the speaker/daughter's]' (227). Both Slatin (141) and Altieri (*Painterly Abstraction* 270) seem to find more resistance than Durham in the speaker's final statement in 'Silence', but both end up arguing that the only form of resistance available to the daughter is to accept silence and to transform it into restraint. The problem with such a reading, it seems to me, is that *transforming* silence into restraint is hard to distinguish from *justifying* the oppression and the arbitrary exercise of power which makes the restraint and silence necessary in the first place. In contrast, *see* Heuving on how the daughter's statement 'ironizes' the father's speech (118) and Cristanne Miller on how the final lines create a 'two-way process of communication' by insisting on the reversibility of the positions of speaker and addressee (*Marianne Moore* 182). Miller is the only critic to stress the importance of the analogy between language and domesticity in this poem (*Marianne Moore* 181).

14 *See* DuPlessis on Moore's more typical strategy of claiming 'the authority of otherness' as symbolized in 'the authority of animals', but without actually claiming to speak as an animal ('No Moore' 17). Hotelling offers a very interesting reading of the nature imagery in Moore's more descriptive poems (78–80), using Donna Haraway's theory of situated knowledges.

15 Gilbert and Gubar are careful not to treat this performative aspect of Moore's poetry as necessarily resistant or subversive. They point out, for example, that 'Moore's originally artful and often ironic female female impersonation ultimately threatened to entrap her in precisely the role she had at first examined with distancing irony' (*No Man's Land*, vol. 3, 108). It is as if the quotation marks that Moore's poetry leads Eliot to put around the word 'feminine', to mark the artificiality of that category, end up becoming a new kind of categorical enclosure.

16 I am quoting Irigaray's famous passage about the production of sexual difference through a strategy of mimicry *(This Sex* 76).

17 This strategy of racial mimicry necessarily has a different meaning from gender mimicry, given the different historical status of blackface minstrelsy as compared to butch/femme or drag performances of gender, famously theorized by Judith Butler as a subversive reiteration and resignification of gender norms. Where gender norms have typically been established through an essentializing rhetoric, most recently the rhetoric of domesticity but also the rhetoric of maternity, racial norms have often been established precisely through practices of denaturalized mimicry, with blackface

minstrelsy functioning to establish the cultural intelligibility of the idea of 'blackness' by defining what kinds of performances will count as 'black', whether the person performing this role has black skin or not; on the implications of minstrelsy, *see* Lott and Rogin.

18 Hotelling argues that the first-person voice in 'Black Earth' moves from being 'unmediated and whole' to 'a radically unfixed voice no longer linked to a self' (89).

19 I am here drawing on Arif Dirlik's terminology; the combination of the local and translocal is necessary to produce a 'critical' or resistant localism.

20 The typical reading of 'Black Earth' accepts the metaphorical nature of the imagery of blackness and darkness. The result is to read the poem as being about the failure to achieve a metaphorical 'illumination' (Costello 57–62; Slatin 66–88, 93–7). Martin differs only in rejecting the idea that the poem dramatizes this failure, that the elephant remains 'in the dark' (Martin 19–21). Miller is the first to read this imagery in a more literal, racial sense. *See* Erickson for a reading of 'Black Earth' as one of the earliest examples of 'armoring' and self-enclosure in Moore's poetry (Erickson 149–57).

21 Cristanne Miller's reading of 'Silence' in terms of speech act theory and as insisting upon the reversibility of structures of address, of speaker and audience is also relevant to these lines from 'Black Earth' (*Marianne Moore* 182).

22 Slatin's reading of 'Black Earth' suggests that Moore is deliberately confusing the distinction between a surface reading and a hermeneutic interpretation intended to get 'under' the text to its true meaning. That is, Moore wants a hermeneutic which arrives precisely at the difficulty of establishing meaning, a hermeneutic that respects obscurity, ambiguity and 'unreason' (66–88, 93–7). *See* a similar claim in Erickson (157).

23 I am alluding here to Jameson's famous definition of postmodernism in terms of its critique of 'depth models', including the interpretive distinctions between latent and manifest meanings, or surface appearance and essential truth (*Postmodernism* 12).

24 *See* Moore's uncollected poem 'Radical' (1919) for a similar set of images. Taking on the first-person voice of a carrot (!), as 'Black Earth' does with the elephant, this poem is a humorous take on the metaphor of being defined by one's roots (the etymological meaning of the word 'radical') or grounded. Especially important is the way that the speaker is described both as possessing 'the secret of expansion' and as 'fused with intensive heat', in a blurring of the categories of 'inner' and 'outer' space. *See* DuPlessis's reading of this poem ('No Moore' 24).

25 This instability of poetic voice is how Moore 'addresses quite specifically the difficult and yet obvious necessity of acknowledging another's perspective while remaining oneself' (Taffy Martin 19).

26 Miller's essay on this poem is an early version of ch. 5 in her book on Moore.

27 The figure of the tourist in this poem prefigures what would become one of the central themes in the poetry of Moore's friend and protégé, Elizabeth Bishop.

5 The Grounding of Modern Women's Fiction: Emily Holmes Coleman's *The Shutter of Snow*

1 *See also* Watt's ch. 6 on 'Private Experience and the Novel'. In 'Building Dwelling Thinking', Heidegger develops his own version of this metaphysical 'homelessness', when he argues that dwelling or being at home in the world means 'that mortals ever search anew for the essence of dwelling, that they *must ever learn to dwell*. What if man's [*sic*] homelessness consisted in this?' (339).

2 Pecora is here describing the same disciplinary and institutional production of subjectivity that Foucault defines as the subject's exteriority and 'dispersion' (*Archeology* 54–5). Stone calls this the 'materialized discursivity' of the modern 'fiduciary subject', in the course of her analysis of the progressive textualization and ultimate virtualization of subjectivity, its dissociation from any particular embodied or social location (39–40).

3 One of the best novelistic examples of this process of the abstraction of space in the first half of the twentieth century is Christina Stead's *House of All Nations* (1938). This novel focuses on a moment of financial crisis, when the Bank of England was expected to go off the gold standard, with the result that the value of money would no longer be tied to any material object and would instead be constituted as a flow of disembodied information (*see* Leyshon and Thrift; in the American context Michaels analyzes the effects of going off the gold standard on the naturalist novel). As the title of the novel implies, with reference to an international banking concern, Stead links this kind of economic transformation to a change in the experience of space, figured metaphorically by the transformation of the idea of 'home' from a fixed space into a boundless one, a house of all nations.

4 *See* Foucault, 'Of Other Spaces' (23) for a similar assimilation of all interiorized spaces to a model of exteriority. Pecora's thesis that stream of consciousness narration encodes an increased vulnerability to techniques of social control is both supported and problematized by Coleman's *Shutter of Snow*, which juxtaposes a stream-of-consciousness style and a story about a woman's struggle with the mental health profession and its efforts to exert its control over her. The question this novel poses is to what extent its own style plays into those efforts and to what extent that style is a kind of antidote or cure to those attempts.

5 On the chronotope, *see* Bakhtin (84–5). De Certeau similarly defines space as 'a practiced place' (117).

6 On Coleman's representation of feminine enclosures, *see* Broe (69), and Marcus, 'Of Method' (3).

7 Barbara Rigney, for example, discusses four feminist writers and their representations of madness, none of whom deal with the collective space of a female asylum.

8 For biographical information on Coleman and the circle of women writers associated with Hayford Hall, *see* Broe's essay and Scott (*Refiguring Modernism*, vol. 1, 229–32). Coleman also figures in memoirs by Guggenheim, Chitty, Hopkinson, and Gascoyne. On Coleman's relationship with Emma Goldman, *see* Alice Wexler (133–4).

9 I am quoting from *Social Science* 7 (January 1932): 85. *See also The American Journal of Sociology* 37 (September 1931): 328–31 and *Social Science* 5 (Aug.–Oct. 1930): 568–9.
10 This untitled statement by Coleman forms part of a group of artists' responses to the journal's invitation to discuss the relation between art and literature; *see transition* 1.4 (Fall 1928): 110–11.
11 *See* Guggenheim's chapter on 'Hayford Hall' and Broe's essay analyzing the relationships among the women.
12 Homans analyzes the role of the representation of motherhood in the establishment of 'the cultural myth of women's place in language' as objects rather than subjects of discourse (*Bearing* 5). Compare Homans's discussion of the Virgin Mary as a figure for this position of exclusion from discourse with Coleman's claim to be Christ, not Mary.
13 Broe uses the paradigm of father–daughter incest to analyze Coleman's novel, especially in terms of how the novel develops a strategy of '*repressing what it must reenact*' (69). There is certainly a strong suggestion of sexual abuse in this passage from Coleman.
14 Kristeva defines the semiotic in relation to the symbolic order in *Revolution* (22–4).
15 Marcus points out that this image of submersion alludes to Ophelia, a traditional literary image for female madness ('Of Method' 2).
16 Coleman's poem 'The Liberator' uses the same imagery of resurrection as release from feminine confinement that we find in the novel.

6 'Can't One Live in More Places Than One?': Virginia Woolf's *The Years*

1 *A Room of One's Own* ironically defines how the confinement of women indoors for 'millions of years' has resulted in the metaphorical identification of femininity and domesticity, so that 'the very walls are permeated by [women's] creative force' (91). While such statements might be read as mystifying the specific history of the ideology of separate spheres and therefore as naturalizing that ideology, it seems to me that Woolf is here dramatizing how domesticity has been turned into a metaphor. Especially important for the tradition of feminist modernism that I define in this book are Woolf's description of how the various rooms women have occupied 'differ so completely' (91) and her assertion that it is no longer necessary for a woman author to 'limit herself' to writing only about 'the respectable houses of the upper middle classes', a statement that demonstrates the way critiques of domesticity lead to a rejection of the false identification of white middle-class domesticity with womanhood in general (92). The space of female subjectivity is thereby rendered indeterminate so that differences among women can emerge, in the same way that Woolf uses the pronoun 'one' instead of 'her' in the title of this text, 'a room of one's own'.
2 Examples include Naremore's book, and vol. 1 of Bonnie Kime Scott's *Refiguring Modernism*; the latter omission is especially surprising given that this book contains chapters on 'Arranging Marriages, Partners, and Spaces' and 'Becoming Professionals', two of Woolf's main themes in *The Years*.

3 The best account of this process of revision is Radin's book. Marcus notes that the novel was one of Woolf's most popular at the time of its publication, practically a bestseller, in contrast to the low critical opinion of it (*Virginia Woolf* 39, 50).
4 Among the critics who focus on textual issues, Transue (163–5) and Rose (213) read *The Years* as a failed experiment, with Woolf ultimately unable to impose a successful form on the material of the novel. *See* Squier, *Virginia Woolf* (166); Marcus's chs 2 and 3 of *Virgina Woolf*; and DuPlessis's ch. 10 for the opposing view. Naremore's essay on *The Years* and Ruotolo's ch. 8 are two of the best examples of the second critical tendency, which situates *The Years* as published in relation to Woolf's other novels. Zwerdling's *Virginia Woolf and the Real World* argues that 'Woolf's strong interest in realism, history, and the social matrix has been largely ignored', although Zwerdling himself offers very little commentary on *The Years* (15).
5 Both Kaivola and DuPlessis argue that this critique of individual isolation provides the precondition for a shift to a more collective notion of subjectivity.
6 *See* Janet Wolff for a feminist critique of the figure of the *flaneur*.
7 Kaivola is here quoting Naremore (*World* 55), in order to suggest that the dissolution of boundaries does not have to be understood purely in individualistic or metaphysical terms, but can also be understood as an attempt to represent social subjects.
8 Wheare offers a detailed inventory of these echoes in *The Years*, but *see also* Naremore's essay on *The Years*, which notes the importance to Woolf's work in general of a scene in which one character 'unknowingly' echoes the separate thoughts of two other characters (258). The party scene that ends *The Years* is an attempt to thematize this migration of words and ideas across the boundaries of individual subjectivities, in contrast to the separate interior monologues that structure other novels, especially *The Waves*. In these earlier novels, the result is to suggest that the limitations of individual subjectivity cannot be overcome in social settings but only through the form of the modernist novel, consumed by private individuals in the comfort of their own homes. In *The Years*, as the characters become aware of these migrations in a specific social setting, Woolf seems to be at least trying to move beyond this limitation.
9 *See* Waugh on Woolf's representation of the discursive construction of the self (95).
10 Marcus (*Virginia Woolf* 65–6) uses Said's concepts of filiation and affiliation to discuss Woolf's narrative technique in *The Years*. *See also* DuPlessis on Woolf's 'invention of a communal protagonist and a collective language' (*Writing* 163) and Marcus's reading of the novel as an 'opera for the oppressed' (*Virginia* 57), with particular attention to its choral features.
11 *See* Gillian Brown on this point (2–3). The phrase 'possessive individualism' derives from C.B. MacPherson's reading of Locke.
12 *See* Ruotolo (ch. 8) on the novel's criticism of its characters' desires for self-enclosure.
13 *See* Squier (*Virginia Woolf* 164–5) for a similar analysis of the effects of urban space. This notion of 'obligatory association' is at the basis of the form of feminist coalition politics that Woolf imagines in this novel.

14 Interruption is the key trope around which Ruotolo's book is organized. *See also* Bowlby on Woolf's use of ellipsis to represent the open-ended character of both historical process and feminine identity (ch. 10). Marcus argues that Woolf's *A Room of One's Own* uses ellipsis as a rhetorical figure to transform 'interruption', a sign of the women's vulnerability to masculine authority, 'into a deliberate strategy' that signifies the gendered nature of her writing (*Virginia Woolf* 187).
15 Armstrong draws on the psychoanalytic model of countertransference to define how Woolf embeds a relation to otherness in the communication situation that her novels represent. *See also* Hussey's chapters on 'Identity and Self' and 'Others'. Benveniste's analysis of subjectivity in language is useful for reminding us that the opposition between speaker and addressee in the communication situation, the grammatical positions of 'I' and 'you', are arranged according to an '"interior/exterior" opposition' (225).
16 On the role of sexual harassment in the novel, *see* de Salvo (184–90).
17 On the children's song, *see* Squier (*Virginia Woolf* 178–9); Marcus, (*Virginia Woolf* 48–50); and Ruotolo (203–4).
18 DuPlessis focuses on Woolf's attempt to define a 'voice that was no one's voice' and to reject 'I' and substitute 'We' (*Writing* 177).

7 Dream Made Flesh: Sexual Difference and Narratives of Revolution in Sylvia Townsend Warner's *Summer Will Show*

1 I am indebted to Susan Stanford Friedman for pointing out this passage to me. *See* her application of it to the analysis of epic poems by women writers ('Gender and Genre Anxiety' 204).
2 Bernstein's book reads Lukacs's famous account of the dialectical production of the working-class's epistemological standpoint, in Lukacs's *History and Class Consciousness*, back into Lukacs's pre-Marxist book *The Theory of the Novel*. This move allows Bernstein to redefine the production of class consciousness as a narrative process. Lukacs's account is the basis for feminist standpoint epistemologies, which Harding also argues should be understood in terms of alternate narratives.
3 The exception here would be Caserio's essay on Warner, which focuses on her association of female couples with revolutionary themes, though his reading of *Summer Will Show* tends to assimilate Sophia and Minna's relationship to the depiction of celibate pairs of women in Warner's work and in other British novels. I read Sophia and Minna not just as a negative critique of heterosexuality through the rejection of sexuality as such but instead as an attempt to imagine and represent alternative sexual arrangements; on this point, I find Castle's reading of the novel more persuasive than Caserio's.
4 This trope of the future perfect tense or *futur antérieur* is widespread in contemporary French theory. Julia Kristeva explicitly reads Lukacs's theory of class consciousness in terms of this type of temporality, in the untranslated section of her *La révolution du language poétique* (364). In his introduction to *Dissemination*, Derrida reminds us that the danger of this temporality is that it might objectify the possibilities of the future and reduce them 'to the

form of manifest presence' (7). In the present context, this passage might be read as identifying the dangers of identity politics or the politics of naming that Roof discusses – that is, the risk that the name taken by an emergent social subject will foreclose on future possibilities for what that name might signify. *See also* Judith Butler ('Imitation' 19).

5 *See also* Bernstein's analysis of *Sentimental Education* and his discussion of its significance for Lukacs (140–6).

6 Castle offers an excellent discussion of *Summer Will Show's* intertextuality. She points out that Sophia's husband has the same name as Flaubert's protagonist and that *Summer Will Show* rewrites Flaubert's homosocial plot, in which Frédéric Moreau 'acts out his emotional obsession with his friend Arnoux by falling in love first with Arnoux's wife, then with his mistress' (Castle 224). As Castle also notes, the last name of Sophia's husband, Willoughby, is the name of the villain in Austen's *Sense and Sensibility*, who abandons one of the sisters (Marianne) for a rich heiress (234, fn. 10). Warner's novel reverses this chain of events, with Frederick Willoughby abandoned by his mistress Minna (who is a rewriting of Marianne) for Sophia, the heiress he married; *Summer Will Show* can therefore be read as a 'comic postlude' to Austen, Castle suggests. Castle also points out that Colette's 1929 novel *L'Autre* (translated into English in 1931) involves a similar narrative of a man's wife and mistress forming a relationship with one another, though that relationship is not explicitly erotic (Castle 234, fn. 11).

7 Harman, pp. 139–76, describes Warner and her lover Valentine Ackland's political activities during this period, as does Mulford. Marcus discusses Warner as a socialist feminist in her essays 'Still Practice' (91–4) and 'Alibis' (285–92).

8 By focusing on how the novel's various narrative strands interrupt one another, I am here arguing that the novel resists closure in a different way from that defined either by Castle or Caserio. Both of those critics of Warner's novel focus on how it leaves open the possibility that the character Minna may have survived the wounds she receives while fighting on the barricades with Sophia during the June uprising (Castle 228–9; Caserio 268–9). *See also* Mulford's reading of the novel's ending, which she takes as a sign of ambivalence toward class issues, marked by a decline in the quality of the writing and a descent into sentimentality and polemic (120–2). The unresolved issue of Minna's fate is clearly a strategy for resisting not only formal closure to the narrative but specifically the typical ideological resolution of narratives of lesbian desire which end with the women's punishment or death. At the end of this ch., I will focus instead on the narrative undecidability introduced by the reappearance of the West Indian mulatto child Caspar.

9 *See* Harman's biography of Warner for an account of this relationship (especially 100–16), and Mulford's book on Warner and Ackland's combination of political and literary activities during the period from 1930–51. Ackland also wrote a memoir about her life with Warner, though this text is primarily a confession by Ackland of her struggle with alcoholism and its effects on her relationship with Warner.

10 Castle is here drawing on Sedgwick's argument about the canonical nature of homosocial relations within literary history (Sedgwick, *Between* 17).

Castle uses *Summer Will Show* to critique Sedgwick's argument that lesbian relationships can be distinguished from male homosexuality because lesbian relationships are subsumed under other types of relations between women and so do not generate the same type of 'homosexual panic' that occurs when male homosociality crosses the line into homosexuality (Sedgwick 2–3). In Warner's novel, the best refutation of this argument comes when Sophia's husband seizes her bank account after Sophia becomes involved with Minna (266).

11 This technique is Warner's version of Woolf's techniques for 'transforming interruption ... into a deliberate strategy as a sign of women's writing' (Marcus, *Virginia Woolf* 187), though Woolf's interruptions took place on the level of interactions between characters rather than the level of the liberation narratives of new social subjects.

12 In an essay entitled 'Women as Writers', Warner suggests that 'a woman has to be most exceptionally secluded if she never goes to her own back door, or is not on visiting terms with people poorer than herself' (272). This passage also suggests Warner's interest in reconceptualizing the domestic novel in a way that privileges women characters for their involvement in 'popular life and its living forces', a characteristic Lukacs attributes to the historical novel (237). Marcus offers a reading of Warner's essay and its attempt to recover class issues within a gendered frame by rewriting Woolf's *A Room of One's Own* in a way that reverses the process Armstrong describes ('Still Practice' 92–4).

13 Mary McCarthy's 1936 review of *Summer Will Show* in *The Nation* responds to this apparent inappropriateness by defending Warner from 'those impatient Marxist critics who assess the value of a revolutionary novel in terms of its potential agitational effect upon the behavior of a steel worker' (191). She describes Warner as 'a more highly trained, more cerebral fiction writer' than the left had previously 'been able to recruit from bourgeois literature' (192). However, McCarthy comments on the lesbian plot only in one brief phrase, when she points out that Sophia goes to work while in Paris in order to support herself and Minna, 'because she loves the Jewess' (192).

14 In a discussion of Marx's techniques for narrating the 1848 revolution, LaCapra argues that Marx's abjection of the *lumpenproletariat* as 'scum, offal, the refuse of all classes' (*Eighteenth Brumaire* 72) and his refusal to acknowledge that there might have been any possibility for shared interests between the workers and the *lumpenproletariat* reflect Marx's own anxieties over 'the possibility that modern societies did not offer a more or less ready-made group analogue to the classical revolutionary subject' (LaCapra 185). In other words, Marx's attitude toward people like Caspar, in Warner's novel (and probably Sophia and Minna as well), represents both his desire to ground his theory of revolution in a form of class essentialism and his anxieties over the necessity of producing that foundational ground rather than finding it in an already existing form.

15 *See* Harper for an account of the structural relationships between the ideology of private property and the threat posed to that ideology by both homosexual desire and miscegenation ('Private Affairs').

16 Caserio comments on the possibility of reading this final passage both as an act of self-erasure in the face of Marx and Engels's text and as an act of 'enwombing' their text 'in a woman's story' (264–5).

8 From Domestic Grounding to Domestic Play: Problems of Reproduction and Subversion in Gertrude Stein and Zora Neale Hurston

1 There is considerable critical debate about the possibility of reading *Tender Buttons* for its domestic themes, given DeKoven's influential argument about the irrelevance of thematic content in Stein's work generally (*Different* 11). The result is to decontextualize domestic imagery; for commentaries on this problem, *see* Perloff's reading of Stein in *The Poetics of Indeterminacy*, Monroe (204), and Chessman. *See* Gubar on how *Tender Buttons* can be read as a 'daemonic' version of the domestic treatise or conduct book ('Blessings' 495–6), and Murphy on how Stein's prose poems 'mimic and undermine' the 'ordinary discourse of domesticity, to create her own new "language"' (391, 383–4). The claim that domesticity can provide the basis for constructing a new language contrasts with North's critique of Stein for basing the 'newness' of her style on the difference between black vernacular and standard English (North 70).

2 Stein offers a somewhat more traditionally coherent account of this transition in the long 'portrait' entitled *Two*. Hadas reads *Tender Buttons* specifically in this biographical context ('Spreading' 61), while Benstock (*Women* 151–8) and Stimpson ('Mind' 493) discuss the more general significance of Toklas's arrival at 27 Rue de Fleurus.

3 All quotations from *Tender Buttons* will be taken from the edition published in Stein's *Selected Writings*. Dickinson's poem 'Races – nurtured in the Dark' (*P* 581) provides one basis for reading this kind of imagery in racialized terms (*see* ch. 2, n. 30), and I have discussed how H.D. and Moore both adopt and problematize this analogy. North criticizes Stein for a similar appropriation of black vernacular speech when Stein adopts a black woman as a viewpoint character in 'Melanctha' from *Three Lives* (North 70); *see* Saldivar-Hull, on 'Melanctha' as a model for the problems feminists of color have with such appropriations. In this respect, we might note Stein's interest in 'the history of the refused' (*Selected Writings* 514–15); *see also* Caramello (6). *See* Ruddick for a reading of *Tender Buttons* in terms of how Stein drew on William James's psychology to define 'the things that every mind suppresses as images connected with femaleness' ('Rosy' 226); *see also* Ruddick (*Reading Gertrude Stein*, ch. 3).

4 The eroticized imagery of entering Stein's text recalls the issues raised by Dickinson's letter to Susan Gilbert, discussed at the beginning of ch. 2, especially the injunction to 'open me carefully'.

5 Stein's phrase for this performative process is making something 'as it is made' (*Selected Writings* 514). In other words, writing is not an act of representing already existing themes but a constitutive act in itself. Compare to Lyotard on the temporality of postmodernism as one in which 'the artist and the writer ... are working without rules in order to formulate the rules of what *will have been done*' (81).

6 There has been a great deal of commentary on Stein's methods for composing *Tender Buttons*, which often invoke her work on automatic writing during her studies with William James; *see* Bridgman (136) and Schmitz ('Gertrude Stein' 1206). Stein's project in *Tender Buttons* responds to James's stream-

of-consciousness metaphor, since that metaphor is a critique of the mind's principles of selection and exclusions, precisely the same habits of thought which Stein tries to overcome. In the context of domesticity and its emphasis on the need for systematic organization within the home as a form of mental hygiene for women, it is particularly suggestive to read James's claim that 'it is ... the reinstatement of the vague and inarticulate to its proper place in our mental life which I am so anxious to press the attention' (254), since the function of domestic economy for women's psyches was to eliminate such vaguenesses. Other discussions of James's influence on Stein include Ruddick; Weinstein; Bridgman (133–4); and Jayne Walker (134–5).

7 Stimpson also comments on this poem as a reference to the effects of Toklas's presence ('Transposition' 3), and Scobie more generally analyzes how Stein metonymically associates Toklas with the objects making up Stein's 'iconography of domestic life' (112–14). There is a lively critical debate on the topic of how Stein's writing encodes lesbian references and whether her experimental techniques can be read as stylistically dramatizing a lesbian idiolect. *See* Fifer on the existence of such codes, and Stimpson ('Mind' 496–506) and Benstock (*Women* 161–9, 187–90) for more skeptical readings. Both Stimpson ('Transposition' 12) and Gilbert and Gubar (*Sexchanges* 246) also express skepticism about Stein and Toklas's gender role-playing or claims to identificatory mobility.

8 *See also* Schmitz (*Of Huck* 162). 'That' is an example of what Beveniste calls a shifter, a word which refers not to 'real objects, to "historical" times and places', but instead to 'the *present* instance of discourse' (218–19).

9 Bridgman (xiv–xv) also discusses this poem, as an example of how important context is for understanding Stein's writing.

10 This split in Stein's work, between the deconstruction of the public/private dichotomy defining domesticity in *Tender Buttons* and the subsumption of racial difference to a model of gender opposition grounded in the public/private dichotomy, is reflected in a split in recent critical assessments of Stein. In the 1996 special issue of *Modern Fiction Studies* devoted to Stein, one group of essays focuses on how Stein's critique of identity can be read as a form of resistance to Stein's own sexual and ethnic marginality; *see* Charles Bernstein (485) and Damon, on Stein's Jewish ethnicity and the instability of 'home' in Jewish diasporic traditions (499). In contrast, another set of essays critiques Stein's reproduction of racial stereotypes in her attempt to resist gender and sexual stereotypes; *see* Hovey, on Stein's use of 'racial drag' as a means to express female desire (548), and Smedman (570–1).

11 In addition to Alice Walker's classic essay on Hurston, 'In Search of Our Mother's Gardens', *see* Mary Helen Washington's essay '"I Love the Way Janie Crawford Left Her Husbands": Emergent Female Hero' (Gates and Appiah 98–109); Barbara Christian's chapter on Hurston; Susan Willis (Gates and Appiah 110–29); Baker on Janie's gaining her blues voice (*Blues* 59); Callahan's argument about how the novel weaves together Hurston and Janie's voices (145); Awkward's analysis of how the novel presents Janie as gaining 'a cultural voice' but deferring the narration of her story in favor of a collective voice rather than 'individual textual control' (13); and Wall's

reading of Hurston's 'physical and spiritual journey' (*Women of the Harlem Renaissance* 195). In contrast, Carla Kaplan offers a provocative reading of the novel as dramatizing Hurston's skepticism toward 'the Harlem Renaissance's politics of voice' (*Erotics of Talk* 103, 108).

12 While Carla Kaplan lists both Johnson and Gates among the critics who read *Their Eyes Were Watching God* as a story of Janie's finding her voice, it seems to me that Johnson and Gates are pointing toward the way of Janie's discovery that she has an inside and an outside, her discovery of the conceptual framework of an expressive epistemology, is problematized in Hurston's novel.

13 For example, *see* Gates, *Signifying* (191), Johnson (160), and Wall's reading of how 'Tea Cake delights in Janie's pleasure' (*Women* 188).

14 Wall offers an excellent reading of how *Their Eyes Were Watching God* is not organized so much around a romance plot but instead around 'the journey from store porch to jook to muck mapped in *Mules*', – that is, *Mules and Men*, Hurston's ethnographic study of African-American folk tales (*Women* 179).

15 Wall reads this scene as dramatizing the connection between domestic violence and 'the capitalist, racist, and elitist values' of the character of Mrs Turner, who encourages Tea Cake's jealousy and who urges Janie to take a lighter-skinned lover (*Women* 190), though this reading minimizes the self-conscious theatricality of the beating, emphasized by the structural parallel to Tea Cake's metaphorical reference to being unable to beat a woman. Washington cites the presentation of the beating scene as an example of how Janie is denied voice (since the scene is narrated from the point of view of the community and its interpretation is privileged), until she is speaking to another black woman – that is, Janie has voice only in the frame-tale, not in the narrative itself (Gates and Appiah 99). In contrast, Collins focuses on Janie's participation in black vernacular practices of 'specifying', especially the famous scene in which Janie is presented as precipitating Joe Starks's death by publicly engaging in an exchange of insults with him (25).

16 The scene in which Janie is forced to shoot Tea Cake, after he's been bitten by a rabid dog and as a result suffers changes in personality that make him dangerous to Janie, is another example of this type of denaturalized performance of violence. This scene is designed to put Janie into a situation where her actions mimic those of a woman taking revenge on an abusive man, though the novel is careful to explain that this is not what Janie is doing; the entire sequence of events is presented as a set of chance occurrences for which neither character is responsible, an act of God like the flood in which the two are caught during this scene. It is also clear that the effects of Tea Cake's rabies, including delusions and irrational anger, are also intended to mimic sexist aggression. The rabies turns Tea Cake into an extreme form of the kind of man Joe Starks is revealed to be when Starks slaps Janie.

17 In her book on 'migrations of the subject' in African-American women's writing, Davies suggests that the African diaspora provides another historical source for Hurston's imagery, since it ambivalently combines both positive 'fluidity' with 'displacement and uprootedness' (128).

18 *See* Gates, *Signifying* (213), for a similar reading of the ending of the novel.
19 Kaplan's reading of the frame-tale, in which Janie narrates her story to Pheoby, is particularly interesting for its argument that Hurston intends to dramatize 'the impossibility of the social situation she depicts', specifically Janie's finding an ideal audience (*Erotics of Talk* 118). In Kaplan's view, 'Hurston very deliberately figures Phoeby's "comprehensive listening" as a hard act to follow', in order to make readers reflect upon our own shortcomings in living up to this 'exaggerated idealization', especially 'coming as it does from a black woman writer who we know had such good reasons to distrust her own reception and to doubt the motives of her audience(s), as much when they chose to celebrate her as when they chose to vilify her' (118).

Works Cited

Abraham, Julie. 'Summer Will Show', *The Nation*, 19 March 1989, 389–90.

Ackland, Valentine. *For Sylvia: an Honest Account*, London: Methuen, 1986.

Adelson, Leslie A. 'Racism and Feminist Aesthetics: the Provocation of Anne Duden's *Opening of the Mouth*' in Micheline R. Malson, Jean F. O'Barr, Sarah Westphal-Wihl and Mary Wyen (eds), *Feminist Theory in Practice and Process*, Chicago: University of Chicago Press, 1989.

Adorno, Theodor W. *Aesthetic Theory*, trans. C. Lenhardt, New York: Routledge & Kegan Paul, 1984.

Allen, Polly Wynn. *Building Domestic Liberty: Charlotte Perkins Gilman's Architectural Feminism*, Amherst: University of Massachusetts Press, 1988.

Althusser, Louis. 'Ideology and Ideological State Apparatuses' in Louis Althusser, *Lenin and Philosophy and Other Essays*, trans. Ben Brewster, New York: Monthly Review Press, 1971.

Altieri, Charles. *Painterly Abstraction in Modernist American Poetry: the Contemporaneity of Modernism*, New York: Cambridge University Press, 1989.

Ardis, Ann. *New Women, New Novels: Feminism and Early Modernism*, New Brunswick: Rutgers U. Press, 1990.

Armstrong, Nancy. *Desire and Domestic Fiction: a Political History of the Novel*, New York: Oxford University Press, 1987.

Austin, J.L. *How to Do Things with Words*, 2nd ed., J.O. Urmson and Marina Sbisa (eds), Cambridge: Harvard University Press, 1975.

Awkward, Michael. *Inspiriting Influences: Tradition, Revision, and Afro-American Women's Novels*, New York: Columbia University Press, 1989.

Bachelard, Gaston. *The Poetics of Space*, trans. Maria Jolas, Boston: Beacon, 1969.

Baker, Houston A., Jr. *Blues, Ideology, and Afro-American Literature: a Vernacular Theory*, Chicago: University of Chicago Press, 1984.

——. *Workings of the Spirit: the Poetics of Afro-American Women's Writing*, Chicago: U. of Chicago Press, 1991.

Bakhtin, M.M. *The Dialogic Imagination: Four Essays*, trans. Caryl Emerson and Michael Holquist, Austin: University of Texas Press, 1981.

Barker, Wendy. *Lunacy of Light: Emily Dickinson and the Experience of Metaphor*, Carbondale: Southern Illinois University Press, 1987.

Barrett, Michele. *Women's Oppression Today: Problems in Marxist Feminist Analysis*, London: Verso, 1980.

Barthes, Roland. 'From Work to Text', in Barthes, *Image-Music-Text*, trans. Stephen Heath, New York: Hill and Wang, 1977.

Baudrillard, Jean. *The Ecstasy of Communication*, trans. Bernard and Caroline Schutze, New York: Semiotext(e), 1988.

Bauerly, Donna. 'Emily Dickinson's Rhetoric of Temporality', *The Emily Dickinson Journal* 1.2 (1992): 1–7.

Baym, Nina. *Woman's Fiction: a Guide to Novels by and about Women in America, 1820–1870*, Ithaca: Cornell University Press, 1978.

Beauvoir, Simone de. *The Second Sex*, trans. H.M. Parshley, New York: Vintage, 1974.

Beecher, Catherine. *Treatise on Domestic Economy for the Use of Young Ladies at Home and at School*, Boston: Thomas H. Webb & Co., 1842.

Bennett, Paula. '"By a Mouth That Cannot Speak": Spectral Presence in Emily Dickinson's Letters', *The Emily Dickinson Journal* 1.2 (1992), 76–99.

——. '"The Descent of the Angel": Interrogating Domestic Ideology in American Women's Poetry, 1858–1890', *American Literary History* 7.4 (Winter 1995), 591–610.

Benstock, Shari. 'Expatriate Modernism: Writing on the Cultural Rim' in Mary Lynn Broe and Angela Ingram (eds), *Women's Writing in Exile*, Chapel Hill: University of North Carolina Press, 1989.

——. *Women of the Left Bank: Paris, 1900–1940*, Austin: University of Texas Press, 1986.

Benveniste, Emile. *Problems in General Linguistics*, trans. by Mary Elizabeth Meek, Miami: University of Miami Press, 1971.

Berger, Peter L., Brigitte Berger and Hansfried Keller. *The Homeless Mind: Modernization and Consciousness*, New York: Random House, 1973.

Bergson, Henri. *An Introduction to Metaphysics*, trans. T.E. Hulme, New York: Bobbs-Merrill, 1955.

Berman, Marshall. *All That is Solid Melts into Air: the Experience of Modernity*, New York: Penguin, 1988.

Bernstein, Charles. 'Stein's Identity', *Modern Fiction Studies* 42.3 (Fall 1996); 485–8.

Bernstein, J.M. *The Philosophy of the Novel: Lukacs, Marxism and the Dialectics of Form*, Minneapolis: University of Minnesota Press, 1984.

Berry, Ellen E. *Curved Thought and Textual Wandering: Gertrude Stein's Postmodernism*, Ann Arbor: U. of Michigan Press, 1992.

Bishop, Elizabeth. *The Collected Prose*, New York: Farrar, Straus and Giroux, 1984.

——. *The Complete Poems 1927–1979*, New York: Farrar, Straus and Giroux, 1983.

Blankley, Elyse. 'Beyond the "Talent of Knowing": Gertrude Stein and the New Woman', in Michael J. Hoffman (ed.), *Critical Essays on Gertrude Stein*, Boston: G.K. Hall, 1986.

Blasing, Mutlu Konuk. *American Poetry: the Rhetoric of Its Forms*, New Haven: Yale University Press, 1987.

Bowlby, Rachel. *Virginia Woolf: Feminist Destinations*, New York: Basil Blackwell, 1988.

Bradbury, Malcolm. 'The Cities of Modernism', in Malcolm Bradbury and James McFarlane (eds), *Modernism, 1890–1930*, New York: Penguin, 1976, 96–104.

Bridgman, Richard. *Gertrude Stein in Pieces*, New York: Oxford University Press, 1970.

Broe, Mary Lynn. 'My Art Belongs to Daddy: Incest as Exile, the Textual Economics of Hayford Hall', in Mary Lynn Broe and Angela Ingram (eds), *Women's Writing in Exile*, Chapel Hill: University of North Carolina Press, 1989.

Brown, Gillian. *Domestic Individualism: Imagining Self in Nineteenth-Century America*, Berkeley: U. of California Press, 1990.

Burke, Carolyn. 'Supposed Persons: Modernist Poetry and the Female Subject', *Feminist Studies* 11 (Spring 1985), 131–48.
Butler, Judith. *Bodies That Matter: on the Discursive Limits of 'Sex'*, New York: Routledge, 1993.
——. *Gender Trouble: Feminism and the Subversion of Identity*, New York: Routledge, 1990.
——. 'Imitation and Gender Insubordination', in Diana Fuss (ed.), *Inside/Out: Lesbian Theories, Gay Theories*, New York: Routledge, 1991, 13–31.
Callahan, John. *In the African-American Grain: the Pursuit of Voice in Twentieth-Century Black Fiction*, Urbana: University of Illinois Press, 1988.
Cameron, Sharon. *Choosing Not Choosing: Dickinson's Fascicles*, Chicago: University of Chicago Press, 1992.
——. *Lyric Time: Dickinson and the Limits of Genre*, Baltimore: Johns Hopkins University Press, 1979.
Caramello, Charles. 'Gertrude Stein as Exemplary Theorist', in Shirley Neuman and Ira B. Nadel (eds), *Gertrude Stein and the Making of Literature*, Boston: Northeastern University Press, 1988.
Carby, Hazel. *Reconstructing Womanhood: the Emergence of the Afro-American Woman Novelist*, New York: Oxford University Press, 1987.
Caserio, Robert L. 'Celibate Sisters-in-Revolution: towards Reading Sylvia Townsend Warner', in Joseph A. Boone and Michael Cadden (eds), *Engendering Men: the Question of Male Feminist Criticism*, New York: Routledge, 1990.
Castle, Terry. 'Sylvia Townsend Warner and the Counterplot of Lesbian Fiction', *Textual Practice* 4 (Summer 1990), 213–35. Reprinted in Castle, *The Apparitional Lesbian: Female Homosexuality and Modern Culture*, New York: Columbia University Press, 1993.
Chatterjee, Partha. 'The Nationalist Resolution of the Women's Question', in *Recasting Women: Essays in Colonial History*, New Delhi: Kali for Women, 1989.
Cherniavsky, Eva. *That Pale Mother Rising: Sentimental Discourses and the Imitation of Motherhood in 19th-Century America*, Bloomington: Indiana U. Press, 1995.
Chessman, Harriet Scott. *The Public Is Invited to Dance: Representation, the Body, and Dialogue in Gertrude Stein*, Stanford: Stanford University Press, 1989.
Chisolm, Diane. *H.D.'s Freudian Poetics: Psychoanalysis in Translation*, Ithaca: Cornell U. Press, 1992.
Chitty, Susan. *Now to My Mother: a Very Personal Memoir of Antonia White*, London: Weidenfeld and Nicolson, 1985.
Christian, Barbara. *Black Women Novelists: the Development of a Tradition, 1892–1976*, Westport: Greenwood Press, 1980.
Clark, Suzanne. *Sentimental Modernism: Women Writers and the Revolution of the Word*, Bloomington: Indiana U. Press, 1991.
Clifford, James. 'Notes on Theory and Travel', *Inscriptions* 5 (1989): 177–88.
Coleman, Emily Holmes. 'Grave Song', *transition* 1.10 (January 1928), 92.
——. 'The Liberator', *transition* 1.7 (October 1927), 124–5.
——. 'Poem', *transition* 1.10 (January 1928), 93.
——. *The Shutter of Snow*, London: George Routledge & Sons, 1930; rpt. New York: Penguin, 1986.

Collins, Patricia Hill. *Black Feminist Thought: Knowledge, Consciousness, and the Politics of Empowerment*, Boston: Unwin Hyman, 1990.
Colomina, Beatriz. *Privacy and Publicity: Modern Architecture as Mass Media*, Cambridge, MA: MIT Press, 1996.
Costello, Bonnie. 'The "Feminine" Language of Marianne Moore', in Sally McConnell-Ginet, Ruth Barker and Nelly Furman (eds), *Women and Language in Literature and Society*, New York: Praeger, 1980.
——. *Marianne Moore: Imaginary Possessions*, Cambridge, MA: Harvard University Press, 1981.
Cott, Nancy F. *The Bonds of Womanhood: 'Woman's Sphere' in New England, 1780–1835*, New Haven: Yale University Press, 1977.
——. *The Grounding of Modern Feminism*, New Haven: Yale University Press, 1987.
Cowley, Malcolm. *Exile's Return: a Literary Odyssey of the 1920s*, New York: Penguin, 1982.
Crang, Mike and Nigel Thrift (eds). *Thinking Space*, New York: Routledge, 2000.
Damon, Maria. 'Gertrude Stein's Jewishness, Jewish Social Scientists, and the "Jewish Question"', *Modern Fiction Studies* 42.3 (Fall 1996), 489–507.
Davidoff, Leonore. *Worlds Between: Historical Perspectives on Gender and Class*, New York: Routledge, 1995.
Davidoff, Leonore and Catherine Hall. *Family Fortunes: Men and Women of the English Middle Class, 1680–1850*, London: Hutchinson, 1987.
Davies, Carole Boyce. *Black Women, Writing, and Identity: Migrations of the Subject*, New York: Routledge, 1994.
De Certeau, Michel. *The Practice of Everyday Life*, trans. Steven Rendall, Berkeley: University of California Press, 1984.
Degler, Carl. *At Odds: Women and Family in America from the Revolution to the Present*, New York: Oxford University Press, 1980.
DeKoven, Marianne. *A Different Language: Gertrude Stein's Experimental Writing*, Madison: University of Wisconsin Press, 1983.
——. 'Gendered Doubleness and the "Origins" of Modernist Form', *Tulsa Studies in Women's Literature* 8 (Spring 1989), 19–42.
de Lauretis, Teresa. 'Feminist Studies/Critical Studies: Issues, Terms, Contexts', in Teresa de Lauretis (ed.), *Feminist Studies/Critical Studies*, Bloomington: Indiana University Press, 1986.
——. 'Sexual Indifference and Lesbian Representation', *Theatre Journal* 40 (May 1988), 155–77.
——. 'The Technology of Gender', in Teresa de Lauretis, *Technologies of Gender: Essays on Theory, Film, and Fiction*, Bloomington: Indiana University Press, 1987.
Derrida, Jacques. *Archive Fever: a Freudian Impression*, trans. Eric Prenowitz, Chicago: University of Chicago Press, 1996.
——. *Dissemination*, trans. Barbara Johnson, Chicago: University of Chicago Press, 1981.
——. *Writing and Difference*, trans. by Alan Bass, Chicago: University of Chicago Press, 1978.
DeSalvo, Louise. *Virginia Woolf: the Impact of Childhood Sexual Abuse on Her Life and Work*, Boston: Beacon Press, 1989.
Deutsche, Rosalyn. 'Uneven Development: Public Art in New York City', *October* 47 (Winter 1988), 3–76.

Dhareshwar, Vivek. 'Marxism, Location Politics, and the Possibility of Critique', *Public Culture* 6.1 (1993), 41–54.

Diamond, Irene and Lee Quinby. 'American Feminism and the Language of Control', in Irene Diamond and Lee Quinby (eds), *Feminism and Foucault: Reflections on Resistance*, Boston: Northwestern U. Press, 1988, 193–206.

Diamond, Irene and Lee Quinby (eds). *Feminism and Foucault: Reflections on Resistance*, Boston: Northwestern U. Press, 1988.

Dickinson, Emily. *The Letters of Emily Dickinson*, 3 vols, ed. by Thomas Johnson and Theodora Ward, Cambridge, MA: Belknap Press of Harvard University Press, 1958.

——. *The Poems of Emily Dickinson*, 3 vols, ed. by Thomas Johnson, Cambridge, MA: Belknap Press of Harvard University Press, 1958.

Diggory, Terence. 'Armored Women, Naked Men: Dickinson, Whitman, and Their Successors', in Sandra M. Gilbert and Susan Gubar (eds), *Shakespeare's Sisters: Feminist Essays on Women Poets*, Bloomington: Indiana University Press, 1979.

Dirlik, Arif. 'The Global in the Local', in Rob Wilson and Wimal Dissanayake (eds), *Global/Local: Cultural Production and the Transnational Imaginary*, Durham: Duke U. Press, 1996.

Dobson, Joanne. 'Emily Dickinson and the "Prickly Art" of Housekeeping', in Suzanne Juhasz and Cristanne Miller (eds), *Emily Dickinson: a Celebration*, New York: Gordon and Breach, 1989.

Duncan, Nancy (ed.) *Bodyspace: Destabilizing Geographies of Gender and Sexuality*, New York: Routledge, 1996.

DuPlessis, Rachel Blau. *H.D.: the Career of That Struggle*, Bloomington: Indiana University Press, 1986.

——. 'No Moore of the Same: the Feminist Poetics of Marianne Moore', *William Carlos Williams Review* 14 (Spring 1988), 6–32.

——. *Writing Beyond the Ending: Narrative Strategies of Twentieth-Century Women Writers*, Bloomington: Indiana University Press, 1985.

DuPlessis, Rachel Blau and Susan Stanford Friedman. '"Woman Is Perfect": H.D.'s Debate with Freud', *Feminist Studies* 7 (Fall 1981), 417–30.

Durham, Carolyn. 'Linguistic and Sexual Engendering in Marianne Moore's Poetry', in Temma F. Berg, Anna Shannon Elfenbein, Jeanne Larsen and Elisa Kay Sparks (eds), *Engendering the Word: Feminist Essays in Psychosexual Poetics*, Urbana: Illinois University Press, 1989.

Easthope, Anthony. *Poetry as Discourse*, New York: Methuen, 1983.

Eberwein, Jane Donahue. *Dickinson: Strategies of Limitation*, Amherst: University of Massachusetts Press, 1985.

Edmunds, Susan. *Out of Line: History, Psychoanalysis, and Montage in H.D.'s Long Poems*, Stanford: Stanford U. Press, 1994.

Eliot, T.S. 'Tradition and the Individual Talent', in Eliot, *The Sacred Wood: Essays on Poetry and Criticism*, New York: Methuen, 1960. Originally published 1920.

Engels, Frederick. 'Introduction to Karl Marx's Work *The Class Struggles in France, 1848–1850*', in Karl Marx and Frederick Engels, *Selected Works*, New York: International Publishers, 1968.

Erickson, Darlene Williams. *Illusion is More Precise Than Precision: the Poetry of Marianne Moore*, Tuscaloosa, AL: U. of Alabama Press, 1992.

Erkkila, Betsy. 'Emily Dickinson and Class', *American Literary History* 4.1 (Spring 1992): 1–27.

Farr, Judith. 'The Encoding of Homoerotic Desire: Emily Dickinson's Letters and Poems to Susan Dickinson, 1850–1886', *Tulsa Studies in Women's Literature* 9.2 (Fall 1990): 251–72.

Felski, Rita. *Beyond Feminist Aesthetics: Feminist Literature and Social Change*, Cambridge, MA: Harvard University Press, 1989.

Fifer, Elizabeth. '"In Conversation": Gertrude Stein's Speaker, Message, and Receiver in *Painted Lace and Other Pieces (1914–1937)*', *Modern Fiction Studies* 34 (Autumn 1988), 465–80.

——. 'Is Flesh Advisable?: the Interior Theater of Gertrude Stein', *Signs* 4 (Spring 1979): 472–83.

——. *Rescued Readings: a Reconstruction of Gertrude Stein's Difficult Texts*, Detroit: Wayne State U. Press, 1992.

Flax, Jane. 'Postmodernism and Gender Relations in Feminist Theory', *Signs* 12 (Summer 1987), 621–43.

Fletcher, John and Malcolm Bradbury. 'The Introverted Novel', in Malcolm Bradbury and James McFarlane (eds), *Modernism: 1890–1930*, New York: Penguin, 1976.

Foster, Thomas. 'History, Critical Theory, and Women's Social Practices: "Women's Time and *Housekeeping*"', *Signs* 14 (Autumn 1988), 73–99.

——. '"The Very House of Difference": Gender as Embattled Standpoint', *Genders* 8 (Summer 1990), 17–37.

Foucault, Michel. *The Archeology of Knowledge*, trans. A.M. Sheridan Smith, New York: Pantheon, 1972.

——. *Discipline and Punish: the Birth of the Prison*, trans. Alan Sheridan, New York: Vintage, 1979.

——. 'Of Other Spaces', trans. Jay Miskowiec, *Diacritics* 16.1 (Spring 1986): 22–7.

——. *Power/Knowledge: Selected Interviews and Other Writings, 1972–1977*, New York: Pantheon, 1980.

Fox-Genovese, Elizabeth. 'Placing Women's History in History', *New Left Review* 133 (May–June 1982), 5–29.

Fox-Genovese, Elizabeth and Eugene Genovese. *Fruits of Merchant Capital: Slavery and Bourgeois Property in the Rise and Expansion of Capitalism*, New York: Oxford University Press, 1983.

Freud, Sigmund. *Beyond the Pleasure Principle*, trans. and ed. by James Strachey, New York: Norton, 1961.

——. *The Interpretation of Dreams*, trans. and ed. James Strachey, New York: Avon, 1965.

——. 'A Note Upon the "Mystic Writing-Pad"', in James Strachey (ed.) and others (trans.), *The Standard Edition of the Complete Psychological Works of Sigmund Freud*, vol. 19, London: Hogarth Press, 1961.

——. 'A Note Upon the Unconscious in Psycho-Analysis', in James Strachey (ed.) and others (trans.), *The Standard Edition of the Complete Psychological Works of Sigmund Freud*, vol. 19, London: Hogarth Press, 1961.

——. 'Project for a Scientific Psychology', in James Strachey (ed.) and others (trans.), *The Standard Edition of the Complete Psychological Works of Sigmund Freud*, vol. 1, London: Hogarth Press, 1966.

Friedman, Susan Stanford. 'Exile in the American Grain: H.D.'s Diaspora', in Mary Lynn Broe and Angela Ingram (eds), *Women's Writing in Exile*, Chapel Hill: University of North Carolina Press, 1989.

——. 'Gender and Genre Anxiety: Elizabeth Barrett Browning and H.D. as Epic Poets', *Tulsa Studies in Women's Literature* 5 (Fall 1986), 203–28.

——. *Mappings: Feminism and the Cultural Geographies of Encounter*, Princeton: Princeton University Press, 1998.

——. 'Modernism of the "Scattered Remnant": Race and Politics in the Development of H.D.'s Modernist Vision', in Michael King (ed.), *H.D.: Woman and Poet*, Orono, ME: National Poetry Foundation, 1986.

——. *Penelope's Web: Gender, Modernity, and H.D.'s Fiction*, New York: Cambridge U. Press, 1990.

——. *Psyche Reborn: the Emergence of H.D.*, Bloomington: Indiana University Press, 1981.

Friedman, Susan Stanford and Rachel Blau DuPlessis. '"I Had Two Loves Separate": the Sexualities of H.D.'s *Her*', *Montemora* 8 (1981), 7–30.

Fritz, Angela DiPace. *Thought and Vision: a Critical Reading of H.D.'s Poetry*, Washington, DC: Catholic University of America Press, 1988.

Fuss, Diana. *Essentially Speaking: Feminism, Nature, and Difference*, New York: Routledge, 1989.

Gascoyne, David. *Journal 1936–37*, London: Enitharmon Press, 1980.

Gates, Henry Louis, Jr. *The Signifying Monkey: a Theory of African-American Literary Criticism*, New York: Oxford U. Press, 1988.

Gates, Henry Louis, Jr. and K.A. Appiah (eds). *Zora Neale Hurston: Critical Perspectives Past and Present*, New York: Amistad, 1993.

Gelpi, Albert. *A Coherent Splendor: the American Poetic Renaissance, 1910–1950*, Cambridge: Cambridge University Press, 1987.

——. 'Emily Dickinson and the Deerslayer: the Dilemma of the Woman Poet in America', in Sandra M. Gilbert and Susan Gubar (eds), *Shakespeare's Sisters: Feminist Essays on Women Poets*, Bloomington: Indiana University Press, 1979.

——. *The Tenth Muse: the Psyche of the American Poet*, Cambridge, MA: Harvard University Press, 1975.

George, Rosemary Marangoly. *The Politics of Home: Postcolonial Relocations and Twentieth-Century Fiction*, New York: Cambridge University Press, 1996.

Giddings, Paula. *When and Where I Enter: the Impact of Black Women on Race and Sex in America*, New York: Bantam, 1985.

Gilbert, Sandra M. 'The Wayward Nun beneath the Hill: Emily Dickinson and the Mysteries of Womanhood', in Suzanne Juhasz (ed.), *Feminist Critics Read Emily Dickinson*, Bloomington: Indiana University Press, 1983.

——. 'The American Sexual Politics of Walt Whitman and Emily Dickinson', in Sacvan Bercovitch (ed.), *Reconstructing American Literary History*, Cambridge, MA: Harvard University Press, 1985.

Gilbert, Sandra M. and Susan Gubar. *The Madwoman in the Attic: the Woman Writer and the Nineteenth-Century Literary Imagination*, New Haven: Yale University Press, 1979.

——. *No Man's Land: the Place of the Woman Writer in the Twentieth Century*. Vol. 1: *The War of the Words*, New Haven: Yale University Press, 1988.

——. *No Man's Land: the Place of the Woman Writer in the Twentieth Century*. Vol. 2: *Sexchanges*, New Haven: Yale University Press, 1989.

——. *No Man's Land: the Place of the Woman Writer in the Twentieth Century*. Vol. 3: *Letters from the Front*, New Haven: Yale U. Press, 1994.

Gilman, Charlotte Perkins. *Women and Economics: a Study of the Economic Relation between Men and Women as a Factor in Social Evolution*, ed. Carl N. Degler, New York: Harper and Row, 1966.

Gilmore, Leigh. 'The Gaze of the Other Woman: Beholding and Begetting in Dickinson, Moore, and Rich', in Temma F. Berg *et al.*, *Engendering the Word: Feminist Essays in Psychosexual Poetics*, Urbana: University of Chicago Press, 1989.

Gilroy, Paul. *The Black Atlantic: Modernity and Double Consciousness*, Harvard University Press, 1993.

Goldman, Emma. *Living My Life*, 2 vols, New York: Dover, 1970.

Gollin, Gillian Lindt. *Moravians in Two Worlds: a Study of Changing Community*, New York: Columbia University Press, 1967.

Grahn, Judy. *Really Reading Gertrude Stein: a Selected Anthology with Essays*, Freedom, CA: Crossing Press, 1989.

Gregory, Eileen. 'Rose Cut in Rock: Sappho and H.D.'s *Sea Garden*', *Contemporary Literature* 27 (Winter 1986), 525–52.

Gregory, Elizabeth. '"Silence" and Restraint', in Patricia C. Willis (ed.), *Marianne Moore: Woman and Poet*, Orono, ME: National Poetry Foundation, 1990, 169–83.

Grewal, Inderpal. *Home and Harem: Nation, Gender, Empire, and the Cultures of Travel*, Durham: Duke U. Press, 1996.

Gubar, Susan. 'Blessings in Disguise: Cross-Dressing as Re-Dressing for Female Modernists', *Massachusetts Review* 22 (Autumn 1981), 477–508.

——. 'The Echoing Spell of H.D.'s *Trilogy*', in Sandra M. Gilbert and Susan Gubar (eds), *Shakespeare's Sisters: Feminist Essays on Women Poets*, Bloomington: Indiana University Press, 1979.

Guggenheim, Peggy. *Out of This Century*, New York: Dial, 1946.

H.D. *Borderline–a Pool Film with Paul Robeson* (1930). Reprinted in *Sagetrieb* 7 (Fall 1987), 29–50.

——. *Collected Poems 1912–1944*, ed. by Louis L. Martz, New York: New Directions, 1983.

——. *End to Torment: a Memoir of Ezra Pound*, eds. Norman Holmes Pearson and Michael King, New York: New Directions, 1979.

——. *The Gift: the Complete Text*, ed. Jane Augustine, Gainesville: University of Florida Press, 1998.

——. *HERmione*, New York: New Directions, 1981.

——. *Notes on Thought and Vision*, San Francisco: City Lights Books, 1968.

——. *Tribute to Freud*, New York: New Directions, 1974.

Habermas, Jürgen. 'The Public Sphere', trans. Sara Lennox and Frank Lennox, *New German Critique* 1 Fall (1974), 49–55.

——. *The Structural Transformation of the Public Sphere: an Inquiry into a Category of Bourgeois Society*, trans. Thomas Burger, with Frederick Lawrence, Cambridge: MIT Press, 1989.

Hadas, Pamela White. *Marianne Moore: Poet of Affection*, Syracuse: Syracuse University Press, 1977.

Hadas, Pamela. 'Spreading the Difference: One Way to Read Gertrude Stein's *Tender Buttons*', *Twentieth Century Literature* 23 (Spring 1978), 57–75.

Haraway, Donna. *Simians, Cyborgs, and Women: the Reinvention of Nature*, New York: Routledge, 1991.

Harding, Sandra. 'Conclusion: Epistemological Questions', in Sandra Harding (ed.), *Feminism and Methodology: Social Science Issues*, Bloomington: University of Indiana Press, 1987.

Harman, Claire. *Sylvia Townsend Warner: a Biography*, London: Chatto & Windus, 1989.

Harper, Philip Brian. *Framing the Margins: the Social Logic of Postmodern Culture*, New York: Oxford U. Press, 1994.

——. 'Private Affairs: Race, Sex, Property, and Persons', *GLQ* 1.2 (1994), 111–33.

Harrison, Victoria. *Elizabeth Bishop's Poetics of Intimacy*, New York: Cambridge University Press, 1993.

Hartsock, Nancy C.M. 'The Feminist Standpoint: Developing the Ground for a Specifically Feminist Historical Materialism', in Sandra Harding (ed.), *Feminism and Methodology: Social Science Issues*, Bloomington: University of Indiana Press, 1987.

Harvey, David. *The Condition of Postmodernity: an Enquiry into the Origins of Cultural Change*, Cambridge, MA: Blackwell, 1990.

Hayden, Dolores. *The Grand Domestic Revolution: a History of Feminist Designs for American Homes, Neighborhoods, and Cities*, Cambridge, MA: MIT Press, 1982.

Heidegger, Martin. 'Building Dwelling Thinking', trans. Alfred Hofstadter, in David Farrell Krell (ed.), *Martin Heidegger, Basic Writings*, New York: Harper & Row, 1977.

Hekman, Susan. 'Truth and Method: Feminist Standpoint Theory Revisited', *Signs* 22.2 (Winter 1997), 341–65.

Henneberg, Sylvia. 'Neither Lesbian nor Straight: Multiple Eroticisms in Emily Dickinson's Love Poetry', *The Emily Dickinson Journal* 4.2 (1995), 1–19.

Herrmann, Anne. *The Dialogic and Difference: 'An/Other Woman' in Virginia Woolf and Christa Wolf*, New York: Columbia University Press, 1989.

Heuving, Jeanne. *Omissions Are Not Accidents: Gender in the Art of Marianne Moore*, Detroit: Wayne State U. Press, 1992.

Higonnet, Margaret R. 'New Cartographies, an Introduction', in Margaret R. Higonnet and Joan Templeton (eds), *Reconfigured Spheres: Feminist Explorations of Literary Space*, Amherst: University of Massachusetts Press, 1994.

Hoffman, Michael J. *The Development of Abstractionism in the Writings of Gertrude Stein*, Philadelphia: University of Pennsylvania Press, 1965.

Hollenberg, Donna Krolik. *H.D.: the Poetics of Childbirth and Creativity*, Boston: Northeastern U. Press, 1991.

Holley, Margaret. *The Poetry of Marianne Moore: a Study in Voice and Value*, Cambridge: Cambridge University Press, 1987.

Homans, Margaret. *Bearing the Word: Language and Female Experience in Nineteenth-Century Women's Writing*, Chicago: University of Chicago Press, 1986.

——. *Women Writers and Poetic Identity: Dorothy Wordsworth, Emily Bronte, and Emily Dickinson*, Princeton: Princeton University Press, 1980.

Honig, Bonnie. 'Difference, Dilemmas, and the Politics of Home', In Seyla Benhabib (ed.), *Democracy and Difference: Contesting the Boundaries of the Political*, Princeton: Princeton U. Press, 1996.

Honigsblum, Bonnie. 'Marianne Moore's Revisions of "Poetry"', in Patricia C. Willis (ed.), *Marianne Moore: Woman and Poet*, Orono, ME: National Poetry Foundation, 1990, 185–202.

Hopkinson, Lyndall Passerini. *Nothing to Forgive: a Daughter's Story of Antonia White*, London: Chatto & Windus, 1988.

Hotelling, Kirstin. '"The I of each is to the I of each, a kind of fretful speech which sets a limit on itself": Marianne Moore's Strategic Selfhood', *Modernism/Modernity* 5.1 (January 1998), 75–96.

Hovey, Jaime. 'Sapphic Primitivism in Gertrude Stein's *Q.E.D.*', *Modern Fiction Studies* 42.3 (Fall 1996), 547–68.

Howe, Susan. *My Emily Dickinson*, Berkeley: North Atlantic Books, 1985.

Hull, Gloria T. 'Living on the Line: Audre Lorde and *Our Dead Behind Us*', in Cheryl Wall (ed.), *Changing Our Own Words: Essays on Criticism, Theory, and Writing by Black Women*, New Brunswick: Rutgers University Press, 1989.

Hurston, Zora Neale. *Mules and Men: Negro Folktales and Voodoo Practices in the South*, New York: Perennial Library, 1970.

——. *Their Eyes Were Watching God*, New York: Perennial Library, 1990.

Husserl, Edmund. *Ideas: General Introduction to Pure Phenomenology*, trans. W.R. Royce Gibson, New York: Collier, 1962.

Hussey, Mark. *The Singing of the Real World: the Philosophy of Virginia Woolf's Fiction*, Columbus: Ohio State University Press, 1986.

Irigaray, Luce. *This Sex Which Is Not One*, trans. Catherine Porter, Ithaca: Cornell University Press, 1985.

Isenberg, Nancy. *Sex and Citizenship in Antebellum America*, Chapel Hill: University of North Carolina Press, 1998.

Jackson, Laura (Riding). *The Word Woman and Other Related Writings*, eds Elizabeth Friedmann and Alan J. Clark, New York: Persea Books, 1993.

Jaggar, Alison. *Feminist Politics and Human Nature*, Totowa, NJ: Rowman & Allanheld, 1983.

Jakobson, Roman. 'What Is Poetry', in Ladislav Matejka and Irwin R. Titunik, *Semiotics of Art: Prague School Contributions* (eds), Cambridge, MA: MIT Press, 1984.

James, William. *The Principles of Psychology*, Vol. 1, New York: Dover, 1950.

Jameson, Fredric. '*History and Class Consciousness* as an "Unfinished Project"', *Rethinking Marxism* 1 (Spring 1988), 49–72.

——. *Postmodernism, or, The Cultural Logic of Late Capitalism*, Durham: Duke U. Press, 1991.

Jan Mohamed, Abdul R. 'The Economy of Manichean Allegory: the Function of Racial Difference in Colonialist Literature', in Henry Louis Gates, Jr.,*'Race', Writing, and Difference*, Chicago: University of Chicago Press, 1986.

Jehlen, Myra. 'Archimedes and the Paradox of Feminist Criticism', in Nannerl O. Keohane, Michelle Z. Rosaldo and Barbara C. Gelpi (eds), *Feminist Theory: a Critique of Ideology*, Chicago: University of Chicago Press, 1982.

Johnson, Barbara. *A World of Difference*, Baltimore: Johns Hopkins U. Press, 1987.

Jones, Kathleen B. 'On Authority: Or, Why Women Are Not Entitled to Speak', in Irene Diamond and Lee Quinby (eds), *Feminism and Foucault: Reflections on Resistance*, Boston: Northwestern U. Press, 1988.

Juhasz, Suzanne. *The Undiscovered Continent: Emily Dickinson and the Space of the Mind*, Bloomington: Indiana University Press, 1983.

Kaivola, Karen. *All Contraries Confounded: the Lyrical Fiction of Virginia Woolf, Djuna Barnes and Marguerite Duras*, Iowa City: U. of Iowa Press, 1991.

Kamuf, Peggy. 'Replacing Feminist Criticism', *Diacritics* 12 (Summer 1982), 42–7.

Kaplan, Caren. *Questions of Travel: Postmodern Discourses of Displacement*, Durham: Duke U. Press, 1996.

Kaplan, Carla. *The Erotics of Talk: Women's Writing and Feminist Paradigms*, New York: Oxford University Press, 1996.

Keith, Michael and Steve Pile (eds). *Place and the Politics of Identity*, New York: Routledge, 1993.

Keller, Karl. *The Only Kangaroo among the Beauty: Emily Dickinson and America*, Baltimore: Johns Hopkins University Press, 1979.

Kelley, Mary. *Private Woman, Public Stage: Literary Domesticity in Nineteenth-Century America*, New York: Oxford University Press, 1984.

Kenner, Hugh. *A Homemade World: the American Modernist Writers*, New York: Knopf, 1975.

——. *The Pound Era*, Berkeley: University of California Press, 1971.

Kern, Stephen. *The Culture of Time and Space, 1880–1918*, Cambridge, MA: Harvard University Press, 1983.

Kirby, Kathleen M. *Indifferent Boundaries: Spatial Concepts of Human Subjectivity*, New York: Guilford, 1996.

Kristeva, Julia. 'The Ethics of Linguistics', in Julia Kristeva, *Desire in Language: a Semiotic Approach to Literature and Art*, trans. Thomas Gora, Alice Jardine and Leon S. Roudiez, New York: Columbia University Press, 1980.

——. *Revolution in Poetic Language*, trans. Margaret Waller, New York: Columbia University Press, 1984.

——. *La révolution du langage poétique*, Paris: Edition du Seuil, 1974.

Lacan, Jacques. *Ecrits: a Selection*, trans. by Alan Sheridan, New York: Norton, 1977.

LaCapra, Dominick. *Rethinking Intellectual History: Texts, Contexts, Language*, Ithaca: Cornell University Press, 1983.

Laity, Cassandra. 'H.D., Modernism, and the Transgressive Sexualities of Decadent-Romantic Platonism', in Margaret Dickie and Thomas Travisano (eds), *Gendered Modernisms: American Women Poets and Their Readers*, Philadelphia: University of Pennsylvania Press, 1996. 45–68.

Leder, Sharon with Andrea Abbott. *The Language of Exclusion: the Poetry of Emily Dickinson and Christina Rossetti*, New York: Greenwood Press, 1987.

Lefebvre, Henri. *The Production of Space*, trans. Donald Nicholson-Smith, Cambridge, MA: Blackwell, 1991.

Lerner, Gerda. *The Majority Finds Its Past: Placing Women in History*, New York: Oxford University Press, 1979.

Levin, Harry. *Refractions: Essays in Comparative Literature*, New York: Oxford University Press, 1966.

Leverenz, David. *Manhood and the American Renaissance*, Ithaca: Cornell University Press, 1989.

Leyshon, Andrew and Nigel Thrift. *Money/Space: Geographies of Monetary Transformation*, New York: Routledge, 1997.

Lipking, Joanna. 'Looking at the Monuments: Woolf's Satiric Eye', *Bulletin of the New York Public Library* 80 (Winter 1977): 141–5.

Loeffelholz, Mary. *Dickinson and the Boundaries of Feminist Theory*, Urbana: U. of Illinois Press, 1991.

Lorde, Audre. *The Black Unicorn*, New York: Norton, 1978.

Lott, Eric. *Love and Theft: Blackface Minstrelsy and the American Working Class*, New York: Oxford U. Press, 1995.

Lukacs, Georg. *The Historical Novel*, trans. Hannah and Stanley Mitchell, Lincoln: University of Nebraska Press, 1983.

——. *History and Class Consciousness: Essays in Marxist Dialectics*, trans. by Rodney Livingstone, Cambridge, MA: MIT Press, 1971.

——. *The Theory of the Novel: a Historico-Philosophical Essay on the Forms of Great Epic Literature*, trans. Anna Bostock, Cambridge, MA: MIT Press, 1971.

Lyotard, Jean-François. *The Postmodern Condition: a Report on Knowledge*, trans. Geoff Bennington and Brian Massumi, Minneapolis: University of Minnesota Press, 1984.

MacKinnon, Catherine A. 'Feminism, Marxism, Method, and the State: an Agenda for Theory', in Nannerl O. Keohane, Michelle Z. Rosaldo and Barbara C. Gelpi (eds), *Feminist Theory: a Critique of Ideology*, Chicago: University of Chicago Press, 1982.

MacPherson, C.B. *The Political Theory of Possessive Individualism: Hobbes to Locke*, New York: Oxford University Press, 1962.

Mani, Lata. 'Multiple Mediations: Feminist Scholarship in the Age of Multinational Reception', *Inscriptions* 5 (1989): 1–24.

Marcus, Jane. 'Alibis and Legends: the Ethics of Elsewhereness, Gender and Estrangement', in Mary Lynn Broe and Angela Ingram (eds), *Women's Writing in Exile*, Chapel Hill: University of North Carolina Press, 1989.

——. 'Of Madness and Method', *The Women's Review of Books* 3 (August 1986): 1, 2–3.

——. 'Still Practice, A/Wrested Alphabet: toward a Feminist Aesthetic', *Tulsa Studies in Women's Literature* 3 (Spring/Fall 1984): 79–97.

——. 'Thinking Back through Our Mothers', in Jane Marcus (ed.), *New Feminist Essays on Virginia Woolf*, Lincoln: University of Nebraska Press, 1981.

——. *Virginia Woolf and the Languages of Patriarchy*, Bloomington: Indiana University Press, 1987.

——. 'A Wilderness of One's Own: Feminist Fantasy Novels of the Twenties: Rebecca West and Sylvia Townsend Warner', in Susan Merrill Squier (ed.), *Women Writers and the City: Essays in Feminist Literary Criticism*, Knoxville: University of Tennessee Press, 1984.

Martin, Biddy and Chandra Talpade Mohanty. 'Feminist Politics: What's Home Got to Do with It?', in Teresa de Lauretis (ed.), *Feminist Studies/Critical Studies*, Bloomington: Indiana University Press, 1986.

Martin, Taffy. *Marianne Moore, Subversive Modernist*, Austin: University of Texas Press, 1986.

Martin, Wendy. *An American Triptych: Anne Bradstreet, Emily Dickinson, and Adrienne Rich*, Chapel Hill: University of North Carolina Press, 1984.

Marx, Karl. *Capital*, Vol. 1, trans. Ben Fowkes, New York: Vintage, 1977.

——. *The 18th Brumaire of Louis Napoleon*, New York: International Publishers, 1963.

Massey, Doreen. *Space, Place, and Gender*, Minneapolis: University of Minnesota Press, 1994.

Massumi, Brian. *A User's Guide to Capitalism and Schizophrenia: Deviations from Deleuze and Guattari*, Cambridge, MA: MIT Press, 1992.

Matthews, Glenna. *'Just a Housewife': the Rise and Fall of Domesticity in America*, New York: Oxford University Press, 1987.

Matthiessen, F.O. 'The Private Poet: Emily Dickinson', in Caesar R. Blake and Carlton F. Wells (eds), *The Recognition of Emily Dickinson: Selected Criticism since 1890*, Ann Arbor: University of Michigan Press, 1965.

McCarthy, Mary. 'Paris, 1848', *The Nation* 143 (14 August 1936): 191–2.

Deborah McDowell. *'The Changing Same': Black Women's Literature, Criticism, and Theory*, Bloomington: Indiana U. Press, 1995.

McDowell, Linda. 'Spatializing Feminism: Geographic Perspectives', in Nancy Duncan (ed.), *Bodyspace: Destabilizing Geographies of Gender and Sexuality*, New York: Routledge, 1996.

McNeil, Helen. *Emily Dickinson*, New York: Virago/Pantheon, 1986.

Meyrowitz, Joshua. *No Sense of Place: the Impact of Electronic Media on Social Behavior*, New York: Oxford U. Press, 1985.

Michaels, Walter Benn. *The Gold Standard and the Logic of Naturalism: American Literature at the Turn of the Century*, Berkeley: University of California Press, 1987.

Miller, Cristanne. *Emily Dickinson: a Poet's Grammar*, Cambridge, MA: Harvard University Press, 1987.

——. *Marianne Moore: Questions of Authority*, Cambridge, MA: Harvard U. Press, 1995.

——. 'Marianne Moore's Black Maternal Hero: a Study in Categorization', *American Literary History* 1 (Winter 1989): 786–815.

Miller, D.A. *The Novel and the Police*, Berkeley: University of California Press, 1988.

Miller, Nancy K. 'The Text's Heroine: a Feminist Critic and Her Fictions', *Diacritics* 12 (Summer 1982): 48–53.

Mohanty, Chandra Talpade. 'Feminist Encounters: Locating the Politics of Experience', *Copyright* 1 (Fall 1987): 30–44.

Monroe, Jonathan. *A Poverty of Objects: the Prose Poem and the Politics of Genre*, Ithaca: Cornell University Press, 1987.

Montefiore, Jan. *Feminism and Poetry: Language, Experience, Identity in Women's Writing*, New York: Pandora, 1987.

Moore, Marianne. *Collected Poems*, New York: Macmillan, 1951.

——. *The Complete Poems of Marianne Moore*, New York: Penguin, 1982.

——. *The Complete Prose of Marianne Moore*, New York: Viking, 1986.

——. 'Radical', *Others* 5 (March 1919): 15.

——. *Selected Poems*, ed. and intro. by T.S. Eliot, New York: Macmillan, 1935.

Morris, Adelaide. 'The Concept of Projection: H.D.'s Visionary Powers', *Contemporary Literature* 25.4 (Winter 1984): 411–36.

——. '"The Love of Thee–a Prism Be": Men and Women in the Love Poetry of Emily Dickinson', in Suzanne Juhasz (ed.), *Feminist Critics Read Emily Dickinson*, Bloomington: Indiana University Press, 1983.

——. 'A Relay of Power and of Peace: H.D. and the Spirit of the Gift', *Contemporary Literature* 27 (Winter 1986): 493–524.

Mossberg, Barbara Antonina Clarke. *Emily Dickinson: when a Writer Is a Daughter*, Bloomington: Indiana University Press, 1982.

Mudge, Jean. *Emily Dickinson and the Image of Home*, Amherst: University of Massachusetts Press, 1975.

Mulford, Wendy. *This Narrow Place. Sylvia Townsend Warner and Valentine Ackland: Life, Letters, and Politics 1930–1950*, London, Pandora, 1988.

Murphy, Margueritte. '"Familiar Strangers": the Household Words of Gertrude Stein's *Tender Buttons*', *Contemporary Literature* 32.3 (Fall 1991): 383–402.

Naremore, James. 'Nature and History in *The Years*', in Ralph Freedman (ed.), *Virginia Woolf: Revaluation and Continuity*, Berkeley: U. of California Press, 1980.

——. *The World without a Self: Virginia Woolf and the Novel*, New Haven: Yale U. Press, 1973.

Newton, Judith. *Women, Power, and Subversion: Social Strategies in British Fiction, 1778–1860*, Athens: University of Georgia Press, 1981.

Nicholson, Linda. 'Feminism and Marx: Integrating Kinship with the Economic', in Seyla Benhabib and Drucilla Cornell (eds), *Feminism as Critique: on the Politics of Gender*, Minneapolis: U. of Minnesota Press, 1987, 16–30.

Nielsen, Aldon L. *Reading Race: White American Poets and the Racial Discourse in the Twentieth-Century*, Athens: University of Georgia Press, 1988.

North, Michael. *The Dialect of Modernism: Race, Language, and Twentieth-Century Literature*, New York: Oxford U. Press, 1994.

Ostriker, Alicia. *Stealing the Language: the Emergence of Women's Poetry in America*, Boston: Beacon Press, 1986.

——. 'What Do Women (Poets) Want: H.D. and Marianne Moore as Poetic Ancestresses', *Contemporary Literature* 27 (Winter 1986): 475–92.

Pecora, Vincent P. *Self and Form in Modern Narrative*, Baltimore: Johns Hopkins University Press, 1989.

Perloff, Marjorie. *The Poetics of Indeterminacy: Rimbaud to Cage*, Princeton: Princeton University Press, 1981.

——. 'Postmodernism and the Impasse of Lyric', *Formations* 1 (Fall 1984): 43–63.

Peterson, Jeffrey D. 'Notes on the Poem(s) "Poetry": the Ingenuity of Moore's Poetic "Place"', in Patricia C. Willis (ed.), *Marianne Moore: Woman and Poet*, Orono, ME: National Poetry Foundation, 1990, 223–41.

Phelan, Peggy. 'Weapons and Scalpels: the Early Poetry of H.D. and Marianne Moore', in Patricia C. Willis (ed.), *Marianne Moore: Woman and Poet*, Orono, ME: National Poetry Foundation, 1990, 403–18.

Philo, Chris. 'Foucault's Geography', in Mike Crang and Nigel Thrift (eds), *Thinking Space*, New York: Routledge, 2000, 205–38.

Phillips, Elizabeth. *Emily Dickinson: Personae and Performance*, University Park: Pennsylvania State University, 1988.

Pollak, Vivian. *Dickinson: the Anxiety of Gender*, Ithaca: Cornell University Press, 1984.

Pondrom, Cyrena N. 'H.D. and the Origins of Imagism', *Sagetrieb* 4 (Spring 1985): 73–97.

——. 'Marianne Moore and H.D.: Female Community and Poetic Achievement', in Patricia C. Willis (ed.), *Marianne Moore: Woman and Poet*, Orono, ME: National Poetry Foundation, 1990 371–402.

Poovey, Mary. *Uneven Developments: the Ideological Work of Gender in Mid-Victorian England*, Chicago: University of Chicago Press, 1988.

Pound, Ezra. *Literary Essays of Ezra Pound*, ed. T.S. Eliot, New York: New Directions, 1968.

——. *Personae: Collected Shorter Poems*, New York: New Directions, 1971.

——. *Selected Letters of Ezra Pound, 1907–1941*, ed. D.D. Paige, New York: New Directions, 1971.

Quinones, Ricardo J. *Mapping Literary Modernism: Time and Development*, Princeton: Princeton University Press, 1985.

Radin, Grace. *Virginia Woolf's The Years: the Evolution of a Novel*, Knoxville: University of Tennessee Press, 1981.

Reagon, Bernice Johnson. 'Coalition Politics: Turning the Century', in Barbara Smith (ed.), *Home Girls: a Black Feminist Anthology*, New York: Kitchen Table: Women of Color Press, 1983, 356–68.

Rich, Adrienne. *Blood, Bread, and Poetry: Selected Prose 1979–1985*, New York: Norton, 1986.

——. 'Vesuvius at Home: the Power of Emily Dickinson', in Adrienne Rich, *On Lies, Secrets, and Silence: Selected Prose 1966–1978*, New York: Norton, 1979.

Riddel, Joseph N. 'H.D. and the Poetics of "Spiritual Realism"', *Contemporary Literature* 10 (1969): 447–73.

Rigney, Barbara Hill. *Madness and Sexual Politics in the Feminist Novel: Studies in Bronte, Woolf, Lessing, and Atwood*, Madison: University of Wisconsin Press, 1978.

Robinson, Marilynne. *Housekeeping*, New York: Farrar, Straus & Giroux, 1980.

Rogin, Michael. *Blackface, White Noise: Jewish Immigrants in the Hollywood Melting Pot*, Berkeley: University of California Press, 1996.

Romero, Lora. *Home Fronts: Domesticity and Its Critics in the Antebellum United States*, Durham: Duke University Press, 1997.

Rommetveit, Ragnar. *On Message Structure: a Framework for the Study of Language and Communication*, New York: John Wiley & Sons, 1974.

Ronell, Avital. *The Telephone Book: Technology, Schizophrenia, Electric Speech*, Lincoln: Nebraska U. Press, 1989.

Roof, Judith. 'Lesbians and Lyotard: Legitimation and the Politics of the Name', in Laura Doan (ed.), *The Lesbian Postmodern*, New York: Columbia U. Press, 1994.

Rose, Gillian. 'As If Mirrors Had Bled: Masculine Dwelling, Masculine Theory, and Feminist Masquerade', in Nancy Duncan (ed.), *Bodyspace: Destabilizing Geographies of Gender and Sexuality*, New York: Routledge, 1996, 56–74.

——. *Feminism and Geography: the Limits of Geographical Knowledge*, Minneapolis: U. of Minnesota Press, 1993.

Rose, Phyllis. *Woman of Letters: a Life of Virginia Woolf*, New York: Oxford University Press, 1978.

Ross, Andrew. *The Failure of Modernism: Symptoms of American Poetry*, New York: Columbia University Press, 1986.

Rowbotham, Sheila, Lynne Segal and Hilary Wainwright. *Beyond the Fragments: Feminism and the Making of Socialism*, Boston: Alyson Publications, 1981.

Rowbotham, Sheila. *Woman's Consciousness, Man's World*, Harmondsworth: Penguin, 1973.

Ruddick, Lisa. *Reading Gertrude Stein: Body, Text, Gnosis*, Ithaca: Cornell U. Press, 1990.

——. 'A Rosy Charm: Gertrude Stein and the Repressed Feminine', in Michael J. Hoffman (ed.), *Critical Essays on Gertrude Stein*, Boston: G.K. Hall, 1986.

——. 'William James and the Modernism of Gertrude Stein', in Robert Kiely (ed.), *Modernism Reconsidered*, Cambridge, MA: Harvard University Press, 1983.

Ruotolo, Lucio P. *The Interrupted Moment: a View of Virginia Woolf's Novels*, Stanford: Stanford University Press, 1986.

Ryan, Mary P. *Womanhood in America: from Colonial Times to the Present*, 3rd ed., New York: Franklin Watts, 1983.

Said, Edward W. *Beginnings: Intention and Method*, Baltimore: Johns Hopkins University Press, 1974.

——. *The World, the Text, and the Critic*, Cambridge, MA: Harvard University Press, 1983.

Saldivar-Hull, Sonia. 'Wrestling Your Ally: Stein, Racism, and Feminist Critical Practice', in Mary Lynn Broe and Angela Ingram (eds), *Women's Writing in Exile*, Chapel Hill: University of North Carolina Press, 1989.

Sanchez-Eppler, Karen. 'Raising Empires Like Children: Race, Nation, and Religious Education', *American Literary History* 8.3 (Fall 1996): 399–425.

——. *Touching Liberty: Abolition, Feminism, and the Politics of the Body*, Berkeley: University of California Press, 1993.

Schmitz, Neil. 'Gertrude Stein as Post-Modernist: the Rhetoric of *Tender Buttons*', *Journal of Modern Literature* 3 (July 1975): 1203–18.

——. *Of Huck and Alice: Humorous Writing in American Literature*, Minneapolis: University of Minnesota Press, 1983.

Scobie, Stephen. 'The Allure of Multiplicity: Metaphor and Metonymy in Cubism and Gertrude Stein', in Shirley Neuman and Ira B. Nadel (eds), *Gertrude Stein and the Making of Literature*, Boston: Northeastern University Press, 1988.

Scott, Bonnie Kime. *Refiguring Modernism*, Vol. 1: *The Women of 1928*, Bloomington: Indiana U. Press, 1995.

Scott, Bonnie Kime (ed.), *The Gender of Modernism: a Critical Anthology*, Bloomington: Indiana U. Press, 1990.

Scott, Patricia Hill. *The World Their Household: the American Woman's Foreign Mission Movement and Cultural Transformation, 1870–1920*, Ann Arbor: University of Michigan Press, 1985.

Sedgwick, Eve Kosofsky. *Between Men: English Literature and Male Homosocial Desire*, New York: Columbia University Press, 1985.

——. *Epistemology of the Closet*, Berkeley: University of California Press, 1990.

Sewall, Richard B. (ed.), *The Lyman Letters: New Light on Emily Dickinson and Her Family*, Amherst: U. of Massachusetts Press, 1965.

Short, Bryan C. 'Stowe, Dickinson, and the Rhetoric of Modernism', Arizona Quarterly 47.1 (Autumn 1991): 1–16.

Sibley, David. *Geographies of Exclusion: Society and Difference in the West*, New York: Routledge, 1995.

Simmel, Georg. *On Individuality and Social Forms: Selected Writings*, ed. Donald N. Levine, Chicago: University of Chicago Press, 1971.

Sklar, Kathryn Kish. *Catherine Beecher: a Study in American Domesticity*, New Haven: Yale University Press, 1973.

Slatin, John M. *The Savage's Romance: the Poetry of Marianne Moore*, University Park, PA: Pennsylvania State University Press, 1986.

Smedman, Lorna J. '"Cousin to Cooning": Relation, Difference, and Racialized Language in Stein's Nonrepresentational Texts', *Modern Fiction Studies* 42.3 (Fall 1996): 569–88.

Smith, Dorothy E. 'Women, the Family, and Corporate Capitalism', in Marylee Stephenson (ed.), *Women in Canada*, Toronto: New Press, 1973.

Smith, Martha Nell. *Rowing in Eden: Rereading Emily Dickinson*, Austin: U. of Texas Press, 1992.

Smith, Neil and Cindi Katz. 'Grounding Metaphor: towards a Spatialized Politics', in Michael Keith and Steve Pile (eds), *Place and the Politics of Identity*, New York: Routledge, 1993, 67–83.

Smith, Paul. *Discerning the Subject*, Minneapolis: University of Minnesota Press, 1988.

——. 'H.D.'s Flaws', *Iowa Review* 16 (Fall 1986): 77–86.

——. 'H.D.'s Identity', *Women's Studies* 10 (1984): 321–37.

——. *Pound Revised*. London: Croom Helm, 1983.

Smith, Valerie. '"Loopholes of Retreat": Architecture and Ideology in Harriet Jacobs's *Incidents in the Life of a Slave Girl*', in Henry Louis Gates, Jr (ed.), *Reading Black, Reading Feminist: a Critical Anthology*, New York: Meridian, 1990, 212–26.

Soja, Edward. *Postmodern Geographies: the Reassertion of Space in Critical Social Theory*, New York: Verso, 1989.

Spivak, Gayatri Chakravorty. 'Can the Subaltern Speak?', in Cary Nelson and Lawrence Grossberg (eds), *Marxism and the Interpretation of Culture*, Urbana: University of Illinois Press, 1988.

——. 'Displacement and the Discourse of Woman', in Mark Krupnick (ed.), *Displacement: Derrida and After*, Bloomington: Indiana University Press, 1983.

——. 'Feminism and Deconstruction, Again: Negotiating with Unacknowledged Masculinism', in Teresa Brennan (ed.), *Between Feminism and Psychoanalysis*, New York: Routledge, 1989.

——. 'Imperialism and Sexual Difference', *Oxford Literary Review* 8 (1986): 225–40.

——. 'The New Historicism: Political Commitment and the Postmodern Critic', in H. Aram Veeser (ed.), *The New Historicism*, New York: Routledge, 1989.

——. 'Three Women's Texts and a Critique of Imperialism', *Critical Inquiry* 12 (Autumn 1985): 243–61.

Squier, Susan M. 'A Track of Our Own: Typescript Drafts of *The Years*', in Jane Marcus (ed.), *Virginia Woolf: a Feminist Slant*, Lincoln: Nebraska University Press, 1981.

——. *Virginia Woolf and London: the Sexual Politics of the City*, Chapel Hill: University of North Carolina Press, 1985.

Stead, Christina. *House of All Nations*, New York: Simon and Schuster, 1938.

Stein, Gertrude. *Bee Time Vine and Other Pieces (1913–1927)*, Yale Edition of the Unpublished Writings of Gertrude Stein, Vol. 3, New Haven: Yale University Press, 1953.

——. *How to Write*, New York: Dover, 1975.

——. *Lectures in America*, Boston: Beacon Press, 1957.

——. 'Lifting Belly', in Richard Kostelanetz (ed.), *The Yale Gertrude Stein*, New Haven: Yale University Press, 1980.

——. *Narration: Four Lectures*, Chicago: University of Chicago Press, 1935.

——. *A Primer for the Gradual Understanding of Gertrude Stein*, ed. Robert Bartlett Haas, Los Angeles: Black Sparrow Press, 1974.

——. *Selected Writings of Gertrude Stein*, ed. Carl van Vechten, New York: Vintage, 1972.

——. *Two: Gertrude Stein and Her Brother and Other Early Portraits (1908–12)*, Yale Edition of the Unpublished Writings of Gertrude Stein, Vol. 1, New Haven: Yale University Press, 1951.

——. *Wars I Have Seen*, New York: Random House, 1945.

Steiner, George. *Extra-Territorial: Papers on Literature and the Language Revolution*, New York: Atheneum Press, 1971.

Stevens, Wallace. *The Collected Poems of Wallace Stevens*, New York: Alfred A. Knopf, 1981.

Stimpson, Catherine R. 'Gertrice/Altrude: Stein, Toklas, and the Paradox of the Happy Marriage', in Ruth Perry and Marine Watson Brownley (eds), *Mothering the Mind: Twelve Studies of Writers and Their Silent Partners*, New York: Holmes & Meier, 1984.

——. 'Gertrude Stein and the Transposition of Gender', in Nancy K. Miller (ed.), *The Poetics of Gender*, New York: Columbia University Press, 1986.

——. 'The Mind, the Body, and Gertrude Stein', *Critical Inquiry* 3 (Spring 1977): 489–506.

——. 'The Somagrams of Gertrude Stein', in Susan Rubin Suleiman (ed.), *The Female Body in Western Culture: Contemporary Perspectives*, Cambridge, MA: Harvard University Press, 1986.

——. 'Zero Degree Deviancy: the Lesbian Novel in English', in Elizabeth Abel (ed.), *Writing and Sexual Difference*, Chicago: University of Chicago Press, 1982.

Stone, Allucquere Rosanne. *The War of Desire and Technology at the Close of the Mechanical Age*, Cambridge, MA: MIT Press, 1995.

Tate, Claudia. *Domestic Allegories of Political Desire: the Black Heroine's Text at the Turn of the Century*, New York: Oxford University Press, 1992.

Tillyard, E.M.W. 'The Nature of the Epic', in Anthony C. Yu (ed.), *Parnassus Revisited: Modern Critical Essays on the Epic Tradition*, Chicago: American Library Association, 1973.

Tomlinson, Charles (ed.), *Marianne Moore: a Collection of Critical Essays*, Englewood Cliffs, NJ: Prentice-Hall, 1969.

Tompkins, Jane. *Sensational Designs: the Cultural Work of American Fiction, 1790–1860*, New York: Oxford University Press, 1985.

Transue, Pamela J. *Virginia Woolf and the Politics of Style*, Albany: State University of New York Press, 1986.

Vicinus, Martha. *Independent Women: Work and Community for Single Women, 1850–1920*, Chicago: U. of Chicago Press, 1985.

Vidler, Anthony. *The Architectural Uncanny: Essays in the Modern Unhomely*, Cambridge: MIT Press, 1992.

Walker, Jayne L. *The Making of a Modernist: Gertrude Stein from Three Lives to Tender Buttons*, Amherst: University of Massachusetts Press, 1984.

Walker, Nancy. '"Wider Than the Sky": Public Presence and Private Self in Dickinson, James, and Woolf', in Shari Benstock (ed.), *The Private Self: Theory*

and Practice of Women's Autobiographical Writings, Chapel Hill: University of North Carolina Press, 1988.
Wall, Cheryl A. *Women of the Harlem Renaissance*, Bloomington: Indiana U. Press, 1995.
Warner, Michael. *The Letters of the Republic: Publication and the Public Sphere in Eighteenth-Century America*, Cambridge, MA: Harvard University Press, 1990.
Warner, Sylvia Townsend. *Letters*, ed. William Maxwell, New York: Viking, 1982.
——. *Lolly Willowes; or, The Loving Huntsman*, New York: Viking, 1926.
——. *Summer Will Show*, London: Chatto & Windus, 1936; rpt. New York: Penguin, 1987.
——. 'Women as Writers', in Sylvia Townsend Warner, *Collected Poems*, ed. Claire Harman, New York: Viking, 1982.
Watson, Sophie and Katherine Gibson (eds), *Postmodern Cities and Spaces*, Cambridge: Blackwell, 1995.
Watt, Ian. *The Rise of the Novel: Studies in Defoe, Richardson and Fielding*, Berkeley: University of California Press, 1959.
Waugh, Patricia. *Feminine Fictions: Revisiting the Postmodern*, New York: Routledge, 1988.
Weinstein, Norman. *Gertrude Stein and the Literature of the Modern Consciousness*, New York: Frederick Ungar, 1970.
Wexler, Alice. *Emma Goldman in Exile: from the Russian Revolution to the Spanish Civil War*, Boston: Beacon, 1989.
Wexler, Laura. 'Tender Violence: Literary Eavesdropping, Domestic Fiction, and Educational Reform', in Shirley Samuels (ed.), *The Culture of Sentiment: Race, Gender, and Sentimentality in 19th Century America*, New York: Oxford University Press, 1992.
Wheare, Jane. *Virginia Woolf: Dramatic Novelist*, New York: St. Martin's Press, 1989.
Wiegman, Robyn. *American Anatomies: Theorizing Race and Gender*, Durham: Duke University Press, 1995.
Wigley, Mark. *The Architecture of Deconstruction: Derrida's Haunt*, Cambridge: MIT Press, 1993.
Wolff, Janet. 'The Invisible Flaneuse: Women and the Literature of Modernity', *Theory, Culture, Society* 2 (1985): 37–46.
Wolff, Cynthia Griffin. *Emily Dickinson*, New York: Alfred A. Knopf, 1986.
Wollstonecraft, Mary. *A Vindication of the Rights of Women*, ed. Carol H. Poston, New York: Norton, 1988.
Woolf, Virginia. 'Modern Fiction', in Mitchell A. Leaska (ed.), *The Virigina Woolf Reader*, New York: Harcourt Brace Jovanovich, 1977.
——. *The Pargiters: the Novel-Essay Portion of The Years*, ed. Mitchell A. Leaska, New York: Harcourt Brace Jovanovich, 1977.
——. *A Room of One's Own*, New York: Harcourt, Brace & World, 1957.
——. *Three Guineas*, New York: Harcourt, Brace & World, 1966.
——. *The Waves*, New York: Harcourt Brace Jovanovich, 1959.
——. *A Writer's Diary*, ed. Leonard Woolf, New York: Harcourt Brace Jovanovich, 1954.
——. *The Years*, New York: Harcourt, Brace & World, 1937; rpt. New York: Harcourt Brace Jovanovich, 1965.

Yoshimoto, Mitsuhiro. 'Real Virtuality', in *Global/Local: Cultural Production and the Transnational Imaginary*, eds. Rob Wilson and Wimal Dissanayake, Durham: Duke U. Press, 1996.

Young, Iris Marion. *Throwing Like a Girl and Other Essays in Feminist Philosophy and Social Theory*, Bloomington: Indiana University Press, 1990.

Zach, Natan. 'Imagism and Vorticism', in Malcolm Bradbury and James McFarlane (eds), *Modernism, 1890–1930*, New York: Penguin, 1976.

Zwerdling, Alex. *Virginia Woolf and the Real World*, Berkeley: University of California Press, 1986.

Index

Abraham, Julie, 117
Adorno, Theodor, 137
Althusser, Louis, 16
Armstrong, Nancy, 4, 5, 85–6, 89, 106
Austen, Jane, 119–20
Austin, J.L., 145

Baker, Houston, A., Jr., 146, 150
Bakhtin, Mikhail, 87
Barnes, Djuna, 90, 91
Baym, Nina, 7
Beauvoir, Simone de, 75
Beecher, Catherine, 17–19, 85, 89
Benveniste, Emile, 67, 107
Berman, Marshall, 14
Bernstein, J.M., 84, 116, 117, 128, 136
Berry, Ellen, 141
black women's writing, 11, 145–54
blackface minstrelsy, 54, 72, 176–7 n. 17
Bowlby, Rachel, 100, 101, 107, 110
Bradbury, Malcolm, 84, 116
Broe, Mary Lynn, 91
Brown, Gillian, 7, 8
Burke, Carolyn, 17, 75
Butler, Judith, 17, 144

Cameron, Sharon, 35, 41
Carby, Hazel, 13
Castle, Terry, 116, 118, 120, 122, 125–6
Chitty, Susan, 91
class
  and gender, 5, 43–4, 89–90, 94–5, 104–5, 134–5
  and sexuality, 89, 94, 116–18, 124–5, 128, 132–5
coalition politics, 9, 12, 25, 111, 112, 139
Coleman, Emily Holmes
  autobiographical basis of novel, 90
  and Emma Goldman, 90–1
  expatriatism, 90
  female body, 94
  female voice, 92–3, 97
  figure of the madwoman, 89–90
  and Hayford Hall, 91
  housework, 95–7
  'Poem', 90
  racial and class differences, 88–9, 94–5
  redefining home, 88–9
  Shutter of Snow, 87–97
Costello, Bonnie, 75
Cott, Nancy, 7, 9, 54, 139
counter-public sphere, 24
cross-class identification, 124
cross-racial identification, 53–5, 72–3, 144–5

Damon, Maria, 144
de Beauvoir, Simone, 75
deconstruction of domestic oppositions, 5, 8, 9, 12, 24, 32, 36, 48, 62, 74, 101, 103, 114, 117
DeKoven, Marianne, 142
de Lauretis, Teresa, 24, 129
Derrida, Jacques, 47
Dickinson, Emily
  'Alone and in a Circumstance' (*P* 1157), 40
  'At last, to be identified!' (*P* 174), 40–1
  'Dimple in the Tomb, A' (*P* 1489), 34–5, 42
  'Ditch is dear to the Drunken man, The' (*P* 1645), 42–4
  'Fashioning what she is' (*P* 1573), 35–6
  'Forever – is composed of Nows' (*P* 624), 37
  home, meanings of, 32–3
  'How many times these low feet staggered' (*P* 187), 38–40

'If I should die' (*P* 54), 39
'I heard a Fly buzz – when I died' (*P* 465), 41–2
'I Years had been from Home' (*P* 609), 44
'One need not be a Chamber – to be Haunted' (*P* 670), 49
as private poet, 27
'Races – nurtured in the Dark' (*P* 581), 53
letter to sister-in-law, 26–32
mother, 35–6
same-sex desire, 29–30
'Up Life's Hill with my little Bundle' (*P* 1010), 37–8
'What shall I do when the Summer troubles' (*P* 956), 44
'Who occupies this House' (*P* 892), 32
Dobson, Joanne, 32
domestic economy, 17–18, 21, 39
domesticity (*see also* ideology of separate spheres; *see also* home)
as alternative to the capitalist marketplace, 7
as cultural framework for modernist women, 6, 22
and democracy, 19
as extension of the marketplace, 8
as falsely universalised, 5, 11, 23
first wave of feminist criticism, 7
as generalized oppositional structure, 4–5, 7–9, 33, 43, 107
as internalized self-discipline, 8, 17–19, 43, 44, 88, 97, 146, 148
and the modern individual, 4, 8, 17–18
as performance, 131, 142, 152, 162–3 n. 51
post-colonial critiques of, 157 n. 11
as 'protection', 109, 153
second wave of feminist criticism, 8
self-critique, by white middle-class women, 11–13, 23, 43, 52–4, 136–40, 150, 153
third wave of feminist criticism, 156 n. 7
Doolittle, Hilda (*see* H.D.)
DuPlessis, Rachel Blau, 47, 61

Eliot, T.S., 71
Engels, Frederick, 120, 133–4
Erkkila, Betsy, 4
essentialism, 11, 21, 56, 60, 66–7, 69, 75, 82
expanding 'woman's sphere', 8–10, 20, 52, 57, 102, 104 (*see also* social housekeeping)
expatriatism, 5, 13, 45, 48

Felski, Rita, 24, 158 n. 17
femininity
and domesticity, 7, 17, 28, 31, 34, 37–9
as spatialized, 4, 30–1
flaneur, 100, 109
Flaubert, Gustave, 119
Fletcher, John, 84, 116
Foucault, Michel, 3, 6, 18, 20
Fox-Genovese, Elizabeth, 18, 33, 122
Friedman, Susan Stanford, 46, 48, 53
Fuss, Diana, 16

Gates, Henry Louis, Jr., 146–7
gender
as performative, 72
as space of indeterminacy, 6, 27, 56, 58, 67, 117
as spatially bounded, 4, 5
Genovese, Eugene, 18, 33, 122
Gilbert, Sandra, 71, 84, 89
Gilman, Charlotte Perkins, 21–2
Grahn, Judy, 141–2
Gubar, Susan, 71, 84, 89
Guggenheim, Peggy, 90, 91

Habermas, Jürgen, 21
Haraway, Donna, 2, 3, 6, 15–16
Harman, Claire, 121
Hartsock, Nancy, 7
Hayden, Dolores, 7
H.D.
bisexuality, 48
and Emily Dickinson, 48–9, 53
expatriatism, 45, 48
and Ezra Pound, 173 n. 32

fourth dimension, 46, 51
and Freud, 46–7
'Garden', 58–9
Gift, The (autobiography), 46, 49–55
'The Gift' (poem), 57–8
'Hermes of the Ways', 55, 59–60
HERmione, 58
and Imagism, 45, 47
photographic metaphor, 50
and Paul Robeson, 53
'Pursuit', 60–2
Sea Garden, 47, 55–62, 64
'Sheltered Garden', 56–7
theatrical metaphor, 52
transcendence, 45, 59–61, 64
Tribute to Freud, 48, 50
and *Uncle Tom's Cabin*, 50–5
historical novel
after modernism, 86–7, 116
lesbian, 117
home (*see also* domesticity; ideology of separate spheres)
called into question by modernism, 6
as enunciative modality, 18, 20
as model for political separatism, 7, 9
as performance, 52
as racially and class-specific position, 8
relation to concept of private self, 4, 8
homelessness at home, 2–3, 9–12, 16, 20, 32, 35–8, 47, 63, 69, 73, 101, 109, 138, 141, 153–4
homosociality, 120, 122, 125
Honig, Bonnie, 111
Hotelling, Kirstin, 70
Hurston, Zora Neale
free indirect discourse, use of, 147
and Gertrude Stein, 147, 153
relation to white women's modernist writing, 139, 148, 152–4
sexual violence, 146–7, 150–3
Their Eyes Were Watching God, 24–5, 139, 145–54
thematics of play, 148–52

ideology of separate spheres, 2, 4, 5, 9–12, 14–16, 26, 32, 50, 63–4, 67, 98–9 (*see also* public/private distinctions)
individualism (*see also* interiority)
domestic, 4, 8, 103, 111
in novel, 84–6, 119
possessive, 103
interiority (*see also* individualism)
critique of, 8, 18–19, 77–8, 101
domestic femininity as model of, 6, 85–7, 100
and selfhood, 4, 17–18, 41, 46, 47, 50, 63, 69–70, 105, 146–8
Irigaray, Luce, 60

Jakobson, Roman, 58, 78
JanMohamed, Abdul, 71
Jehlen, Myra, 85
Johnson, Barbara, 146–7

Kaivola, Karen, 101
Kaplan, Caren, 10
Kaplan, Carla, 154
Katz, Cindi, 4, 16, 19
Kelley, Mary, 33
Kern, Stephen, 13, 160 n. 3
Kristeva, Julia, 20, 22, 93, 113–14, 162 n. 43

Lacan, Jacques, 16
language
conventionality of, 101, 102
of interiority, 17–18
performative, 107, 145
women's relation to, 18, 20, 24, 30, 64, 67–70, 82, 138
Lauretis, Teresa de 24, 129
Lefebvre, Henri, 15, 84
lesbianism, 116–18
Lorde, Audre, 1, 11
Lukacs, Georg, 84, 115–18, 121, 133, 134, 136
Lyotard, Jean François, 117, 118

male readers of women's texts, 31, 124, 154, 159 n. 26
Marcus, Jane, 49, 99, 106, 115, 122, 159 n. 24

Martin, Biddy, 157 n. 14
Marx, Karl, 14, 130, 135
Miller, Cristanne, 71–4, 76, 79–81
Miller, D.A., 86
modernism (*see also* expatriatism)
  anticipation of postmodern critiques, 2–4, 6, 10, 14
  anti-foundational philosophy, 137
  concepts of space, 13–14, 16
  continuities with nineteenth century, 6
  defamiliarization, techniques of, 65, 137–8, 152
  defined against modernity, 14–15
  defined against romanticism, 6, 17
  impersonality, 17, 19, 161 nn. 36 and 40
  Kristeva's theory of, 20, 22
  primitivism, 71–3
  psychologising tendencies, 121
  redefining conventional language, 57–9
  tension between realism and experimentation, 137–8
  women's traditions defined in contrast to men's, 6
  and women's writing, 3, 5, 6, 10, 17, 19–22, 137–9
Mohanty, Chandra Talpade, 157 n. 14
Monroe, Jonathan, 140
Moore, Marianne
  ambivalent relation to modernism, 65–6
  'Black Earth', 70–80
  Collected Prose, 63–5
  and Emily Dickinson, 63–5, 69, 72
  'England', 73
  experience, problematizing of, 66–7
  and Ezra Pound, 70
  'feminine' qualities of her poetry, 71
  and H.D., 63–4, 72, 75, 76
  'Hero, The', 80–2
  'Jerboa, The', 71
  and liberal attitudes toward race, 72–3
  'Monkeys, The', 70–1
  'Poetry', 65–7, 82
  quotation, techniques of, 68–9
  race, 70–80, 80–2
  redefinition of home, 69–70, 74
  resistance of being 'placed', 66–7, 74
  representation of animals, 70–1
  'Silence', 67–70, 82
  transcendence and immanence, 71, 74–7
  and T.S. Eliot, 71
Morris, Adelaide, 45
Mulford, Wendy, 129

Naremore, James, 98
North, Michael, 145, 149
novel, 24, 83–7, 138

Pankhurst, Sylvia, 144–5
Pecora, Vincent, 84–5
performativity, 17, 24, 72, 142, 145, 149–53
poetess, stereotype of, 64
poetry, 23–4, 58, 78, 138
politics of location, 5, 67, 156 n. 10
Pondrom, Cyrena, 55
Poovey, Mary, 156 n. 9
positionality, 24, 48, 60, 73, 160 n. 32
postmodern geography movement, 3, 14, 19
postmodernism
  as periodizing concept, 2, 3, 14
  as privileging mobility, 6
  as return to realism in fiction, 84
  and spatial boundaries, 12, 15–17
  and temporality, 118
poststructuralism, 18–19
Pound, Ezra, 56, 58, 70–1
prolepsis, 34, 44, 63, 118, 127
prose poetry, 24, 145
public/private distinctions, 6, 8, 15, 17–18, 24, 26–7, 86, 103 (*see also* ideology of separate spheres)

race
  and class, 149–50
  and gender, 5, 24–5, 52–5, 70–80, 95, 104, 111–12, 134–5, 144–6, 148

Reagon, Bernice Johnson, 9
revolution in France (1848), 118–19, 125–6, 133
Rich, Adrienne, 5 (*see also* politics of location)
Romero, Lora, 4, 8, 9, 12, 16
Rommetveit, Ragnar, 144
Ronell, Avital, 15, 109
Roof, Judith, 117
Rose, Gillian, 4–5
Rowbotham, Sheila, 44

Said, Edward, 102–3
Sanchez-Eppler, Karen, 53, 54
Schmitz, Neil, 144
Sedgwick, Eve Kosofsky, 120, 161 n. 34
sentimental culture, 6, 7, 15
Simmel, Georg, 105–6
Slatin, John, 72, 78
Smith, Neil, 4, 16, 19
social housekeeping, 8, 104–5
Soja, Edward, 14
space
  abstraction of, 15
  and capitalism, 15–16
  metaphors of, 4, 9–10, 16, 32, 45, 46, 65, 67, 82, 101, 136
  redefinitions of, 9
  shared social, 107–8, 144–5
Spivak, Gayatri Chakravorty, 20, 33
Squier, Susan, 103, 105, 108–9
standpoint epistemologies, 5, 7, 119, 156 n. 10, 181 n. 2
Stein, Gertrude
  and Alice, B. Toklas, 138, 142–4
  Bee Time Vine and Other Pieces (1913–1927), 142, 144–5
  'Composition as Explanation', 149
  Lectures in America, 141, 142
  lesbianism, 144
  'Lifting Belly', 137
  Primer for the Gradual Understanding of Gertrude Stein, A, 138, 141
  relation to other modernist women writers, 139
  Tender Buttons, 138–45
  transformation of domesticity, 140–3
  Wars I Have Seen, 83, 86
Stepto, Robert, 149
Stimpson, Catherine, 142
Stone, Allucquere Rosanne, 110, 111
stream-of-consciousness techniques, 85, 87, 107, 161–2 n. 42
subjectivity
  black women's, 145, 147
  dispersed, 18, 20, 100
  enunciative modalities (Foucault), 18
  expressive, 17, 20
  female, 17, 18, 141–2
  in language, 16–17, 60–1, 67, 141, 160 n. 33
  in the novel, 85–6
  poststructuralist critiques of, 18–19
  and space, 16–17, 65

temporality
  as a defining concern of modernism, 14, 142
  in Emily Dickinson's poetry, 34, 44 (*see also* prolepsis)
  of housekeeping, 22
  and postmodernism, 118
Thomson, Virgil, 144–5
Tillyard, E.M.W., 115, 119
Tompkins, Jane, 7

Vicinus, Martha, 7
virtualization, 109–11, 160 n. 30, 178 n. 2
voice
  in black women's writing, 145–8
  novelistic, 92–3
  poetic, 26, 40, 47, 60–2, 65, 70, 76, 79, 83

Warner, Michael, 164 n. 8
Warner, Sylvia Townsend
  communism, 121
  lesbian representations, 116–19, 122, 125–8
  Letters, 121, 122, 133
  Lolly Willowes, 122
  reversal of male homosocial relations, 125
  revolution in France (1848), 118–19, 125–6

Summer Will Show, 87
technique of narrative interruption, 129–30, 134
transformation of domesticity, 130–2
and Valentine Ackland, 121–2
Wexler, Alice, 91
Wexler, Laura, 9
Wheare, Jane, 99, 102
whiteness, 23, 73, 138–9
Wiegman, Robyn, 172 n. 24
Wollstonecraft, Mary, 56
Wolff, Maria Tai, 149
Woolf, Virginia
and Emily Holmes Coleman, 106, 112
family chronicle, 101–3, 114
'Modern Fiction', 19–20, 51
Mrs. Dalloway, 107, 113
Pargiters, The, 103, 109
place, 100–1
privatisation, problem of, 99, 101
redefining domesticity, 105, 114
racial and class differences, 104–5, 111–12
Room of One's Own, A, 49
sexual violence, 108–9
shift from print to electronic communication, 108–9
status of modern individual, 99
telephone, figure of, 100, 107–11
Three Guineas, 99, 103
Waves, The, 99, 101, 102, 106
Writer's Diary, A, 98, 106
Years, The, 87, 98–114